CHILDHOOD INTO A

This book is about the lives of 11-year-old children growing up in a Midlands city in the late 1960s and early 1970s. Based on interviews with their parents, it describes family life at the time, as well as the experiences, hopes and concerns of the children as they themselves become adolescents. The book reflects upon the changes that occur for children in the transitional period between childhood and adolescence. It looks at the friendship patterns of 11-year-olds, their special interests and activities and how they spend their leisure time as well as describing the children's worries and concerns as perceived by their parents. It also considers family life and parental issues in the context of children's growing independence and their developing sexual maturity.

Originally written in the 1980s but recently discovered and published now for the first time, this is the fifth book in the series of long-term investigations of child upbringing by John and Elizabeth Newson, distinguished child psychologists at the University of Nottingham. Their research began in the late 1950s when the cohort of children was a year old; their mothers were subsequently interviewed at intervals as the children grew up. This fifth volume draws links between the material from interviews with parents when their sons and daughters were 7, 11, 16 and 19 years, and also invites comparison with the lives of children growing up now. The final chapter reviews the book series and the Newsons' research programme.

This exceptional book will be of interest to psychologists and other academics interested in child development, as well as professionals involved in work with children and adolescents such as teachers, doctors, nurses and social workers. It also has great historical significance with its potential for comparisons between the lives of children and adolescents now with those growing up some 50 years ago.

John and **Elizabeth Newson** were both Professors of Developmental Psychology at the University of Nottingham. In 1967 they established the Child Development Research Unit in the Department and were its Co-Directors. Their research study of child-rearing practices in a sample of 700 families in Nottingham is well known in the field and is highly respected and widely cited. In 1994 the Early Years Diagnostic Centre was renamed the Elizabeth Newson Centre. In 1999 Elizabeth Newson was appointed an OBE for her services to children on the Autistic Spectrum.

Peter Barnes was Research Officer in the Child Development Research Unit at the University of Nottingham from 1970 to 1977, working closely with John and Elizabeth Newson. He subsequently worked at The Open University, where he became Director of the Centre for Childhood, Development and Learning.

Susan Gregory was a student and then Research Officer in the Child Development Research Unit at the University of Nottingham with John and Elizabeth Newson. Following a senior lecturer post at the Open University, she was appointed Reader in Deaf Education at the University of Birmingham.

CHILDHOOD INTO ADOLESCENCE

Growing up in the 1970s

By John and Elizabeth Newson
Edited by Peter Barnes and Susan Gregory

Routledge
Taylor & Francis Group

LONDON AND NEW YORK

First published 2019
by Routledge
2 Park Square, Milton Park, Abingdon, Oxon OX14 4RN

and by Routledge
711 Third Avenue, New York, NY 10017

Routledge is an imprint of the Taylor & Francis Group, an informa business

British Library Cataloguing-in-Publication Data
A catalogue record for this book is available from the British Library

Library of Congress Cataloging-in-Publication Data
A catalog record for this book has been requested

ISBN: 978-1-138-56594-4 (hbk)
ISBN: 978-1-138-56596-8 (pbk)
ISBN: 978-1-315-12326-4 (ebk)

Typeset in Bembo
by Out of House Publishing

CONTENTS

ACKNOWLEDGEMENTS

Editors' note

This book is the posthumous publication of a manuscript by John and Elizabeth Newson, part of their series of books about growing up in the urban environment of Nottingham. How it came to be published is described in Chapter 1. The book has been edited for publication by Peter Barnes and Susan Gregory, both of whom were members of the Child Development Research Unit at Nottingham University from its early days and who worked with John and Elizabeth Newson.

Chapter 1 has been written by Peter Barnes and Susan Gregory. Chapters 2 to 8 closely follow the manuscript authored by John and Elizabeth Newson. Chapter 9 is a reflection by Charlie Lewis (University of Lancaster), who also studied and worked with the Newsons between 1977 and 1983.

What follows is our best effort to recreate the form of acknowledgements that John and Elizabeth Newson would have written, based on their practice in previous books. Many of the names have been taken straight from the equivalent section in the 7-year-old books. We are aware that unnamed others were involved when the later fieldwork was carried out and the results analysed; we hope that they, too, will feel duly appreciated.

Acknowledgements as they might have appeared in 1984

The research programme, of which the fourth stage – and elements of later stages – is reported in this book, was financed by a generous grant from the Social Science Research Council. We should also like to acknowledge our gratitude to the

University of Nottingham which has given the research that measure of financial security which all long-term projects hope for and too few achieve.

In order to follow a large group of children through time, we are very dependent on the goodwill and cooperation of local authority departments, on whose efficient record-keeping we rely for sampling purposes and for tracing children who have moved. The City of Nottingham Health and Education Departments have actively given us their help over many years now; that we have come to expect their cooperation does not mean that we are less aware of our good fortune in having chosen to work in a city with a research-minded authority. Especial thanks are due to past and present Medical Officers of Health, Dr William Dodd and Dr Wilfred Parry, and to past and present Directors of Education, Mr W.G. Jackson, Mr D.J.W. Sowell and Mr James Stone. To Mr B.O. Neep, Chief Education Welfare Officer, and his staff, we are part icularly grateful for their unfailing kindness and friendliness on the many occasions when we have interrupted their work to check a new batch of addresses.

We probably demand far more than is reasonable of our interviewers: they not only have to maintain a very high level of interviewing skill, and code the results in rather complicated ways, but they are expected to contribute ideas, insights and expertise in long work sessions during the gestation of new interview schedules. If we seem to take their talents for granted, it must be because they offer them with such apparently effortless generosity; but we are endlessly appreciative of their efficiency as colleagues and their niceness as friends. Our warmest thanks to Diane Barnes, Jean Crossland, Jean Jacobs, Dady Key and Margaret Rose.

780 recordings could result in a roomful of untranscribed audio-cassettes; that our interviews are condensed into a manageable number of fat books of typed quotations is due to the energy of our transcribers and typists. Thanks to all of them, but particularly to Julia Hibbitt, Beryl West and Joy Rayner.

Special thanks to our research colleagues Peter Barnes and Dady Key who have contributed both creatively and in terms of organisation of data gathering and sheer hard work on data processing, to the success of this research programme. The personal commitment they have brought to the project has given us incalculable support. Thanks are not quite appropriate from one half of a team to the other: we can only say that we have found working with them exciting and satisfying.

People occasionally comment that our books must be easy to write because the mothers contribute so many of the paragraphs. We must, however, claim considerable industry and effort in choosing amid so much vivid material; often we feel truly self-denying in leaving out some pertinent illustration. Once again, the only possible dedication is to the families who allow us this privileged glimpse of their private lives.

Acknowledgments regarding the publication of this book in 2018

The penultimate paragraph of the original Acknowledgements section in *Seven Years Old in an Urban Community* reads:

> Although our own children say that they are now too old to be mentioned by name, we would still like to record our debt to them for giving us the practice to set beside the theory; and especially for teaching us about the total emotional involvement which is a part of the parental condition.

Doubtless John and Elizabeth would have penned something in a similar vein had they written their own acknowledgements for this book. However, now that the three 'children' are even older, it is appropriate both to name them and place on record an additional debt.

As described in Chapter 1, Carey Newson discovered the manuscript of this book in 2014 when sorting through her parents' effects and, in due course, she brought it to our attention. There followed a series of meetings, email exchanges and telephone conversations involving Jo Newson and Roger Newson in which we discussed the desirability of publishing it and the practicalities of finding a publisher. Similar exchanges have continued during the course of preparing the text for publication, in an effort to ensure, as far as possible, that their parents' intentions were being respected at the same time as being sensitive to the issues of going into print after 34 years when social attitudes have changed to a significant degree. Between the five of us we hope we have been able to produce a book that will be of interest to followers of this research project and at the same time respects the academic integrity and insights of two people whom we have had the privilege of knowing in many different ways.

Professor Charlie Lewis (University of Lancaster) added his support to the discussions from an early stage and, in a final chapter, has contributed his reflections on this book and the significance of the Newsons' work for the wider realms of developmental psychology and social policymakers and practitioners.

Robin Key, Timothy Key and Penny Whitmore have been generous with their support and their recollections of their mother's much-valued roles in the project.

Professor Neil Frude (University of Cardiff) recalled details of his contact with the Newsons, which resulted in chapters in books that he edited in the early 1980s.

Sir David Greenaway, then Vice Chancellor of the University of Nottingham, gave his valuable endorsement to our wish to honour the reputation of two distinguished former members of staff who had appeared in the list of the university's '100 Heroes', published in 2014. In the Department of Psychology, Professor Paul McGraw, Dr Anthea Gulliford and Dr Nick Durbin responded very positively to our early plans and ambitions over a convivial Christmas lunch in the Staff Club where John and Elizabeth used to take their own guests and in the very room where their memorial gatherings were held in 2010 and 2014 respectively. At a later stage, we are also grateful to Professor Peter Mitchell in the Nottingham department for his encouragement and practical support.

Access to the data stored in the Economic and Social Research Council archive enabled us to retrieve information on the sample size and composition at successive stages of the study, together with a scanned version of the 11-year interview schedule (Appendix 1), of which no paper copies could be traced. Roger Newson, who had assisted his parents in preparing the data for the archive, provided valuable help in accessing it.

Gill Gowans, Materials Procurement Executive at the Open University, helped us on the way to Routledge and once that contact was established we have been very grateful to Lucy Kennedy, Alex Howard, Hannah Kingerlee, Sarah Willis and Kelly Winter for their encouragement, support and advice in what was recognised at the outset as being a project with unusual challenges. Their willingness and ability to have the original typescript scanned into an editable format was essential to progress, as has been their flexibility over the production of a handover that is unusual in significant respects.

Finally, we would like to thank the three anonymous reviewers whose positive response was instrumental in Routledge's commitment to this project. We hope that the finished product justifies their collective enthusiasm.

1

SETTING THE SCENE

Peter Barnes and Susan Gregory

How this book came to be published

John and Elizabeth Newson were developmental psychologists, whose professional careers covered many areas. They met as undergraduate students at University College London in the late 1940s and married in 1951, on the same day that they received the notification of their degree results. Shortly afterwards they moved to Nottingham where John had been offered an assistant lectureship in the university's Department of Psychology. Elizabeth worked for a time as a primary school teacher before joining John at the department.

Together, they founded the Child Development Research Unit at Nottingham University in 1967. Their interests in developmental psychology were wide and varied, including toys and playthings and the training of educational and clinical child psychologists. In addition, John had a particular focus on mother–infant interaction and intersubjectivity, while Elizabeth developed an expertise in the assessment and management of autism. She was awarded an OBE for that work in 1999.

Their main body of work, however, was a longitudinal study of children growing up in Nottingham. For this, they studied a large cohort of around 700 children, carrying out interviews with the parents, usually the mother, when the children were 1, 4, 7, 11, 16 and 22 years of age. The findings of the study of 1-, 4- and 7-year-olds were published in the 1960s and 1970s:

> *Infant Care in an Urban Community* – hardback in 1963 and paperback (as *Patterns of Infant Care in an Urban Community*) in 1965;
> *Four Years Old in an Urban Community* – hardback in 1968 and paperback in 1970;
> *Seven Years Old in the Home Environment* – hardback in 1976 and paperback in 1978; and
> *Perspectives on School at Seven Years Old* (with Peter Barnes) – hardback in 1977.

One of the main features of this research was the emphasis on involving parents as a source of information, rather than professionals. The idea for the study arose following the birth of their first child, Roger, in 1955. They found that few, if any, of the existing child care manuals provided information about what parents actually *do* and how they cope. As psychologists, it seemed to them that it was important to find out what really went on in families and what the parental experience was. That interest, which began in infancy, continued as the children grew older, still with the focus on the parents' perspectives.

Inevitably, a proliferation in commitments later in their careers, their otherwise busy lives and subsequent ill health had implications for the demands of the longitudinal study. At the time of their deaths, John in 2010 and Elizabeth in 2014, only the above books relating to 1-, 4- and 7-year-olds had been published, although much of the later data had been analysed and selected parts had appeared in edited books and journals (Newson and Newson, 1980; Newson, Newson and Mahalski, 1982; Newson and Newson, 1984; Newson, Newson and Adams, 1993).

Following Elizabeth's death in 2014, their daughter Carey was looking through the many cases of material relating to their professional careers that were stored in the basement of the house in Oxford to which they had retired. There she came across a 237-page typescript describing the findings from the 11-year-old interviews, bound between orange card covers. In many aspects this appeared complete, giving references and additional notes, but in other respects it seemed unfinished. There is some evidence that the work was finalised in 1984 and submitted to a publisher, probably George Allen & Unwin who had produced the four previous hardbacks, but for reasons unknown it never saw the light of day in print.

The newly discovered manuscript was shared with a number of people familiar with the research. It provided, for the first time, information about this group of children at 11 years of age, plus a final chapter that discussed more longitudinal aspects of the research, bringing together the early information with findings from interviews conducted at 16 years. It seemed important that it was published, despite some reservations about the implications of the passage of time. How would an audience in the 21st century make sense of reports of 11-year-old children's lives in the late 1960s and early 1970s? Would people be sufficiently interested? Who would fund it and who would publish it?

After some discussion, it was decided to approach a publisher and for the University of Nottingham to ascertain the likely response to the proposal to publish. The decision to go ahead was based on the positive reactions received.

The origins of the research and how it took shape

As already described, the origins of the longitudinal study lay in the seemingly mundane experience of John and Elizabeth Newson as first-time parents in suburban Nottingham in the mid-1950s. Here is how they described it many years later:

We were finding that our academic training [...] was rather less than adequate to answer the questions that naturally seemed to arise in the day-to-day prac- tice of parenthood; and we were curious to know whether our own ways of dealing with quite ordinary issues were in fact typical. We just didn't know whether most people fed their babies on schedule or demand. We didn't know whether they potted the baby from the second day or the second year, nor what difference it made. When our son cried in the night and we hauled him into bed with us and sleepily sang him a song or muttered a nursey rhyme, we wondered whether we were quite alone in such indulgence. [...]

Over and above our curiosity, on an anthropological level, to know where we stood in the cultural scheme of things, we were intrigued by the degree of authority with which 'professional' advice on child rearing was vested. Words like 'ought' and 'should' seemed to be bandied about on issues which we were gradually coming to believe were matters of opinion; value judgements in terms of 'good', 'best', 'correct', 'harmful', 'faulty' were made with an assurance which, naively, we first assumed must stem from a well-established body of knowledge. [...] It took us some time to realise that if we seriously wanted answers to our questions, we would have to undertake some of the basic research ourselves.

Newson and Newson, 2001: 413–14

Who were the children?

That 'basic research' took shape in 1957. The immediate aim was to interview 700 Nottingham mothers about how they were bringing up their 1-year-old child. The initial sample was drawn from the records of the City of Nottingham Health Department. This meant that at the time of the child's birth and during the first year of life the families were resident within the city boundaries. As the total interviewing programme was spread out over a period of two years, batches of names were drawn month by month in an effort to ensure that interviews took place within a fortnight either way of the child's first birthday. As a consequence, the dates of birth of the children in the sample ranged from late 1957 to late 1959.

Certain exclusions were made: illegitimate children; children known to have gross disabilities; children not in the care of their mother; and children whose parents were recent immigrants. These exclusions did not imply that such children and their families were not of interest in their own right; several were the subject of subsequent studies at the Child Development Research Unit, using similar meth- odology and drawing on data from the core sample for comparative purposes. These included: children with cerebral palsy (Hewett, 1970); blind children (Wood, 1970); fatherless children (Canning, 1974); deaf children (Gregory, 1976); Punjabi children (Dosanjh, 1976); and West Indian children (Grace, 1983).

Names were drawn at random from the Health Department records until a total of 500 interviews had been completed. At that point a further random sample was scrutinised in terms of the fathers' occupation in order to increase the representation of those social class groups, as defined by the Registrar General's classification (see p. 13), which were less well represented in the initial random sample. It thus became a stratified random sample (Newson and Newson, 1963, Appendix 1).

How were the data collected?

In total, 709 mothers were interviewed. Elizabeth Newson conducted 184 of them herself, 16 were carried out by 'other university people' and the majority (509) was undertaken by health visitors from the Health Department. Elizabeth recorded her interviews on the sole reel-to-reel tape recorder available in the Department and then transcribed excerpts from what the mothers said, in longhand. The health visitors' interviews were not recorded.

The data from the completed schedules were then transferred to yellow Cope-Chat cards, one for each child. The 8 inch by 5 inch cards (it was still the late 1950s!) had 116 punched holes around the margin. Each hole was assigned a characteristic or attribute – social class, gender, temperament, method of feeding – and, depending on the response, the hole was either left intact or clipped open. So, for example, if the record was of a child with a father in a skilled manual occupation, the designated hole was clipped. When it came to analysis, the completed cards were stacked and a knitting needle passed through that line of holes and jiggled about. All of the Class III manual clipped cards fell out and those left on the needle could then be further sorted to end up with separate piles for the five social class categories that formed the basis of the analysis. These cards could then be sorted according to other variables of interest and the numbers recorded. For a pair of researchers juggling the demands of jobs and a growing family – there were now three children under the age of 7 – this technology, seemingly primitive by today's standards, had advantages:

> [I]f one wanted to try out some hunch of correlation, all one needed was the box of cards and one's homely knitting needle, and the hypothesis could be checked there and then – no booking ten minutes' computer time some day next week!
>
> *Newson and Newson, 1976: 28*

It was in this fashion that the findings of the 1-year-old study came together and the resulting book produced (Newson and Newson, 1963).[1]

Although the health visitors who carried out the majority of the interviews were experienced at interviewing in the course of their jobs, there was a perceived problem in that the professional relationship they had had with the families prior to carrying out the interviews ran the risk of generating responses from the mothers that were closer to what they judged the health visitor would *want to hear* rather than what they *actually did*. Subsequent analysis of the data found evidence that that was indeed the case, which had implications for what became the next stage in the research.

What happened next?

The 1-year-old study may have been embarked upon as a one-off, but there was a grander ambition, as stated in 1968:

> Integral in itself, we nevertheless planned, with more hope than confidence, that this should be dovetailed into a much more ambitious investigation which should follow children through their childhood and adolescence, and indeed into early adulthood, if this proved practicable.
>
> *Newson and Newson, 1968: 16*

The 4-year-old research built on the lessons learned from its predecessor. It also enjoyed the significant support of a generous grant from the Nuffield Foundation, which, among other benefits, meant that it was possible to engage a team of six part-time interviewers in addition to Elizabeth Newson herself. Between them, these interviewers visited 275 of the mothers who had been seen at 1, together with 425 first-time interviewees, randomly selected from the same Health Department records that had been used in 1957. These families replaced those who had been interviewed by the health visitors.

As the research programme progressed through the 7- and 11-year stages there was inevitable further drop out and replacement. It was not possible to follow up 83 of the 700 interviewed at 4 when the child was 7; just over half declined to take part and the remainder had moved away and could not be contacted. A further top-up sample was drawn of children born in 1960, resulting in a total of 697 interviews.

A similar pattern can be seen at 11: a proportion of those interviewed at 7 years could not be followed up four years later and additional numbers were recruited such that 780 interviews were completed. The data presented in the following chapters are based on that number. Further details of the composition of the sample at the later age-stages are provided in Appendix 2.

Who were the interviewers?

There was a welcome continuity in the team of interviewers from stage to stage. It is possible to account for ten over the duration of the research, based on a combination of the acknowledgements in the published books and personal memory. The Newsons summarised their significance in a retrospective account of the project. From the outset

> Elizabeth's genuine role as a young mother was enormously in her favour: when we were financially able to employ a team of interviewers, a prime qualification was their motherhood, so that this could be mentioned in the introductory letter; once contact had been made, we could all grow older together! The nature and length of the encounter (two to four hours, or more) seemed to have a bonding effect, as did the intimacy of the topic; and training new

interviewers in achieving the skills we wanted was made possible by taping and thus closely supervising their first few (non-sample) interviews – not everyone could manage the degree of flexibility and sensitivity, nor the abrogation of status. Our favourite quotation (and we salute our long-term assistant, Dady Key, for getting so right the deceptive simplicity of the approach) was this one: 'I can sew ... I don't say I'm clever ... I'm not a *brainy* person ... I couldn't do clerical work ... I probably couldn't even do *your* job ...'.

Newson and Newson, 2001: 419

The Newsons were powerful advocates of the interview as a means of gathering informed and informative data. When writing about the technique in a reflective account, first published in 1976 (Newson and Newson, 1976), they quote their own description from *Four Years Old in an Urban Community*. The fundamental properties remain relevant to all the subsequent age-stages of the research:

Our basic tool of investigation has been and remains the interview: primarily because it seems to give exceptionally good value in terms of detailed data on both behaviour and the attitudes underlying behaviour. In any human activity the factual event and its associated feelings are of equal importance for our understanding. For instance, it may be a fact that a mother regularly smacks her child in certain situations, and it may also be true that this mother feels guilty whenever she thinks about smacking her child: it is the *conjunction* of these two things which is important. In the assessment of the socialization process, it may be very misleading to rely on either behaviour or attitude taken in isolation: even a 4-year-old child is aware that slaps of the same objective force have totally different meanings according to the feelings and intentions which lie behind them.

It is the normal function of conversation to probe such subtleties if one really wished to know about the opinions and motives of those with whom one converses. Once talk is flowing freely, in fact, it will be very difficult indeed for the participants to discuss their own behaviour without expressing any attitude towards it: and it is from such expressions of feeling, as much as from a knowledge of events, that the hearer is enabled to predict behaviour in future situations. Thus if we want to predict how A will behave when next he meets B, the most obvious thing to do is talk to A about B. From this conversation, *provided that we are not personally involved in the A/B relationship*, we may expect to gain a very fair idea both of what happened in previous encounters and of how A feels about B. Conversation is by far the most economical means, in terms of time and effort, of arriving at a valid assessment of a situation.

Newson and Newson, 1968: 18–19

When asked what qualities they looked for in a good interviewer, their response was '*intelligence; flexibility*; but, above all, *niceness*' (Newson and Newson, 1968: 7).

For more detail on the techniques of interviewing in the Nottingham research, see Newson and Newson (1976).

The context of the research

Advice to parents and child psychology

Although John and Elizabeth were both part of the Nottingham Psychology Department at the time of the birth of their first child, they found that neither the study of psychology nor the conventional advice to parents addressed the issues that concerned them in their day-to-day life.

That conventional advice was largely influenced by male doctors, often psychoanalysts. Dr Truby King was still significant with his views on the need for a rigid routine with babies, especially with respect to feeding (Truby King, 1937, republished 1945). Dr Donald Winnicott (1957), a paediatrician and psychoanalyst, published a number of books about parenting in the period 1945–71. However, in the late 1950s and 1960s a gradual shift was beginning away from the authoritative expert perspective on child-rearing to mothers being their own expert. The American paediatrician Dr Benjamin Spock (1945, revised and reprinted many times) was becoming an extremely influential figure and his basic advice to mothers was underpinned by the notion that 'you know more than you think you do' (Newson and Newson, 1974).

Developmental (also known as child) psychology was a very young discipline at this time, and a small part of psychology. It seemed of little relevance to the new parent. The influence of behaviourism was very strong as psychology, as a discipline, was concerned with its right to be considered a science. A standard textbook used on many university psychology courses was *Introduction to Psychology* by Ernest Hilgard and Richard Atkinson (4th edition 1967, first published in 1953). The status of the early years may be apparent from the fact that only 59 of its 686 pages focused on developmental psychology. The topics dealt with in those pages largely discussed controlled observation of behaviour, often described in terms of stages of development. In the chapter on infancy and childhood, there were many comparisons of the development of human babies with that of animals, including guinea pigs, ducks, dogs, chimpanzees, rats, monkeys and hamsters (Hilgard and Atkinson, 1967: 60–90).

Further illustration comes from the questions asked in end-of-course examinations. The following come from the Child Psychology – note, not yet Developmental Psychology – paper in the final year of the psychology degree course that one of us sat at Nottingham University in 1967. John Newson, who taught the course, may well have written them.

1. Describe and briefly discuss the principles that should be observed in the scientific observation of the human infant at the preverbal level.
2. Compare and contrast the typical behaviour of the human infant at the age of six months and twelve months under the headings: sensory, motor and personal-social development.

It seemed to John and Elizabeth Newson that there was a large gap between the nature of the study of child psychology and their parental experience.

What are longitudinal studies?

As already noted, the Newsons' 'grander ambition' at the outset of this research was to follow the development of the children in the sample through their childhood, into adolescence and maybe through to adulthood. That ambition fitted a developing style of research that was slowly taking shape in the UK and elsewhere, what is known as a longitudinal study. An important early entry to the field began as a survey of the experience of maternity services shortly after the end of the Second World War. The sample comprised all children born in England, Wales and Scotland in a single week in March 1946 – around 17,000. The ground-breaking research was conducted, with limited resources, by a medical doctor, James Douglas, working with a team of health visitors. Seventy years on, the story of the project has been retold by Helen Pearson in *The Life Project* (Pearson, 2016).

As Douglas was writing up the results of the maternity study with his co-researcher, demographer David Glass, an idea came to them: 'Wouldn't it be wonderful to keep following these thousands of children all through the course of their lives? In other words, would it be possible to turn their maternity study into a cohort study?' (Pearson, 2016: 33).

They were interested to see whether the inequalities related to social class that their survey had revealed would persist as the children grew up or whether the 'wounds' were only shallow and would heal and fade over time. Douglas was able to return to the same children again and again during the school years and recruited teachers and school doctors to provide updates on their progress. The data gathering continued into the adult years.

The positive response to Douglas's early work led to a second nationwide survey of British births, begun in 1958 and prompted by concerns over high levels of infant deaths and a desire to appraise the maternity services that had been running under the NHS for six years. That, too, developed into a longitudinal study, the National Child Development Study, with a sample of 16,000 or so. The children were tested again at the ages of 7, 11 and 16 and through into adulthood. Between them, these major pieces of research informed, in unique ways, the development of health, education and social policies.

How does the Nottingham research sit alongside these national studies? Here are the Newsons' own reflections from a chapter in an edited volume on disruptive behaviour in schools:

> Longitudinal studies offer an exceptional opportunity to trace the development of a child's school career from one stage to the next, giving equal regard to what was going on at each stage. The massive national studies offer us broadly based statistical data covering the achievements of thousands of children at different focal points in their schooling, together with various

measures of parental situation and attitude. More limited longitudinal studies such as the Nottingham one cannot compete with the coverage of the national studies in terms of breadth; however the Nottingham study has its own advantages (which indeed complement those of the national studies). Thus it can take a closer view of both parents and children, using in the main interviewers who already know the family well and are trained to follow through their questions in some depth, and thus eliciting the kind of data which allow us to get the *feel*, as well as the facts, about what 'getting an education' means in day-to-day terms to children and their parents.

Newson and Newson, 1984: 99–100

What was Nottingham like as these children were growing up?

The Nottingham where these families lived and where the children grew up was very different from the city as it is today, in the second decade of the 21st century. The sample children reached the age of 11 in and around 1970. In many respects their environment had changed little during the course of their lives.

Nottingham was a prosperous city with a wide variety of established and successful businesses, including several household names: Player's cigarettes, Raleigh cycles and Boots the chemist. There was a thriving clothing trade, with lacemaking and lingerie a speciality. There had long been coal mines in the vicinity and, taken together, there were many opportunities for skilled, semi-skilled and unskilled workers alike.

In the late 1960s the unemployment rate was around 2.5%, similar to that for England and Wales as a whole. The average salary of £1,101 was in line with that across the East Midlands but lower than the national average of £1,164. That difference may have been accounted for by the high proportion of female workers – 38% – whose pay would have been lower than the men's (Newson and Lowinger, 1970).

In 1970 the population of Nottingham was just over 300,000. Much of the old inner-city housing was in decline, notably St Ann's, the Meadows and Radford. St Ann's, just north of the city centre, was the subject of a research project that attracted a lot of attention, both locally and nationally (Coates and Silburn, 1968, 1970). In the first of their reports it was described as:

> A large, deteriorated district, geographically distinct, with a certain sense of identity and community; [...] an area of manifest environmental and social deprivation, in which general amenities are at the most rudimentary level: where there are almost no trees; where until recently there have been no adequate play facilities; [...] where the schools are old and decrepit; with dingy buildings and bleak factories and warehouses, functionally austere chapels, a host of second-hand shops stacked out with shabby, cast-off goods; overhung throughout the winter by a damp pall of smoke.

Coates and Silburn, 1968: 13

St Ann's was also overcrowded, with 62.6 persons per acre compared with a density of 17.0 persons per acre for the city as a whole (Newson and Lowinger, 1970). Some of the families in the sample lived there, many fiercely protective of the sense of community that prevailed, despite the depressing physical conditions.

By 1970 the post-war housing estates were well-established. A third of the city's population lived in council-built houses (Newson and Lowinger, 1970). Those in Aspley, Bilborough and Broxtowe were started in the 1930s and added to in 1947–52. The Clifton estate was one of the largest of its kind in Europe. Built between 1951 and 1958 on the southern edge of the city, it featured nearly 7,000 spacious houses, gardens, wide streets, trees and woodlands. It was home to 30,000 people, among them families who feature in this book.

The predominantly middle-class, owner-occupied housing areas such as Wollaton and Mapperley were also well-established and offered substantial detached and semi-detached properties with gardens.

The following chapters include references to named places around Nottingham. Sometimes these are where the child or the family as a whole go to spend leisure time or in pursuit of cultural activities: Wollaton Hall, a 16th-century Elizabethan mansion housing a natural history museum and set in a large park, with a lake; Nottingham Castle, high on a rock near the city centre, with its terraced gardens and art gallery; and the Embankment alongside the River Trent, near the football and cricket grounds at Trent Bridge. Elsewhere in the text the names relate to the limits of the range where the child is allowed to go on his or her own or parts of the city that are strictly off-limits. Appendix 3 has a section listing the places referred to, with a brief description to help put them in context.

Appendix 3 also provides a short glossary of some of regional terms that appear in the transcribed interviews, together with an explanation of the Nottingham institutions that are referred to from time to time in the chapters.

The final component of Appendix 3 is notes of explanation of some of the features of daily life in the early 1970s that were significant then but may not make much sense to readers who were not around at the time. The explanations may help to bridge that divide.

The world of technology was very different in 1970 to the way it is today. There were no mobile phones, no personal computers, no internet, no email, no social media. There were three television stations: BBC1, BBC2 and ITV. The first transmissions in colour were made in 1967 and although by 1970 all three stations were regularly broadcasting in colour, to receive those programmes a new set was required and they were expensive. The large majority of the families in the study would have been viewing in black-and-white. And when the set was turned off at the end of the day some would watch until 'the spot on the television goes …' (Chapter 7).

Radio Nottingham had begun broadcasting in the late 1960s as one of the first wave of local radio stations in the UK. There were two local daily newspapers, *The Guardian Journal* (which closed in 1973) and the *Nottingham Evening Post*.

The commercial hub of the city radiated from the market square, known locally as 'slab square', dominated by the Council House, a mix of large department stores – Jessops (part of John Lewis), Pearsons, Hopewells – high-street regulars such as Woolworth's, Marks & Spencer, British Home Stores, C&A, Boots and WHSmith, plus more specialist shops. This traditional pattern was starting to change. Between 1967 and 1972 the Victoria Centre was built on the site of the former Nottingham Victoria railway station and was one of the early large indoor shopping centres in the UK, quickly becoming popular venue. Out-of-town shopping centres remained in the realms of fantasy.

Within the home, much of what might be regarded as standard domestic equipment today – microwave cookers, dishwashers, freezers, washing machines – was, in 1970, either at an early stage of development or too expensive for many to contemplate buying. Launderettes located in the community offered an alternative to washing clothes in the kitchen sink or the dolly tub, and the proximity of the corner shop meant that food could be purchased as and when required rather than in a weekly trip to the supermarket.

A further constraint on such shopping trips was transport. Car ownership was on a much reduced scale compared to today, a second car in the family even more so. This also affected when and how children moved around and what constraints there were on how far they could travel and to where. It could be said, however, that an extensive bus service and the use of bicycles afforded these 11-year-olds more opportunities for independence than their 21st-century counterparts.

These comparisons are general and by no means exhaustive. They are intended merely to alert the reader to the need to make sense of the lives of these 11-year-olds and their families in terms of the environment they inhabited, which is, in significant respects, different from that of today.

Education in Nottingham

The education system in Nottingham – and in the UK as a whole – was very different in 1970 to that of the second decade of the 21st century. The large majority of Nottingham children spent their time between the ages of 5 and 16 in primary and secondary schools run by the Nottingham Local Education Authority (LEA). At the age of 11, the children in our sample were in transition between the junior schools, of which there were 70 across the city in 1968/9, and secondary schools, of which there were 39, plus two fee-paying high schools, one for boys and one for girls (Newson and Lowinger, 1970).

Approximately 18% of the secondary school population attended a grammar school on the strength of their performance on two tests of verbal reasoning taken in the final year of primary school. The judgement of headteachers also entered the equation and parents might have a significant say in the outcome if they contested the initial recommendation and sought a second opinion from an educational psychologist.

Given that most of the interviews in this research were carried out after the children's eleventh birthday, the likelihood is that most had already started at secondary school by the time their mothers talked to the interviewers. The interview schedule (Appendix 1) has a whole section – questions 95–121 – about the experience of school but only a limited amount of it features in the following pages, mostly in Chapter 8. At this distance in time we cannot know why. When writing up the findings from the 7-year-old stage of the research the Newsons opted to publish them in two books: *Seven Years Old in the Home Environment* (1976) and *Perspectives on School at Seven Years Old* (1977). Given the seven-year interval between the appearance of those two books and the likely hoped-for publication of the 11-year data – 1984 or thereabouts – it is probable that any plans for a fuller consideration of the findings from the school questions had been put to one side and efforts concentrated instead on bringing together the other components of the interviews. The net result is that the children's experience of school and the relationship between the world of school and the world of home and family has only limited coverage in the following pages.

Issues in publishing work carried out in the 1970/1980s in 2018

Issues relating to content

We decided from the outset that our editing should involve as light a touch as possible in order to retain the tone and emphases of the original draft, as well as respecting the interviewees. This means that we have, for the most part, retained the Newsons' words, even when, occasionally, some might not be deemed appropriate in a work written now. We have also retained their use of the generic 'he' when both genders are being referred to. We have likewise kept their use of 'his' for 'his' and 'hers', and 'him' for both 'him' and 'her'.

However, there is one area in which we *have* made significant changes, namely in the attribution of the verbatim quotations. In the original, every quote is preceded by a descriptor of the speaker, starting with her husband's occupation, for example:

> Asphalter's wife, a part-time cleaner
> Engineer's wife, not at work

Our discomfort was twofold. First, we were uneasy that the husband's occupation was the first element to be described in the attribution, even though the words quoted were almost always those spoken by the mothers. That ordering replicated the style established in the earlier books and was driven by the fact that the social class categorisation, which features strongly in the narrative, was determined by the man's occupation (discussed further in the following section), but it is significantly at odds with present-day practice. In any event, the reversed order, giving prominence to the mother as speaker, does not change the ability to relate occupation to social class category. Second, we felt, consistent with current practice, that 'not in paid work' was a more acceptable way to describe those mothers who were not in receipt of some form of income from employment. Thus, the two examples above become:

Part-time cleaner, husband an asphalter
Not in paid work, husband an engineer

We felt comfortable about taking this step as the Newsons themselves had made such changes elsewhere in their later work and had they overseen the publication of this manuscript they might well have done likewise.

The emphasis on social class

To the reader in the 21st century, the use of social class based on occupation to classify and compare families and children may seem somewhat strange. This may reflect changing attitudes over the past 40 years to the notion of social class and to the far greater flexibility in working patterns in general. The British Social Attitudes Survey, which has recorded aspects of social class since 1983, when describing the situation in 2013 suggests that both the measurement of social class and its ability to predict attitudes have become much weaker (Ormston and Curtis, 2015).

When the Nottingham study began, the use of the Registrar General's classification of occupations (1955) seemed an appropriate system with which to start.

Classification by father's occupation

Class description

I and II *Professional and managerial:* Doctors, solicitors, clergymen, teachers, nurses, company directors, shopkeepers (own business) police officers etc.

III WC *White collar:* Clerical workers, shop assistants etc.; tradesmen in one-man business, foremen and supervisors in industry.

III Man *Skilled manual:* Skilled tradesmen in industry, drivers etc.

IV *Semi-skilled:* Machine operators, bus conductors, window cleaners, drivers' mates, porters etc.

V *Unskilled:* Labourers, refuse collectors, cleaners in industry, messengers etc.; persistently unemployed.

The changes they made were to split Class III into two sections, III WC and III Man. For some analyses they were then able to describe the sample in two main categories: middle class comprising I, II and III WC; and working class, comprising III Man, IV and V.

In Chapter 7 of *Infant Care in an Urban Community* the Newsons discuss the relevance of using social class as a dimension but also the difficulties in its use. From the start, they made some adaptations to the categorisation taking into account the mother's occupation if it was in a higher category than that of the father. They described how they had to use their own judgement where the job title was ambiguous, 'for example an "engineer" may be a professional man with a university degree, engaged on research or engineering design; or he may be a mechanic; a skilled tradesman without any prospect of qualifying for professional status' (Newson and Newson, 1965: 153, paperback edition).

In the second book in the series, *Four Years Old in an Urban Community*, they explain why they have kept social class as a dominant variable:

> [W]e should have been prepared to abandon the factor of social class if we had found it was no longer significantly operative at this stage, and we have looked for other lines of cleavage which might have been gaining in importance, but the reality is that class affiliations remain pervasively powerful even in the minutiae of the four year old's daily life, and we can only report what we find.
>
> *Newson and Newson, 1968: 23*

In writing the 7-year-old book, they still found class a 'pervasive influence' in 'different patterns of child rearing'. While in the earlier books there were no other variables that were considered relevant in terms of the questions they were asking, they felt that '[a]t seven, however, it quickly became clear that both sex and social class were operating at a high level of potency in the child's upbringing experience' (Newson and Newson, 1976: 21) They thus report differences related to both sex and class in that volume.

The use of sex (or gender, as in current usage) and social class continues in the present volume, although the Newsons were still sensitive about the use of the latter. A particular issue they discuss is the fact that 'it is the business of social researchers to empathise very closely with these families, and to suspend any moral judgement', which may make it difficult when the researcher comes to analyse their responses (Chapter 6, p. 127).

Recently, concern about the use of social class as a measure has become part of general research considerations. Two main problems have been discussed. The inadequacies of both the use of occupation alone, and greater mobility and flexibility within the working environment, resulted in the UK Office for National Statistics producing a new socio-economic classification in 2001. This defined class in terms of economic capital, cultural capital and social capital. Economic capital was defined as income and assets; cultural capital as the amount of cultural activity and interests; and social capital as the number and social status of friends, colleagues and acquaintances.

The use of social class would be different were the research to be carried out today. However, in the late 1960s and early 1970s when the 11-year-old interviews were carried out, the Newsons decided, on reflection, that both social class and gender met their needs in terms of providing tools to highlight important comparisons.

Inclusion of potentially sensitive material

If this research were to be carried out now, its planning would have included ethical approval procedures to protect confidentiality of respondents and the children and family members they were describing. The conditions under which the material could be published would be ascertained and any permission needed to publish established. Clearly, this was not carried out at the time the research was planned as there were no such procedures in place. As such, formally, there are no limitations on what can be quoted.

However, we are aware that some of the interviews contain sensitive material. Our concern is less for the parents, as it is possible to argue that they had given implicit consent by agreeing to be interviewed. The books about the research at 1 and 4 years were already in the public domain and there were also occasional articles in the local press. Many of the parents would have been aware of these and thus we may assume they would know that the findings at each stage of the research could be published. Indeed, many of them derived pleasure from knowing that they and their child were part of a project known nationally.

Our concern, however, is greater for the 'young people' themselves, now heading into their sixties. In some instances, it might be possible for them to recognise themselves in quotes, prefaced as they are by the occupations of both parents. The now adult might identify something a parent had said about them that they were previously unaware of, or was a view they did not know the parent had of them, or an occurrence that had been forgotten but might now be recognisable by others. Examples could be that one of the parents had had an affair that was hushed up, that the child was 'difficult to like', or that they had been in trouble with the police.

For that reason, in such instances the relevant part of the quote has been deleted, the identifying part of the parents' occupation changed to something compatible with but less specific, or the quote has been embedded in the text, with no attribution. In practice, there are few such changes in Chapters 2 to 7 and none affect the sense or readability of the text. In Chapter 8, where the material is, by its very nature more sensitive, we have omitted information about parental occupation across the board.

Why Chapter 8 is different

Anyone familiar with the style of the Newsons' writing from previous published reports of the Nottingham research will find that the following six chapters (2–7) are out of the same mould: a mix of straightforward statistical analysis, mostly exploring differences and trends by gender and social class, and the everyday experiences, attitudes and insights that inform these, brought to life through verbatim extracts from what mothers said in the course of the interviews. The authors sometimes likened the writing process to John providing the statistical skeleton of the argument to which Elizabeth then added the flesh, in the shape of judiciously selected illustrations from the volumes of typed transcribed quotations.

Chapter 8 is different in a number of ways. While illustrative quotations are still to be found, the focus of attention is directed to an analysis of the relationships between styles of child-rearing at the age of 11 and aspects of behaviour – in particular, negative ones – when the same children were 16 years old. The fact that such an analysis was feasible is an indication of the extent of the publication lag identified earlier in this chapter. The sample children reached the age of 16 between 1973 and 1976 and so coded data from that stage of the research were available at the time this book about the 11-year-olds was being written.

To the best of our knowledge there are only three other publications that explore the longitudinal dimension in any depth. In 1982 the Newsons published a paper with Pauline Mahalski (formerly Nye), a New Zealand researcher with a long-standing interest in children's attachment behaviour (Newson, Newson and Mahalski, 1982). She had made occasional visits to the Child Development Research Unit from the mid-1970s and analysed data specific to her interests. The paper examined whether relationships could be found between specific comfort habits in early childhood and personality at the ages of 11 and 16. Some reliable statistical associations were identified that suggested that children with a persistent oral habit at 4 years may later be less 'well-adjusted' emotionally and more difficult for their parents to influence and control than other children.

In a chapter in an edited book about disruptive behaviour in schools the Newsons presented an analysis of some of the relationships between children's experiences of school at the age of 11 and their subsequent attitudes and behaviour at 16 (Newson and Newson, 1984). This parallels and to some extent prefigures the content of Chapter 8. We know that the chapter in the earlier book was by invitation of the editors, Neil Frude and Hugh Gault, so the likelihood is that ongoing work at the time was managed in order to fulfil two briefs. Indeed, the existence of *Childhood into Adolescence* was indicated, albeit prematurely, in the list of references.

The third published source appeared in 1993, based on a paper given at a conference of the Royal College of Psychiatrists Forensic Section at York in February 1991 (Newson, Newson and Adams, 1993). It analysed data from 504 7- and 11-year interviews with respect to two outcome measures: 'troublesomeness' at 16 years (the same index to be found in Table 8.3, p. 170) and the acquisition of a criminal record in early adulthood. The findings suggested that there were significant correlations between child-rearing strategies and the child's development of delinquency. In particular, an authoritarian approach to children, a lack of sensitive communication and negotiation between parent and child, and the use of physical punishment were found to predict subsequent delinquency. (Note that the source of the data on criminal records is not provided in the paper but we know that in the late 1970s/early 1980s there was a project conducted in association with the Home Office.)

One final point

We acknowledge that in many ways this book does not have a straightforward format. We do not know why Chapter 8 is so different in style from the others or if John and Elizabeth Newson would have made significant changes to it before publication, and we cannot ask them. We also realise that the present-day reader is encountering a different world for 11-year-olds from the present one and we have done our best to provide adequate background to make it comprehensible.

We nevertheless feel, as we did when we first read the manuscript, that this book provides unique and important material that adds to our understanding of growing up both then and now. We hope you will agree.

When James Douglas, director of the longitudinal study that began in 1946, reviewed *Seven Years Old in the Home Environment* for the *Times Educational Supplement* (9 April 1976) his conclusion read: 'This book discredits many firmly held – and often sentimentally or politically generated – beliefs about social class differences in attitudes to child care in this country. I look forward to reading its sequel.' Forty-two years later, here it is.

Note

1 At the 4- and 7-year stages the interview data were punched on to 80-column Hollerith cards, which were then sorted mechanically. It was only at the 11-year stage that the power of the university's mainframe computer came into play.

References

Canning, F. (1974) 'The socialisation of the child in the fatherless family', unpublished PhD thesis, University of Nottingham.

Coates, K. and Silburn, R. (1968) *Poverty, Deprivation and Morale in a Nottingham Community: St Ann's*, Nottingham: Nottingham University Department of Adult Education.

Coates, K. and Silburn, R. (1970) *Poverty: the Forgotten Englishmen*, Harmondsworth: Penguin Books.

Dosanjh, J. (1976) 'A comparative study of Punjabi and English child-rearing practices with special reference to lower juniors (7–9 years)', unpublished PhD thesis, University of Nottingham.

Grace, A.M. (1983) 'Jamaican immigrant child rearing practices', unpublished PhD thesis, University of Nottingham.

Gregory, S. (1976) *The Deaf Child and his Family*, London: George Allen & Unwin. Republished as *Deaf Children and their Families*, Cambridge: Cambridge University Press, 1995.

Hewett, S., with Newson J. and Newson, E. (1970) *The Family and the Handicapped Child*, London: George Allen & Unwin.

Hilgard, E.R. and Atkinson, R.C. (1967) *Introduction to Psychology, 4th edition*, New York: Harcourt, Brace and World (first published in 1953).

Newson, J. and Lowinger, L. (1970) 'Nottingham', in J.A. Lauwerys and D.G. Scanlon (eds) *The 1970 World Year Book of Education*, London: Evans Bros.

Newson, J. and Newson, E. (1963) *Infant Care in an Urban Community*, London: George Allen & Unwin. Published in paperback as *Patterns of Infant Care in and Urban Community*, Harmondsworth: Penguin Books, 1965.

Newson, J. and Newson, E. (1968) *Four Years Old in an Urban Community*, London: George Allen & Unwin. Published in paperback, Harmondsworth: Penguin Books, 1970.

Newson, J. and Newson, E. (1974) 'Cultural aspects of child rearing in the English-speaking world', in M.P.M. Richards (ed.) *The Integration of a Child into a Social World*, Cambridge: Cambridge University Press.

Newson, J. and Newson, E. (1976) *Seven Years Old in the Home Environment*, London: George Allen & Unwin. Published in paperback, Harmondsworth: Penguin Books, 1978.

Newson, J. and Newson, E. (1976) 'Parental roles and social context', in M. Shipman (ed.) *The Organisation and Impact of Social Research: Six Original Case Studies in Education and Behavioural Sciences*, London: Routledge & Kegan Paul. Reprinted as a Routledge Library Edition, 2017.

Newson, J. and Newson, E., with Barnes, P. (1977) *Perspectives on School at Seven Years Old*, London: George Allen & Unwin.

Newson, J. and Newson, E. (1980) 'Parental punishment strategies with eleven-year-olds', in N. Frude (ed.) *Psychological Approaches to Child Abuse*, London: Batsford.

Newson, J. and Newson, E. (1984) 'Parents' perspectives on children's behaviour at school', in N. Frude and H. Gault (eds) *Disruptive Behaviour in Schools*, Chichester: John Wiley & Sons.

Newson, J. and Newson, E. (2001) 'Taking people seriously: psychology as a listening ear', in G.C. Bunn, A.D. Lovie and G.D. Richards (eds) *Psychology in Britain*, Leicester: BPS Books.

Newson, J., Newson, E. and Adams, M. (1993) 'The social origins of delinquency', *Criminal Behaviour and Mental Health*, 3: 19–29.

Newson, J., Newson, E. and Mahalski, P. (1982) 'Persistent infant comfort habits and their sequelae at 11 and 16 years', *Journal of Child Psychology and Psychiatry*, 23 (4): 421–36.

Ormston, R. and Curtis, J. (eds) (2015) *British Social Attitudes: the 32nd Report*, London: National Centre for Social Research.

Pearson, H. (2016) *The Life Project*, London: Allen Lane.

Registrar General General Register Office (1955) *Census, 1951, Classification of Occupations*, London: HMSO.

Spock, B. (1945) *Baby and Child Care*, New York: Simon and Schuster (republished many times).

Truby King, F. (1937) *Feeding and the Care of Baby*, London: Whitcombe and Tombs (several revisions).

Winnicott, D. (1957) *The Child and the Outside World*, London: Tavistock Publications.

Wood, H. (1970) 'Problems in the development and home care of pre-school blind children', unpublished PhD thesis, University of Nottingham.

2

CONTINUITY AND CHANGE

The 11-year-old in context

When an interviewer returns to a family after an absence of four years, inevitably her thoughts are focused on potential change. We have always tried to keep the same interviewer for any individual family over the years, and usually this has been possible: so the interviewer will have personal knowledge of the family of four years ago, and this will have been refreshed immediately before her visit by re-reading the transcript from the previous visit. Self-briefing of this kind is essential in order to know what individually-tailored follow-up questions need to be asked, but also to maintain the relationship at its peak. The interviewer will set off to see the family, then, with a genuine sense of anticipation and interest to discover what has happened since her last visit, how the child has developed, whether and how problems of last time have been resolved and what new issues now preoccupy the family. Implicit in a person's interest in change must be their assumption of some kind of continuous relationship between themselves and their respondent; and the fact that interviewer and respondent seem effortlessly to take up the dialogue where they left off four years previously is a phenomenon which initially astonished us (though we had consciously worked to make it possible), and which we now regard as a major strength of this kind of interviewing method.[1]

Sometimes there will in fact be immediately noticeable changes in the circumstances in which the family lives. They may have moved house, and this in itself may be significant both as a pointer to how the family has been prospering in material terms, and as having implications for child-rearing in terms of the pressure and potentialities of the new dwelling and its neighbourhood. Is there now a garden, or more room for the children's indoor play? Are the neighbours more tolerant, or less? Are the local schools depressed or attractive (and was this a factor in the decision to move)? Do the children and young people in the street represent a peer group that the mother can feel happy about, or will she find herself caught up in a losing battle against their influence on her children? Sometimes changes will be seen, not in an actual move, but in what is essentially a 'new house' in terms of structural improvements, re-decorating and so on; or change may consist mainly in unchecked decay. In a council house, radical alterations such as wall cladding, a re-built fireplace and chimney breast, or a 'picture window' usually denote a shift from council tenancy to home ownership; and this undoubtedly carries certain implications about the stability of family circumstances, even if it will take 30 years to pay off the mortgage. Here changes have taken place in status and comfort within the old neighbourhood, rather than in the neighbourhood potential itself; but of course, some neighbourhoods have themselves changed in terms of 'coming up' or 'going down', a factor for change which individual families both contribute to and are consciously influenced by.

It may be, too, that an apparent continuity does in fact denote a change in family fortunes or family expectations to anyone knowing their history. It would be difficult to empathise with the hopelessness of a woman's depressed acceptance of the conditions under which she still lives, if one had not heard her evaluation of them in earlier years: 'I can't wait to get out of this house – it's no place to bring up a baby'; 'This area's really rough – you can't keep your kids nice – we're moving out as soon as we can.'

Major changes in circumstances may be in the form of family structure: new babies may have been born, older siblings may have left, or brought an illegitimate baby into the home; where grown siblings have not left, the structure is still changed in terms of the ratio of adults to children. 13% of our families have a sibling over 18 living at home, and 2% a grandparent, and there are no significant social class differences here. One parent may have died or there may have been a separation or divorce between the parents. With the loss of a mother, we have tried to interview the person currently best informed about and having charge of the child, who might be the father, a grown-up sister, a stepmother, or in one case the mother and stepmother in conjunction. Clearly the effect on the child of changes such as these will vary both in degree of loss or gain, and in terms of what history led up to the new condition. Taking children whose fathers have moved out, we find contrasts such as this:

Barmaid, husband a driver:
She's more confident. She's more open, she's not nervous and withdrawn as she was when he was here. There's been a definite change.

Not in paid work, husband a casual labourer:
Well, she's very, very quiet – whether it's with being separated from her Daddy or not I don't know, but she's all Sunday school. She loves the church. She goes to Sunshine Corner on a Tuesday and Sunday school Sunday afternoon. [And this is a change since the separation?] Yes. She wasn't quiet before.

4% of our sample families (all intact when the child was a year old) had suffered separation or divorce by the time the children were 11, rising from 3% throughout the middle class and 4% among skilled and semi-skilled families, to 13% in Class V:

TABLE 2.1 Mothers at work

Age of focus child	Not working	Gainfully employed at home	Part-time outside home	Full-time outside home
	%	%	%	%
7 years	55	6	34	5
11 years	37	4	47	12

Note: For explanation of table conventions, see Appendix 2.

this amounts to a class trend which is significant at 0.01 although middle class and working class as such do not differ significantly.

Other changes affecting the child are brought about by adult occupation: some fathers will have exchanged or lost their job, some will have retired whether through age or disability, and a few are or have been in prison. More important in terms of numbers, mothers are more likely to have jobs of their own when the sample child is 11 than they were at 7. Table 2.1 compares mothers at work at the two age-stages (see also p. 172).

A further change may be in terms of a significant event occurring to the child himself. One such event is the movement on from primary into secondary education, a 'rite of passage' which in a few cases has already happened and in the rest is imminently anticipated.

Another event is, in girls, the onset of menstruation, marking for themselves and others the approach of adulthood. Those 'others' to whom this significant event is made public are limited in this society, and even boy siblings may deliberately be kept in ignorance of their sister's new status (see Tanner, 1978, p. 43). Boys themselves, on the other hand, have no physical happening comparable to first menstruation by which to *mark* the onset of puberty: it is of *psychological* significance that, as Tanner (1978) points out, first ejaculation is almost impossible to date. 6% of the girls in the sample had already menstruated at the time of the interview, rising to 11% in Class I and II and falling to zero in Class V: this apparent class trend is not significant, however, since the percentages in the intermediate social classes do not fall into line.

For a few children, illness has been a significant event in their lives. 11% have spent up to week in hospital since they were 7, and 6% longer than that. Class and sex differences are not significant here; sex differences would have been present a few years earlier as a result of treatment for undescended testicles in boys, but the policy in Nottingham now is to 'catch' these cases before 7, and in fact not one child in the sample had this treatment between 7 and 11, though one had been circumcised. It is perhaps surprising that head injuries, more frequent in boys, do not create a difference, but the incidence is small in terms of the whole population. We have one girl so seriously impaired as a result of a head injury in a traffic accident that our questions are no longer relevant to her, and a boy only slightly less damaged. The proneness of boys to accident does show up in the proportions of children who have suffered an accident since they were 7 which needed outpatient treatment: 28% overall, falling to 21% in girls and rising to 35% for boys (significant at 0.001). One mother had difficulty in enumerating her son's visits to 'casualty':

> **Outworker, husband a window cleaner:**
> He had a very bad sprain so we thought he'd broken his ankle, and he's had two or three injections for dog bites … he's always unlucky. Now what else has there been? Was his broken arm after you came? Then he had stitches in his head, he fell off running along that little wall near the public house and he had stitches. Oh dear … I can't think what else he's done *this* holiday, I know we've been three times, I'm sure we have.

14% have suffered from 'medical difficulties' since the age of 7, these being defined in terms of the question 'Has he had any medical difficulties – asthma, diabetes, anything of that sort?'[2] The effects of such difficulties range from restriction of activities, through repeated pain and discomfort and frequent school absence, to serious if not permanent consequences for the child's personality; no children had died between 7 and 11. Some examples of the consequences of illness for children and their families are given below.

> **Teacher, husband a doctor:**
> I think naturally he would be an outdoor child; but because of this asthma, which is caused by grass in the summer and by mould in the winter, he often has to stay indoors.

> **Not in paid work, husband a machine operator:**
> He's suffered a lot with his head in the last few years. I've had him at the doctor's no end of times. Well first they said it might be diabetes and I went to have his water tested, then they said it could be migraine and they gave him tablets. And he were examined at school a few months ago, the school doctor said his eyesight was perfect, so I don't know. It could be a nervous headache, that's what the doctor said. These last few months he's not been quite so bad. But at one time he had two or three days off most weeks, off school – laying on there all day with his head. He's always suffered with his head, from being quite young.

> **Research worker, husband a lecturer:**
> The biggest worry for me is her physical illness. You wouldn't say she was a delicate child, yet things go wrong – they have done. She had this peritonitis, coming out of the blue – she gets earache – things flare up very easily – I don't know why this should be.

> **Not in paid work, husband a fitter:**
> Well, it's rather awkward [to describe her], with this illness [epilepsy] – her whole personality has changed, yet now she's going back again, she's like she

was before – so it's going to be very difficult to know. Because you'd have thought she was a different child altogether – she got very hard to handle and everything changed, her whole personality seemed to have changed, but this last six months she does seem to be going back as she was – carefree and quite happy. So whether it was the tablets or whether it was the illness or what, I've no idea.

'When they get to 11, they've got a character, a sort of personality of their own …'

It has seemed useful to preface this chapter with a brief look at the changes that may happen *to* a child between his seventh and eleventh birthdays; more significant for the developmental process as a whole are the changes which take place within the child's personality and which have to do with the kind of person he is and will be. Obviously some of these changes will be subject to environmental influence, especially in terms of social relationships; yet it is reasonable for both psychologists and mothers to regard them as 'part of growing up' in a rather different sense from the 'acts of fate' which, with the exception of the onset of menstruation, characterise the factors and events which we have so far discussed.

However, it is a truism of development that any consideration of how children actually change as they grow up is confused and complicated by the fact that different things will be expected of a child *just because* he is getting older. As research workers we may decide to ask the same questions in the same words as we did when the child was 4 or 7; but even if we do so, the implications of our question will not be the same as they were earlier, and indeed the same form of words in the mother's reply may well take on a different overtone of meaning.

This is obvious for topics involving milestones and skills, where such questions as 'Does he ever wet his bed nowadays?' or 'How well can he read?', together with the possible answers to these questions, have very different connotations at different ages in terms of the child's development and the parent's anxiety. But it is almost equally true of questions about the child's activities, and of those less specific questions which explore the child's temperament and personality. For instance, 'Could he earn extra money if he wanted to?' raises somewhat different issues according to the actual competence of the child to give good value for his wages. 'Are you happy about his friendships?', another question asked at both 7 and 11, opens up the topics of sexual activity or delinquency or both for some parents, where a child who is both approaching puberty and ranging further afield is concerned; these hardly arose at 7. Again, descriptive words from parents such as 'responsible', 'generous – matured', 'very deep', 'too sensitive' or 'nasty-tempered' carry a more permanent significance as a judgement of personality when used of a child more mature in years, than when describing a child barely out of the 'infants', and they are accompanied by a correspondingly more urgent sense of satisfaction or anxiety. This will be reflected when we come to consider parents' thoughts on matters of discipline.

We asked mothers to address themselves directly to the question of change in the child, before asking them a series of very similar, sometimes identical questions to those we had asked at 7, probing aspects of the child's temperament as such which we would later be putting into the context of activities and attitudes. The major question was:

1. I'd like to start off by asking you about what N is like now as a person; and some of the questions will be the same as last time, because we're interested in how much children change over the years, and how far they stay the same. Would you say that N has changed a lot since he was 7?

This was followed by 14 'temperament' questions, compared with 10 at 7; their wording can be found in Appendix 1 (questions 2–15). The seven 'temperament' questions which are most closely comparable to those asked at 7 years give us a means of checking whether a mother's overall judgement about change is substantiated by actual shifts of rating in individual areas between 7 and 11 years (see pp. 39–42).

Table 2.2 shows mothers who think their children have changed 'a lot', and those who think there has been no change. The residual group (to 100%) are those who think the child has changed only somewhat. 30% think there has been a lot of change, the same proportion 'some', and 40% detect no real change. However, there are minor class differences indicating that more children are perceived as having changed as we move down the class scale.

Among the mothers whose children had not changed, there was a certain emphasis on pleasant qualities, summed up in 'a happy nature'; for some there was

TABLE 2.2 Change 'as a person' between 7 and 11 years

Changed 'a lot'	Social class					Summary		
	I&II	IIIWC	IIIMan	IV	V	I&II, IIIWC	IIIMan, IV,V	Overall population
	%	%	%	%	%	%	%	%
Boys	24	35	29	30	33	29	30	30
Girls	24	26	31	33	41	25	32	30
Both	24	31	30	31	37	27	31	30

Significance: trend ↗ ★ (p = 0.028);   m.class/w.class n.s.

'No change'								
Boys	52	42	40	41	39	47	40	42
Girls	41	49	33	42	35	45	35	37
Both	46	46	36	41	37	46	37	40

Significance: n.s. (p = 0.08);   m.class/w.class ★

Note: n.s. = not significant.

the explicit corollary that this included a lack of sophistication, an unspoiled quality which included very little maturity in terms of the social facts of life.

Not in paid work, husband a clerical supervisor:
[Would you say that Chrissie has changed a lot since she was 7?] Not really. She's really a most delightful child – course, all my children are in my eyes! But she's got a happy nature, she's always singing. She sings through mealtimes sometimes, we have to tell her it's rude to sing over meals. What else can I say about her? She's very generous. If she's got sweets, she'll give them out to everybody.

Training as a teacher, husband a development engineer:
Not a lot – for this reason, she's a guileless child. If a friend said 'If you don't do such-and-such a thing I won't be your friend', she couldn't really understand it – a friend is a friend for life ... She's rather late learning the lesson; it's hard to explain to a child, you know, that you must play them at their own game – it's very difficult to explain.

A rather different aspect of 'no change' was seen in the consolidation of earlier traits. Mothers were aware of characteristics which had been present in immature or non-dominant form at 7 now having become more firmly established as a major feature in the child's personality – to their gratification or dismay. Problems seen as 'just a passing phase' at 4 or at 7 now had to be recognised as long-term difficulties; the 'high-spirited' little boy who was 'a bit of a lad' at 7 could be 'driving everyone hairless' with real anxiety by the time he was 11: to quote one white-collar mother, 'He's just got a lot worse. He's a shocker – he really is a shocker. He's a torment' (her long-term perspective is indicated by her rejoinder to the final question, 'What do you think he'll be like as a husband?' – 'God help *her*', she said).

The quotations that follow can all be summed up in another mother's words, 'Whatever she had then she's got more of now.' They illustrate vividly the point made earlier, that behaviour and attributes of children inevitably vary in their perceived meaning and significance both according to the age of the child and according to their persistence over time. It is of course possible that research such as this, which deliberately asks mothers to make explicit their children's personality traits on successive occasions, increases their awareness of persistence or transience: with what consequences we cannot at this stage judge.

Secretarial teacher, husband an insurance inspector:
Well, he's always been a sensitive child, and he's still sensitive, he may well be a little more sensitive ... He's sensitive to criticism, he always thinks that ... [long example about relationship with siblings]. We've found that he *is* sensitive, and it's particularly that he doesn't like being *told* ... anything really, he takes this to heart very much. So he was like this always, and I think he's probably more so now than he was then. He is shy, still fairly shy.

Machinist, husband a cook:

She's bossy. She's bossy with Harry [sibling], she's *very* bossy with him. [She was a little bit bossy when she was 7, wasn't she — with the children outside?] Well she's *very* bossy with him. She's a very domesticated child. [I remember she was miles ahead of most children in knitting and things like that, wasn't she?] Yes, well she's *really* domesticated, and of course Harry, he's idle, and now and again if she gets a mood on her, 'he should do this and he should do that', you know, and she gets rather annoyed and if I'm not watching her she'll give him one! Actually I think she takes after me as regards that, because I can remember I was a bit that way inclined — I was always domesticated and always liked to be busy round the house, and all of a sudden you get a mood on you, 'I have to do it all' — 'I do it *all* here'. I think something like that must go round in her head, because she says 'He never does anything'. But she loves doing it, I mean I've never told her, forced her to do anything.

Not in paid work, husband a teacher:

Her personality, no, because I think the personality's formed very young and this is obviously carried through, and I mean it's still outstanding. She's a dominant child, she's very self-possessed. I mean, she doesn't lean on anyone, and this worries me a bit because she's *too* strong. I think I've probably said this before, she's too strong, she's very very powerful in herself. So really she hasn't changed, no. She never is ill, I mean if she is ill she'll put up with it. That's what I meant by her power — she's very powerful.

Teacher, husband a university lecturer:

I think she tends to be very emotional, sort of highly strung. In many ways she's still very babyish. I think her reactions are a little more violent. She's always been rather like this, but she was less likely to burst into a fit of sobs over something.

Dinner-lady, husband a crane driver:

[Shaun was described as 'headstrong' at 7.] Well, he's got more awkward to manage. He tries to make trouble all the while — oh, I don't know, I can't really make it out. You know if he misses something, *somebody* must have took it, he hasn't lost it, somebody must have taken it from him! That's just how he is, a bit more awkward.

'She's getting a more grown-up outlook but she's the same sort of child', said a mother, and another echoed this feeling that change in the sense of development is secondary to a basic personality structure: 'That's difficult because they're changing all the time, but she's always had the same sort of personality so I don't think she's changed a lot.' Veronica's mother expressed an example of subtle and appropriate change from a younger to an older child by describing her as 'less *boisterous*, but still *excitable*'. This kind of maturing process was described by a number of mothers:

Brett was said to have 'settled down – he doesn't get quite so excited now'; Danny 'used to be rather aggressive as a 7-year-old but he's mellowed in the last four years'. For some children with quite well-defined problem areas at 7, the problems continued to be easier to define than the improvement, yet improvement there was, either through 'mellowing' or through compensatory features.

Not in paid work, husband a driver:
I think he's coming more to terms with things. He's very ... what I should imagine you could call a complicated or complex personality. He's either one thing or the other, there's no in between. He's very loving and very affectionate – he's also very aggressive. He never can quite just manage to hit that moderate way of being. The house is either in a turmoil or he's a real pleasure to have around. [He used to get very easily frustrated, didn't he?] Yes. He does seem now to give in earlier, you know. He'll have an outburst but it doesn't go on, and he'll come round and say he's sorry, and you can now talk to him and get him to understand why he shouldn't do things, and that there are other people in the world. You can reason with him more now. I think that's really what ... how I've noticed he's changed – he's beginning to be able to reason things out more than he could.

Clerk, husband a clerk:
I wouldn't say he's *changed,* no. He's always been a very lazy child, but he's become more interesting because he's older. He's still a lazy individual. The laziness covers *everything* – not just single things, but he's lazy in everything. [In what ways is he more interesting?] Well, to be with and talk to. Perhaps he's interesting because *we* can talk to *him* easily and he can understand. Under 7 the conversations are almost non-existent. Now he can talk to us and we can sit round and hold conversations.

'He's more independent, more come up on himself'

Focusing now upon mothers who felt there was real change to be identified, we can distinguish a number of different themes. A major one – *the* major one – is summed up by the quotation that heads this section: a new independence of thought and action which seems to imply that the child has in some sense discovered, caught up with, 'come upon' the person he is to be. A second theme was to do with transition as such: mothers who developed this theme were those who emphasised that whatever was happening now was 'just a stage he's going through', and their perceptions were based on that assumption. A third theme, that of recovery, was naturally paramount in the minds of those who had been preoccupied at 7 with problems which had now been resolved in some way. Fourthly, the reverse of this might apply: the emergence of focal problems which had previously seemed trivial or non-existent. Fifthly, life events were seen as the source of change for some parents: secondary education or its approach, and for girls the onset of menstruation. Because the first theme dominated the discussion of change, we will illustrate the four other themes fairly briefly and then return to consider the first in more detail.

To think of a developing child as *going through stages* has functional usefulness for a parent: it means that change can be anticipated and accommodated to, and it offers reassurance that the bad times are transient. Perhaps this is the reason that almost all the parents who emphasised the concept of 'stage' did so against a background of a 'bad time'.

> **Part-time barmaid, husband a jointer:**
> Her personality's changing at the moment, she's changing to be very moody; but that's just her age, it's a stage I've been through with the boys. Theirs came later in life, but hers is at the moment.

> **Part-time packer, husband a joiner:**
> Yes, she's changed – she's getting older – up to this teen-age what people's always on about. I can see this – you know, sometimes she acts up and sometimes she gets a bit uppity and you've got to slap her down, you know what I mean? I find it anyway – she's probably just asserting herself a bit and I feel as if I must keep her down a bit, whether I'm right or wrong I don't know. We're going through a new phase now. The past few months – she's growing up now.

Other children who were seen as 'going through a stage because of their age' were described as 'very arrogant', 'wanting a lot of attention', 'a bit difficult, comes and goes', 'on the cheeky side' and 'very bossy … a bit spiteful … trying to grow up too quickly'. One mother, though despondent, was at home with the experience: 'When they get to want mini-skirts and tights and that sort of thing – I thought, oh dear, we've got to start all over again – I've had it three times, I don't want it again.' Although it was fairly common for mothers to regret the passing of childhood as a whole, it was much less usual for a child to be seen as now passing through a good stage with a beginning and end to it:

> **Part-time playgroup leader, husband a manager:**
> They reach a sort of peak in the fourth year [of junior school] I think. They really blossom – they just love it. It's quite a shock when they get to secondary school because they're nobody then. [When I was here before, you said you thought 7 was a difficult age.] Did I? Oh, I think 6-year-olds are horrible, perhaps she hadn't grown out of it. I think she gets better and better – I think we've reached a sort of peak. I wonder if it's coming to an end now. I have really enjoyed her in the last couple of years – they have so many skills, for a start … they can knit, they can sew, they can crochet – she can sit down and weave a mat if she wants to, set up the loom and finish the job within a morning. And all the things like skating and riding a bike – they're really lovely. She's still like that, I don't feel I have to entertain her. Oh, it's super – I just hope it lasts a bit longer.

The theme of *recovery from earlier problems* tended to be dominant for those who had experienced them: the 'so lovely when it stops' feeling cast a glow over ordinary living for these mothers. We have already quoted mothers on children who are recovering from the effects of marital discord and from serious illness; but many whose children had been clinging and 'mummyish' over a long period were now feeling a similar sense of release.

> **Part-time launderette attendant, husband a technical manager:**
> Yes, particularly in the last 12 months he's grown up; you can sort of treat him like an adult, he doesn't want treating like a baby and he lets you know it. He had this spell where he didn't want to go to school. Since last September, we've never looked back – he's a proper boy, he is, he's into everything now, he's one of the boys – which he's *not* been, you know, he's worried me a lot. Climbing trees and all that sort of thing – he's had this terrible fear he may fall. *Now* you can't stop him from climbing, which I'm very pleased about. He's awfully happy with himself now, and this is the main thing. He used to worry about nothing, if he got his sums wrong he used to come home crying, because he's a child like this, he must do well. It looks as if it's me that's pushing him, when in actual fact it's him. I tell him he can only do his best, and it isn't the end of the world, we all make mistakes – but none of those problems at the moment are there, he seems to take school work in his stride. He was very highly strung with himself, you know, he was in a terrible state. Oh, it's really marvellous, to me it is, I mean. [Quotation reduced to 25% of original length.]

Micky, who at 7 had appeared to be an incorrigible wanderer (his mother had already involved the police in her efforts to control him), was at 11 still wandering; but now he would at least say to his mother 'I'll not be home till such-and-such a time, so don't worry', which thoughtful attention made her feel he had 'learnt a bit of sense that way'.

The *new problems* which were mentioned in response to the question 'Would you say he has changed a lot since he was 7?' were also those which could be expected to colour the whole of the mother's dealings with the child. One boy had 'gone very quiet – very deep' and it was difficult to get through to him or to discover what was troubling him; another had become 'very emotional these last couple of years'; another seemed 'self-sufficient' in a worrying way, and his mother felt that this was a front put on to hide his nervous tension, since he was inclined to suffer from vomiting under stress.

The two girls described here by their mothers were experiencing and causing a great deal of anxiety. One mother said how she did not know whether the anxiety was linked to moving house or because of starting at a new school. 'Since she's been to this school, she's built up a resentment. She never cried like the other two – you know how they cry [when they start a new school] – well, they cried and got over it, but Jessie never cried, she just *looked* at me and walked in. The look was enough to tell me how she felt … She's very quiet, she doesn't like the limelight very much, Jessie doesn't, and she wears glasses — she's very conscious.' The other mother described how it was horrible. 'Oh, I don't know, this last year she's gone moody, and sometimes she isn't a very nice person altogether. Then sometimes she's very nasty-tempered — oh, I can't understand her really, to be quite honest, I give up. I've noticed in the last year since we came up here [to council estate].'

It is perhaps natural to look for *life events* on which to peg significant changes in personality, but the two mothers above, while wondering about this, are tentative in sorting out cause and effect. Some mothers are more firmly focused on puberty or school as accounting for their children's behaviour, or as the major change in their view of the child. For instance, Marcia's mother said that Marcia had changed a great deal: 'Oh, yes, she's a young woman now — yes, she's developed — she's got a lovely figure.' Another mother gave the fact that 'she's developed now, you see — this is the third month of her periods' as the reason for 'a little bit of spitefulness now and again — *that* you've got to allow for'. Madeleine's mother felt she had *not* changed, and attributed this to a delayed puberty.

> **Teacher, husband a teacher:**
> No, I think it's going to be in the next ... I think all this changing goes with development physically as well, and she's a slower developer than the other one was. I think if you get a girl, say, that started her periods at 11, they are more trying and very different in other ways. I think they're not so loving to us — their parents — as they were before. At the moment Madeleine is still very much attached to us, whereas I think if they develop a bit earlier they break away earlier.

One would not of course wish to underestimate the effect on the child's self-image of a change in her own appearance; and having 'a lovely figure', and one which is appreciated within the family, could well change a child's outlook on life generally. This effect is suggested also in the description of a boy newly started at secondary school.

> **Caretaker, husband a paint sprayer:**
> He seems to have grown up a whole year in two months, somehow. People used to tell me, 'Oh, he'll be different when he goes to the big school' — I couldn't realise this, but oh now — oh — I wouldn't have realised — he's like a little gentleman in some ways, you know in long trousers, all this you know — and he's quite pleased with himself in general, you know, Angus is. He loves the school.

Betty has surprised her mother (in view of her earlier couldn't-care-less attitude) by becoming 'a real young lady' for whom 'everything's got to be just so before she goes out, sort of thing — shoes cleaned and does her hair look all right' — and this too is ascribed to moving into secondary education. For this group of mothers, secondary school is very much thought of as 'bringing them out'.

'I prefer her to have her own mind, even though she argues'

Let us return now to the development which seemed to characterise the majority of the 60% of children whose parents thought their personalities had changed, whether a lot or a little: the development of independence of mind and spirit – what one mother described as 'he's his own gaffer', that is, his own boss.

By the age of 11, even mothers who have been reluctant to concede that their children have distinct personalities in their own right are forced into that recognition. As children grow older, parents are less and less able to exert control over their doings; and this is true not only in matters of 'good' and 'bad' behaviour, but also in terms of children's attitudes and preferences. Often it is in these areas that parents first become aware of the child as his own person, when they realise that he is now exerting a right to think for himself: choosing (or demanding) what to wear and in what manner to wear it, giving away some personal possession to a friend, or deciding to abandon one leisure interest in which his parents may have invested time and money, in favour of another. In some of his attitudes, the child will now be influenced by other people outside the family – teachers, peers, the parents of peers and other relatives; and whereas at 7 parents could afford to be wryly amused at the teacher's charisma for the child ('Everything she says is gospel, it's sickening!'), at 11 they have to accept a certain *right to be influenced* simply because they know that the child is also more capable of exerting a critical appraisal. The argument that the child is too young to know his own mind becomes progressively less tenable.

Parents also have to come to terms with the fact that in the world outside the family their children are able to operate relatively independently as people in their own right. As they always have, children may sometimes behave creditably and sometimes less so, but now their actions are vested with more serious interpersonal significance: they are no longer good or naughty children, but people, who may behave thoughtfully or discourteously or unkindly to other people. Their deference or dismissiveness towards the needs of others are now more than the results of training in politeness: they are perceived as a quality in the child's own personality, transcending mere learned habit. Indeed, parents know that the child has now had many chances to measure the effects of his actions on others beyond the family, and that he must now be more self-conscious of the extent of his powers socially. They are also aware that how he presents to the outside world is separate from, and in some ways different from, the way he is within his own family: 78% of mothers, having described their own view of the child's best points, think that an outsider would name a different 'best quality'.

Part-time shop assistant, husband a decorator:
An outsider would say 'What a nice little girl!' you know the sort of thing. If any of her brothers were asked, they'd give a different opinion altogether – 'horrible little spoilt pig', probably! You see, I think everybody's different, and I've been out with her when people have said 'Is that your little girl? What a

dear little girl!' Mind you, I don't think she's a dear little girl, not really. I mean I love her, cause she's mine, but you know they can be a trial.

Part-time worker in her husband's haulage business:
I don't think outsiders see the best of Cliff, because he's always the one that seems as though he's in trouble outside, you know – he's the one ... you know, he doesn't show his best side outside; because some people used to say – there was a person at the shop up the street, and she used to say '*Jamie's* such a *nice* boy, and Cliff seems to – you know – he couldn't care less.' So I don't think people outside really know him as he is. Course I'm perhaps prejudiced, I don't know.

There is more to this than the question of whether the child is 'behaving himself' in public places. The fact that children form independent relationships with their teachers is hardly surprising, but it can come as a shock to mothers to find that a child is carrying conviction as a person with other adults. Anne's mother has always been notable for her respect for Anne as someone to be reckoned with, yet she is still taken aback to find Anne taking the initiative in checking out her sister-in-law-to-be. Sean's mother, is 'shattered' by Sean offering condolences on his own account: first to his father with empathy for *his father's* lost relationship, then to a neighbour.

Part-time cleaner, husband a packer:
In some things Anne's very juvenile; in her attitude towards teddy-bears it's, oh, infantile! But then she drops out something that really sets you back on your heels, you know. She picked on Mandy, the girl that's marrying Dave. She said to her one day, 'Will you learn to cook when you're married, Mandy?' So Mandy looked a bit, er, you know, didn't know quite how to ... she says, 'I mean real cooking, not this packet business that you're always doing'. Not the most tactful thing to say to your brother's young lady, is it?

Comptometer operator, husband an administrative assistant:
[Father:] He was upset at my mother's death ... [Mother:] But the thing is, Sean came to my husband and said 'I'm sorry *your mum's* died.' A child of 11 – that really shattered me more than anything. That was his automatic reaction, 'I'm sorry *your mum's* died' .... A friend of mine, her father died before Christmas, and I went up to see her, and as we were coming out of the house, he said 'I'm sorry your daddy died, but you know he'll be perfectly happy with Jesus.' My friend couldn't speak for a few minutes – it knocked the wind out of her sails.

These mothers have witnessed their children showing this kind of social initiative, but parents also know that most of their children's social life outside the family goes on when they are not present. This in itself affords the child a degree of self-determination and privacy which it is in his own control to protect if he wishes. Obviously parents may pressurise children to tell what they do not want to tell, but the child himself at 11 is both more conscious of his right to keep certain things private and more skilled at doing so by one tactic or another. This is one reason why the 'deep' children are so worrying to their parents: they know that if total reserve is accompanied by 11-year-old determination, it will be beyond adult capability to penetrate, and that this will leave them incapable of monitoring the child's development.

Not in paid work, husband an engineer:
There's a lot I can't understand in Shona at all. She's very, very deep. And sometimes it frightens me, you know, because sometimes I think, will she be that deep that she could go the wrong way, do you know what I mean?

Not in paid work, ex-husband a dealer:
I started letting him go and see his father on a Saturday dinner-time, he's been going on about it for the past four weeks, so I thought he was old enough now, so I'll not stop him seeing his dad. [What effect did it have on him, seeing his father?] Well, when he comes back I said 'Did your dad say anything?' Turns round and tells me to mind my own business, nothing to do with me what his dad said. 'Oh – sorry I spoke!'

Perhaps another indication of a subtle change in the relationship, in terms of the mother regarding the child as approaching some maturity and permanence of personality structure, is the increased frequency with which mothers compare their children with themselves. Whether that is a source of satisfaction or regret, the fact that they do this seems to imply that the child is now seen as having his own distinct personality which thus invites comparison with that of the parent. Sian's mother, explaining Sian's negativism, says 'She's very much like me in her ways, and we clash'; Marcia's mother, expressing her pleasure in Marcia's self-confidence, says that 'she's got all the push I wish *I'd* got'.

Having 'a mind of his own' also implies that, if an 11-year-old criticises his parent, it is no longer so easy simply to dismiss his judgement as irrational and childish: there is always the possibility that he might just be being objective – or, indeed, reflecting the judgements of other people outside the family circle. And what might once have been seen as a naive comment which accidentally touched on a raw nerve will now be seen as having some knowingness and intentionality behind it.

How, then, do parents react to the evidence their children give them that they are becoming more independent and more detached from parental lines of control? On the whole it was clear that they welcomed, at least in principle, the notion that their children were becoming 'persons'. They appreciated that children needed to be able to question parental authority if they were not to become mere putty in the hands of adults generally, and for this reason they were, often secretly, proud to see their children asserting themselves by resisting adult pressure and beginning to hold their own in an argument. They liked to see in them a certain amount of determination, even 'stubbornness', as a sign that in later life they would not be too easily dominated or pushed about for the convenience of other people; automatic compliance was no longer a goal, even for parents with more authoritarian principles.

Obviously there is in practice a thin dividing line between strength of character and 'bloody-mindedness', between independence and rebellion, between having definite opinions and being cheeky or insolent, between being self-confident or merely selfish. Nonetheless, parents are by no means displeased at being forced to treat their 11-year-olds with more circumspection. When they were asked (Q. 3), 'Is he the sort of child who usually agrees with what you want him to do, or does he tend to object to things quite a lot?', the point was frequently made that this would depend on parents' own tact: that children of this age respond to being *asked* but object to being *told*. This was not seen as unreasonable: rather, it was taken positively as a sign of growing-up, and of the child's need to be respected for his own integrity. On the whole parents saw this as a necessary part of 'learning to stand on your own two feet' in the world beyond childhood. For all these reasons, there was a greater degree of tolerance of non-cooperation, argumentativeness and non-compliance than previously; and the tolerance had a different quality to it in that, where before it had been the indulgence of a fond parent towards a funny little child pretending to be grown-up, now (except in the last-ditch stands) there was more often the feeling of a negotiation with someone of acknowledged and accepted strengths.

Part-time waitress, husband a driver:

Yes, I think he has [changed]. He's got more of a mind of his own that what he used to have. When he was younger, you'd tell him to do something and he'd do it. Now he'll question it. I'm glad really, because you know he's standing up for himself a bit more.

Part-time factory hand, husband a miner:

Yes, I would say so. He was very quiet as a small child, but now he's cheeky – you know how they are – sort of standing up for himself; he was more the other way before, you know, very retiring.

Not in paid work, her husband a social worker:

She's obviously growing up now, yes. Otherwise she hasn't changed, not really. Just a little bit more authoritative and – you know – she was easy to deal with before, whereas now you get a little bit of backchat, which is of course normal, isn't it?

Not in paid work, husband a postman:

He … how can I put it? If you tell him not to do something, if he feels he's *going* to do it, he'll do it openly. Irrespective of whether he's going to be punished for it, he'll do it open and above-board – he's not sly.

Machinist, husband a truck driver:

Oh, not half! She answers back, which she never used to do, she lets everybody know she's grown-up!

There are a few mothers who think that this is all happening a bit too early (though their way of putting it seems to imply that they accept that it will happen *some* time), and of course some who find that it goes too far.

Part-time machinist, husband a milkman:
She's got a very strong will, and although it's very good in some ways, sometimes she's very hard to handle. If she gets something fixed in her mind you find it very hard to budge. Sometimes I could really let go at her, because she's only 11, and I think she shouldn't be like this at the moment.

Not in paid work, husband a joiner:
She's changed in every way. Even mentally she's changed. She was a decent girl where she was a baby. Now she's growing up, she seems to be growing away from me. She's cheeky. I don't like cheeky children. I don't want to smack her – she was my first baby, and the first baby's meant to be the one that clings. I tell you, she's changed such a lot. She was ever such a quiet, respectable girl, and in the Infants they all liked her, but they don't like her at this school.

Not in paid work, husband a sales manager:
Yes, yes, he's more self-confident now – almost to the point of aggression, which isn't a very pleasant trait.

'At one time, she'd have shuddered into the background ...'

We have already pointed out that most of the issues of socialisation will vary in perceived significance according to the age of the child. One aspect of this can be seen in changing emphases on the positive and the negative in the child's development. At 7, much emphasis was placed upon issues of control – how to prevent the child doing things which were not acceptable – and parents were often worried lest they be judged inadequate in their ability to exert such control. At 11, they fear that their children will seem inadequate in terms of positive qualities expected of this age, and the term 'self-confidence' covers a constellation of characteristics seen as having major importance. The child who is too diffident to stand up in public, too bashful to say anything when introduced to a strange adult, too timid to ask for what he really wants in a shop or at someone else's house, is seen to be at a big disadvantage; in contrast, social poise and self-assurance are highly valued.

Not in paid work, husband a labourer:
Yes, well I'll give you an incident. She used to go to pictures *every* Saturday morning, and there was a competition on Prince Charles. Well they had to collect a lot of pictures and the person that got the most got a prize. Well all that week she cut them all out, and she went to pictures on Saturday morning. She wouldn't go and hand it in! She give it to her brother to hand it in, and he won a book and all the new stamps that came out that week. But

he had to collect the prize because it had got his name because she wouldn't hand it in herself. She can be a bit shy of things like that.

Not in paid work, husband a clerk:
This is one thing about him that, you know, does worry me a bit. He doesn't seem to have any confidence when he's talking to grown-ups. You can't get anything out of him at school. He's so quiet. The only person I ever saw him talk to really, and I was amazed – when I went to the Scout place, one of the scout leaders, in his twenties – he stood there chatting away as though he was talking to his brother, and it amazed me really, because as a rule, he's talking, but he's looking at the floor, he won't look you in the face.

Not in paid work, husband a supervisor:
I'd like him to have more confidence in himself and to speak up more. With him not being so interested in talking, he's not so interesting for you to listen to either. If we have company, he can sit there two or three hours and just sit there. I say, you know, 'Go and get your toys out and play – or a book'; but, 'Oh, it's all right', he says. So I'm presuming he's listening and interested – but that's as far as it goes.

Not in paid work, husband a sprayer:
[Father:] He'd sooner really go [to the doctor] on his own than his mother go with him. Right, well a week last Monday, wasn't it, I had to go to the doctor myself, and Jack had a little bald patch grown on his head, and course I took him down to the doctor's. And he explained to *him* himself, like, how long he'd had it and how the kids at school were calling him Baldy, that kind of thing. But, you know, *he* spoke to the doctor, as well as I could have done. [Mother:] He could have gone by himself.

Three different aspects of self-confidence can be discerned in the examples that parents discuss. Firstly, there is the question of moving with confidence in an adult world, and coping with new experiences that involve contact with adults outside the immediate family and classroom. Secondly, there is the kind of confidence that allows the child to relate successfully with his peer group – and this at once raises questions of whether the child is a 'natural leader' or 'easily led', whether he can cope with attempts to tease or bully him or perhaps is inclined to be a tease or a bully himself, and whether he fits easily and flexibly into group situations or is 'a bit of a loner'. Finally, confidence often seems relevant to parents in evaluating how the child is doing, or is likely to do, academically: they are often concerned that the child is not doing himself justice at school because of his diffidence, and they may be especially anxious that the child may fail some important test (mainly, for these children at that time, the '11+' selection procedure for secondary education), on account of a tendency to withdraw or panic under pressure. Failure or success in the 11+ (which its advocates would not have described in those terms, but which were certainly seen as such by parents, children and indeed teachers) in themselves exerted an effect on the self-confidence of many of those children whose results were known at the time of our interview, in one direction or the other.

Possibly the most testing moment for a child's self-confidence comes when he has to cope with a situation which is new to him, and this was referred to directly in Q. 5: Would you say he's a self-confident person, or is he a little bit timid about doing things he isn't used to? 49% overall were judged 'self-confident', 36% were said to be 'timid' and 15% varied. These results show that, despite detailed answers with examples that show variability and situational exceptions to a greater extent than 15%, the children do tend to polarise in terms of being identified as 'generally self-confident' or 'generally timid' by their mothers.

While Question 5 takes the direct approach, it might be equally useful to devise an index which draws on a number of different questions which have in common the element of self-confidence. Our attempts at this were not entirely successful, however. The 'index of self-confidence' was derived from the answers to 15 questions, six of which were specifically concerned with self-confidence in relation to adults, and six in relation to the child's peer group, so that these could be looked at separately and also correlated. One problem was that self-confidence implies the ability to 'keep one's end up' in the course of *relationships* with others. The way in which our questions were phrased (e.g. 'Does he get anxious about whether he's doing exactly what's expected of him, or doesn't he care what grown-ups think?') confused ease of relationship with don't-care attitudes or non-relationships. Our own lack of confidence in this measure persuades us not to present it in detail here. It is worth noting, however, that when mothers rate their children for self-confidence in the non-specific sense posed by Questions 5, 6 and 95, they are thinking more about situations with adults than with children, as shown by a closer correlation between the overall index and the adult-specific sub-index. There is a symmetrical and unimodal distribution between the lowest and highest scores on the overall index. Social class differences are low, but boys are more inclined to be self-confident with peers, while girls are more so with adults.

Because self-confidence is mainly brought to the test in the child's contacts with people outside the family, parents are generally baffled about how to 'teach' it to their children. It is clear from the transcripts that many parents feel peculiarly powerless in their efforts to develop self-confidence in children who lack it. One problem is that, however supportive of the child's independence of spirit the parents may be, they know that the child is now coming under the influence of other fairly long-term relationships; he may be finding himself in the shadow of another sibling (who cannot be discouraged or got rid of!), or repeatedly brought down in self-esteem by a 'best friend' (who can be discouraged only with difficulty), or debilitated by an insensitive teacher (which may cause enormous dilemmas for parents wishing to back up the school positively). Equally, of course, parents know that the right outside relationship at the right time may improve the child's confidence in a way that they are incapable of doing themselves, but feel they have no way of ensuring that such a relationship is available to the child.

Another difficulty for parents is that, although some children have a very general lack of confidence, so that parents can accept that an all-round boosting of their self-esteem is necessary, others show a lack of confidence away from their family which they do not show at home. These parents are at a loss to know how to help a child whose reported behaviour elsewhere is at variance with that of the child they know. For instance, Mr Hargreaves, a van salesman, was perturbed that Don's teacher had told them at open night that Don 'lacked confidence in himself'. Don's father went on: 'Everybody says Don's always got a smile for everybody. He speaks to people, he'll *put himself out* to speak to people. You know, to people that he don't really know. That's why I can't understand people who say he's no confidence – to me that is *all* confidence. If you had no confidence, you wouldn't talk to anyone.' Many children lack confidence under certain conditions: Anne is 'very apprehensive' in case she does things wrong in public, but will 'do remarkable things' by way of rising to an occasion if she doesn't know beforehand that it's going to happen; Roger 'came home in hysterics' when asked to play to the school the violin piece on which he had passed his music exam – his mother said that 'some things you think, oh, Roger'll carry that off with confidence, and then he doesn't. You can't put your finger on Roger at all really.'

Although parents whose children lack confidence are usually prepared to try to help them towards it, and report various attempts at doing so, it is notable that those whose children *are* confident, or confident in certain situations, do not seem to take credit for this happy state of affairs: there is the feeling that for some children self-confidence 'comes naturally'. Conversely, parents trying to bolster their children's confidence often find that anything more than the mildest encouragement is counter-productive, particularly where they themselves are working at a distance from the situation and with only second-hand knowledge of it. Self-confidence is most likely to grow from the experience of social success, and much as parents explicitly wish for and try to manufacture such experience for the child, it may be beyond their power to do so in any substantial way and in 'real' situations. In the end, perhaps, the child must dare to stand on his own feet socially, free from the parental intervention which negates his success; and, realising this, parents tend to find themselves reduced to watching and waiting – often with considerable trepidation – while their child meets new challenges. Indeed, the situation often develops in such a way that any help parents might be tempted to give at the time would only be likely to embarrass the child further. Like learning to ride a bicycle or to swim, the child can only prove himself to be self-supporting to the extent that the parent dares to let go completely.

Often, to start with, the learning of self-confidence is a matter of putting on a would-be convincing act and hoping that the feelings inside will catch up with appearances. At this point it may be only the parents who appreciate, from their intimate knowledge of him, just what the child is going *through*. Certainly mothers who distinguished between the outside show and the inside turmoil were common among the 15% whose children were neither timid nor wholly self-confident in new situations (Q. 5), summed up by Patsy's mother (Class II): 'She's frightened underneath, but she puts on a very good face, I'm glad to say. She's shy of facing new situations, but she'll make a *big* effort – doesn't let people see.' For these children especially, it may well be that it is the people who know them less intimately (and for whom they therefore feel the need to put on an act) who are best placed to help – perhaps by offering encouragement and appreciation at the right moment, or even by making demands which compel the child to rise to the occasion and succeed despite himself.

'I can't really say, but I know she's changed in herself ...'

We can now return to the question of change as such, and ask how far the 60% view that the children have changed since they were 7 can be substantiated in terms of shifts of rating on questions concerning temperament between 7 years and 11 years. For this we can use the answers to questions 2, 3, 4, 6, 13 and 14, which are all matched by identical or almost identical questions at 7, the only change at 11 being where the wording had proved slightly ambiguous at 7 and needed prompting in terms of the wording now used. We may also compare the present Q. 5, which at 7 was worded in a more substantially different way, but which is still comparable with the earlier version.

The questions at 11 are as follows:

2. Is he a calm, placid sort of child, or do you think he's a bit highly strung?
3. Is he the sort of child who usually agrees with what you want him to do, or does he tend to object to things quite a lot?
4. Do you find him easy to manage now he's 11, or is he a bit touchy – do you have to *feel* your way with him?
5. Would you say he's a self-confident person, or is he a little bit timid about doing things he isn't used to?
   (At 7: How does he manage in new situations – does he enjoy them, or is he bothered by what he isn't used to?)
6. In general, does he take things as they come, or is he a bit of a worrier?
13. Would you call him an indoor child or an outdoor child?
14. When he has to amuse himself, is he a busy sort of person, or does he easily get bored?

Each answer was rated on a three-point scale at each age, using the two alternatives posed in the question as the outside points and the category 'varies' as the middle point. Here we are only concerned with frequency and degree of change. Obviously a shift of one point is not of great interest, denoting as it does a movement from 'varies' to one definite identification or the other, or from a firm identification to a 'varies'. The question is whether mothers' assertions that the child has substantially changed are backed up by detailed reference to specific characteristics.

Table 2.3 shows those children who on individual scales have changed by two points: that is, who were earlier firmly identified by one characteristic and are now identified by its opposite. Clearly the possibility of scoring a two-step change at all is limited by having been perceived as firmly in one category at the earlier stage: that is to say, a child might have made a commensurate leap from 'varies' to a particularly marked degree of one or other characteristic, but he would not be capable of scoring within the limitations of this measure. The first percentage given refers to children changing in each direction as a proportion to the 'starters' for that category, as it were; the second refers to the 'changed' children on each scale as a proportion of the total population of 700. It is important to understand that although the changed children may be numerous in relation to the number of starters, they may be of much less importance in relation to the population as a whole. For instance, although 50% of former 'indoor children' have changed into 'outdoor children' compared with only 16% of former outdoor children into indoor children, the indoor children are in such a minority throughout that as a directional trend this is not significant; and in fact the *overall* findings, which include one-step changes, show that there are in fact more indoor children at 11 than at 7 (significant at 0.001). Similarly, the minority/majority effect is such that in fact slightly *more* children overall are rated as 'easily bored' at 11 than at 7 (significant at 0.05). On the other hand there is a significant directional change (Q. 2) towards more ex-temperamental children being rated calm and placid at 11, and this is upheld by the overall results (both significant at the 0.001 level).

Although the numbers for each scale are not very high as a proportion of the total sample, all but two falling between 10% and 20%, we have to remember that these represent *big* changes within the scope of the question asked, and are therefore likely to make a heavy impact on the mother. Furthermore, some children have changed on more than one scale. 10% have in fact shown a two-step change on three or more in the seven comparable scales, ignoring those scales which we cannot compare but which may, of course, also have involved change.

Once again we must make the caveat that parents' evaluation of particular characteristics in their children are not and cannot be absolute, but are to some extent tied to what they see as appropriate for the child at various different ages. One further way of exploring parents' perception of change, and of the developmental stage their child has reached, is actually to make use of this notion of what is appropriate and ask the parent of a child at a transitional stage to choose whether he should be identified more closely with the earlier or the later stage. In this way we can discover what are the limits to suggested change, by pushing those limits forward a little.

We asked two questions with this in mind. The first was placed among the 14 'temperament' questions which followed the opening question on change, and the second came during the last few minutes of the interview, following the long discussion on conflict:

11. In his interests and attitudes generally, would you say he's more like a child or more like a teenager?
193. Small children often seem to think their parents know everything and can't do anything wrong; and teenagers sometimes talk as if parents know nothing and can't do anything right. What stage has N got to?

These questions were certainly meaningful to the children's mothers. Question 11 was answered in terms of whether the child was 'putting away childish things', taking a new interest in appearance (which was directly asked about in the question that followed) and showing increased empathy with adult concerns. Mothers

TABLE 2.3 Children moving from one end of a three-point scale to the other between 7 and 11 years (seven scales, defined by question asked; total N = 700)

Question				at 7:			at 11	% of N
2	Of the 218 children rated	calm/placid	at	21%	were rated	highly strung/temperamental	at 11	18%
	Of the 253 " "	highly strung/temperamental	"	33%	" "	calm/placid	" "	
3	Of the 210 " "	'agreeing'	"	17%	" "	'objecting'	" "	10%
	Of the 149 " "	'objecting'	"	20%	" "	'agreeing'	" "	
4	Of the 289 " "	easy	"	21%	" "	touchy/tricky	" "	16%
	Of the 174 " "	touchy/tricky	"	28%	" "	easy	" "	
5	Of the 374 " "	confident in new situations	"	28%	" "	timid	" "	21%
	Of the 131 " "	timid	"	34%	" "	confident in new situations	" "	
6	Of the 307 " "	'takes as come'	"	18%	" "	worrier	" "	6%
	Of the 176 " "	worrier	"	26%	" "	'takes things as they come'	" "	
13	Of the 94 " "	indoor child	"	50%	" "	outdoor child	" "	14%
	Of the 334 " "	outdoor child	"	16%	" "	indoor child	" "	
14	Of the 426 " "	busy person	"	14%	" "	easily bored	" "	14%
	Of the 92 " "	easily bored	"	47%	" "	busy person	" "	

seemed quite subtly aware of the beginnings of the new phase, often dating it rather precisely, or using phrases such as 'just on the turn' or 'on the boundary'. Some distinguished between *intellectual* maturity and the more self-conscious change that seemed to characterise becoming 'like a teenager', often using the phrase 'more like a child but not childish'; as Madeleine's mother added, 'She's not young for her 11 years, but she's not like a teenager at all.'

> **Secretary, husband a shop manager:**
> She's grown up in this last year tremendously. I mean, if you'd asked me this question a year ago, I should have said she's more like a child, but now … She's really taken an interest in her clothes and things like that; she's not so much bothered about dolls like she used to be. I mean she's got a load of dolls all on the top of her dressing-table – costume dolls and that – but she doesn't seem to *play* with dolls like she used to. She's more for reading and, like I say, doing projects.

> **Not in paid work, husband a miner:**
> I should say he's more like a teenager – to me he is, anyway. He seems to be his own gaffer, you see. And if he thinks he'll not play with the other children, he won't. He'll tell them off.

Q. 193 is obviously a somewhat provocative question, which was intended to, and did, amuse; nonetheless, mothers understood its import and some used it to answer very seriously in terms of democratic ideals. Most mothers recognised at least the possibility of the stages described, and for some they were very real.

> **Part-time clerical worker, husband a sales manager:**
> Oh yes, this is *it*. Christopher thinks I don't know a thing about anything.

> **Not in paid work, husband a foreman:**
> Sheena thinks I know it all – poor thing!

> **Part-time shop assistant, husband a shopkeeper:**
> Oh, I don't think she's reached the stage when she thinks we know nothing. I think she's a bit doubtful about some things – I'm not with it, she says, 'things are a bit different now'. In my time, things were 'olden' then! But she's not so far advanced in that argument as Elspeth [18] and Larry [20] – to them I'm *definitely* stupid. Though actually, now Larry's getting older, he's beginning to come back into the circle to ask advice. They seem to have a phase where they go completely off you: you *know* nothing, you can *tell* them nothing, and if you try to give them advice they don't *want* it. But now he is beginning to see that *some* things we said *did* make sense.

In terms of mothers' perceptions of the child, neither of these questions produced significant class or sex differences. 43% thought their son or daughter 'more like a child', 40% 'more like a teenager', and 17% somewhere in between. There was some indication that Class V girls were more likely than the rest to be thought of as teenagers. 44% of mothers thought their children believed they knew everything and couldn't do anything wrong, 11% thought the opposite, and 45% thought their children had a few doubts but had not reached the proposed stage of total negativism. It is perhaps unsurprising that the middle category is so popular, since many parents explicitly say that they do not expect their children ever to take the third category; and probably this is in fact a realistic judgement as opposed to the provocative suggestions. However, the question succeeded in its purpose of making parents think and talk both about their perceptions of the child and about the principles implicit in the topic.

The age of 11 was deliberately chosen by us as a time which began to bring into sharper focus for the child and his family a number of aspects of his personality, and of his relationships with both 'significant' and 'generalised' others. Children do not enter adolescence without a history; for most Western children, this coming face-to-face with their self-image is foreshadowed in cumulative ways, even before puberty. Perhaps too little has been made of this in studies of adolescence. It is an important strength of longitudinal studies that focal age-stages can be seen in the defining light of both past and future time.

Notes

1 Editors' note: in the original typescript the Newsons direct the reader to earlier publications (Newson and Newson, 1968, 1976a and 1976b) for information about the interviewing method. In this volume some consideration is given in Chapter 1.
2 The associated conditions of asthma, hay fever and eczema form the major group here, occurring in 55 of our 700 children (14 of these are asthmatic). Ear, nose and throat problems have occurred between 7 and 11 to the extent of needing consultant help in 48 cases, and the same number have had problems with sight or hearing. There are 19 bronchitic children, 17 with a 'grumbling appendix' or who have actually had appendectomies, and 3 with orthopaedic or muscular problems. 31 have other serious medical problems, 6 have recurring headaches or migraine, and 4 have been hospitalised for dental treatment. The categories given here are not mutually exclusive, as a few children suffer from two or more problems.

Reference

Newson, J. and Newson, E. (1968) *Four Years Old in an Urban Community*, London: George Allen & Unwin.

Newson, J. and Newson, E. (1976) *Seven Years Old in the Home Environment*, London: George Allen & Unwin.

Newson, J. and Newson, E. (1976) 'Parental roles and social context', in M. Shipman (ed.) *The Organisation and Impact of Social Research: six original case studies in education and behavioural sciences*, London: Routledge Kegan Paul (reprinted as a Routledge Library Edition, 2017).

Tanner, J.M. (1978) *Education and Physical Growth*, London: Hodder and Stoughton.

3

ENDURING FRIENDS AND FOES

Everyone has some notion of what friendship consists of, and yet it might prove difficult to settle on an agreed definition of what is meant when one person is identified as another's friend. Both in informal literary or scientific attempts at definition and in the exchange of daily life, it is usual to distinguish between different levels or depths of friendship. At one extreme we have casual acquaintanceships which may however be either short or very long-lasting; at the other we have 'true' friendships which we regard as permanent, involving people to whom we feel a genuine and willing commitment over a considerable period of time, and who, we hopefully assume, reciprocate that commitment. The difficulty is that, although outsiders to the friendship do normally try to judge the depth of the relationship in behavioural terms such as frequency and persistence of contact, they also know that friendship is more complicated than this, and that indeed subjective evidence may offer its most valid criterion. People may behave in an extremely friendly way within a particular social setting, but fail to keep in touch once they move out of that setting; or they may very seldom meet, yet effortlessly resume an intimate relationship, in terms of confidences exchanged and empathy experienced, on these rare occasions of contact.

It might be agreed, then, that a 'real' friendship is one which persists through time even with only intermittent actual contact and which involves a mutual voluntary commitment unrestricted to the period and place where the friendship was formed. This capability for the depth of feeling to override circumstance and life events is clearly one criterion, but perhaps equally important is that our real friends are those towards whom we *choose* to have obligations: people are not friends *just because* we happen to be required to associate with them by virtue of particular roles assigned to us in life, though they may become so if we are lucky. Thus it is an open question whether colleagues at work will want to share any of their leisure time with one another however friendly they may seem within their work roles – or, indeed, whether husband and wife are also true friends.

If these criteria are correct, then it follows that one must have some power of choice both over one's activities and over people to share them with, before one is in a position to make deep and lasting friendships except by happy accident. Young children, however, have little chance to choose their associates, mainly because they have so little power to make their own decisions about how to organise themselves in time and space. Between 1 and 3 years, although parents may use the words 'her little friend', this is more likely to mean that the children's mothers choose to associate than that the children do. At pre-school age, parents often expect their children to play amicably with other children of similar age, regardless of whether they feel drawn towards them personally, and often regardless of whether they are likely to meet again. If they are lucky, pre-school children may have a choice of playmates in their immediate neighbourhood, but this choice is limited by whether there is suitable communal playspace, whether there are neighbouring children of similar age who are also allowed to 'play out', by the weather, the time of year and so on, particularly if the mother is not prepared to entertain other people's children on her own territory. The phrase 'fair weather friends' has a real meaning for young children, and some cannot exert a choice even on these terms.

Once the child is at school, he has a choice of playmates at least within that setting; however, his friends at school may not be the same as his friends at home, where he is still dependent on luck and his parents' time and goodwill to be able to maintain school friendships through weekends and holidays. If he happens to live across a busy road from most of his schoolmates, or in a group of houses cut off in some way from the rest of the neighbourhood, he may find himself isolated from other members of his group who do have out-of-school contact. This can still be true at 11:

School meals supervisor, husband an administrative assistant:
Ah well, she seems content enough, but I often feel sorry she hasn't got someone she can mix more with. I've always felt sorry about both of them (sibling is 3) not having friends once they're home – not having children to play with.

As children grow older, their geographical range extends, in terms of how far and across what roads they may go on their own, and whether they are limited to walking distance or have the money and permission to use public transport. However, their increasing freedom remains under active parental control, and throughout childhood is relative rather than complete; there are likely to be all sorts of restraints both explicit and implicit imposed by parents.

At 7, these restraints were focused upon 'how far' and 'who with'; but, because the permitted geographical range was so small, usually limited by the nearest 'big road' in each direction and often smaller than that, the potential playmates within that area would be reasonably familiar to the mother and associations could be relatively easily monitored. At 11, the question of 'how far?' is more liberally answered (though still with restraints, as we shall see in Chapter 5), and the immediate consequence of this is that the question 'who with?' becomes more urgent. The other child or children may be quite unknown to the mother, and whatever activities are fostered by the friendship may take place at a distance, possibly in places which the mother would regard as undesirable in themselves. It is perhaps not surprising, then, that most mothers do regard their children's friendships as something in which the child should not yet be granted total freedom. Even local friendships are likely to be subject to value judgement, implicit or explicit, since the child at 11 is more capable of giving and accepting invitations on his own behalf; the mother is more likely to encourage children who 'fit in' with her own family – with whom the rest of the family can feel comfortable – but equally she may not wish her child to visit the house of a child of whom she disapproves, for fear that his family might multiply reflect (and in an attractive way perhaps?) the qualities that she regards as a bad influence.

'He can fall out as quick as he can make friends ...'

In focusing on the making and breaking of friendships, we were interested both in how easily the child make friends in the first place, and in his preference and difficulties in maintaining them. The introductory question (following some discussion of sibling relationships) was 'How does N get on with other children – does he make friends easily?' 80% of children are said to make friends reasonably easily, and the rest divide between 16% who 'don't make friends very easily' and 4% who have real difficulty. Interestingly, there are no class or sex differences here.

Mothers value the ability of the child to make friends (though they may not like him to be totally undiscriminating), and they commonly both express anxiety and look for explanations if the child does not make friends easily. A number of reasons are perceived. Some children are described as unusually self-contained and not really interested in other children: this would, of course, also make them unrewarding to other children. Some would like to have friends, but seem to lack initiative in doing anything about it. Some are aggressive and bossy, without the tact to transform this into acceptable leadership qualities, and potential friends are frightened off. Some have particular difficulties in that they are themselves rather unfriendly (as opposed to uninterested), or are quick-tempered and ready to pick a quarrel. All of these reasons for not making friends easily are illustrated in the transcript extracts that follow.

Not in paid work, husband a teacher:
She doesn't go out of her way to make friends. Friends come and call for her and she's not going out to play, she's not interested in going out to play ... I think if it wasn't for me, I don't think she would bother about it, I think it would probably fizzle out – you see *I* ring Sally up and ask her for tea – I don't feel Laura's particularly bothered one way or another.

Part-time nurse, husband a sales manager:
At the nursery, she didn't mix very well there. She'd *watch* the children, but she never joined in the games and ... anyway, after, as she got older, she ... she always seems to have *got* friends, you know, but she's not a child that ... er ... children talk to her in the street, and she'll say hello, but she wouldn't stop to talk to them, unless they are her personal friends. [So, she *has* friends but doesn't seem to *make* them very easily?] No, she doesn't. She's quiet herself and a little bit timid – she won't mix with anyone that's a bit rough.

Not in paid work, husband an unemployed labourer:
Well it all depends, cause Walter's more or less a bully at times, you know. Cause he used to be frightened of the children, and I told him he'd got to hit them back – they don't like him for it.

Not in paid work, husband a driver:
No, she is not a very friendly person by nature.

Not in paid work, husband a skilled labourer:
She likes other company, but she never finds any. [How is this?] Well, I don't know. She wants friends, but as I say, she's touchy and she's easily upset. If they just say one thing, she's not their friend any more. I mean, it's trivial things that doesn't matter and that happens in everyday life .... She takes offence before offence is meant, and she takes things much too seriously, and then she leaves herself all on her own and she doesn't want to be, and she's sorry after she's done it.

Making friends easily does not necessarily mean that the friends are kept, nor that a deep relationship is established. One child 'can fall out as quick as he can make friends'; another makes them easily 'but doesn't stop friends for long'. Another boy 'doesn't keep them – when the novelty's worn off, that's it – some little thing and the friendship's ended'. Yvonne makes 'acquaintances easily, but not friends' and her mother thinks she's 'too particular'.

Teacher, husband an insurance broker:
She does, but often she antagonises them temporarily; because she's painfully honest, and any deviation she speaks up about. This doesn't make her popular, temporarily at any rate, with others. I don't mean she tells tales, so much as to say to them 'you shouldn't have done that' and so on. I think perhaps she'd be wiser if she were quiet about it – but she's got to develop her own personality.

The question 'does he make friends easily?' gets at the child's ability to make and sustain an approach over the initial period of friendship; it does not distinguish between close individual friendship and the easy integration with a group which might involve having a number of more superficial friendships. We asked: 'Does he like to be one of a crowd, or is he happiest when he's doing things with just one special friend?' 39% preferred to be with a 'special' friend, 37% to be with a crowd and 22% varied between the two; only 2% were said to prefer isolation. Again, social class differences were negligible, but this time there was a tendency for more boys than girls to prefer being one of a crowd (boys 41%, girls 32%, P less than 0.03). This may partly reflect the fact that boys have more opportunity than girls to wander 'out and about' and to associate with others free of adult surveillance; where girls are encouraged to stay at home, it is easier to include a 'special friend' in that surveillance than to invite a crowd into the home.

Extending children's preferences into actual achievement, we asked their mothers to identify the special friend: 'Is there any child who you would say is N's "best friend"?' 65% of the children had one best friend, and a further 8% had two 'equally – best' friends. Not all children who prefer to play with one special friend actually have a 'best friend': sadly, 16% who prefer this do not have a best friend of their own.

Boys and girls do not differ, nor is there a straightforward class difference, but there is an interesting class/sex interaction: middle-class boys are less likely than working-class boys to have a 'best friend'. This is significant at the 0.01 level, and there is no such difference for girls. Working-class literature suggests that there is a special need for working-class boys to have a dependable 'mate' for mutual protection and defence as well as for companionship; indeed, the number of regional words to denote such a relationship – buddy, bunkie, marrer, bully, mucker, pal, butty, nibber, chum, cully, acker, cummer etc. – implies that necessity. It seems unlikely that mothers, as women, would over-identify with such a need and therefore perceive more best friends than actually exist for this group; these results are the more interesting, then, as an indication of a traditional pattern at so early an age.

Best friends are almost universally chosen from the same sex at this age: only 1% had as their one best friend a child of the opposite sex, compared with 64% same-sex best friends. Janey, who interestingly enough and for reasons unknown has for years been known as 'Bill', is one of the 1%, although the friendship has just been terminated by circumstance. One mother described how her daughter made friends with a classmate who lived around the corner:

> They were absolutely inseparable, but he left for Rotherham at Christmas. That made her a bit fidgety [mother had already said that her daughter was going through an unsettled period]. They were quite inseparable – they used to work together, and he used to come down at night when his parents were going out, he was an only child. He used to come and sleep here, and just practically lived here, he just walked in and out when he felt like it. And that went on for about three years, he kept her *completely* amused for the last three years.

We were also interested in the comparative age of playmates (not necessarily best friends) and the child's preferences in this respect. More boys (59%) than girls (46%) were regularly playing with older children than themselves; complementarily, more girls (90%) than boys (78%) were regularly playing with younger children. 9% of children are said to *prefer* the company of older playmates and there are no sex differences; 10% prefer to play with younger children, and here there is a sex difference reflecting actual play with younger ones, 15% of girls preferring younger children compared with only 6% of boys (significant at 0.01). Social class differences do not reach significance.

The ability to make friends, and even the fact that the mother can identify her child's 'best friend', does not guarantee plain sailing. Some children seem to fall in and out of friendship with the ease with which some adults fall in and out of love. In fact, the ability to make (presumably shallow) friendships easily seemed to cushion certain children against needing to work at their friendships. We asked: 'Does he seem happy in this friendship [his friendships], or does he often seem to get upset about it?' Some mothers made precisely the point that there was no need for the child to get upset, because he made friends so easily that there were always more where the last one came from. Gordon's mother said that he and his friends 'often fall out, but he's got lots of friends so he just goes with different ones': Josette's mother made the related point that *not* having a best friend saved one a certain amount of agonising.

Not in paid work, husband a banker:
She's happy to be with a crowd. She doesn't seem to attach herself to any child. She seems to blend in with them all on the surface, but she's not deeply involved with one friend. She just seems to blend in with whoever's coming home from · school, sort of thing … She seems to avoid any trouble with other kiddies. She doesn't get too deeply involved with them – not particularly having one deep friend. She just comes and goes with whoever's wandering along.

However, like ripples on the surface of a happy marriage, tiffs and quarrels between friends were not upsetting to some children because of their own confidence in the overriding permanence of the friendship.

Office worker, husband a dancing instructor:
[Tim and Barry have been close friends for five years.] Not upset, but they argue terribly and part company, and then one or the other of them goes back again – they're always falling out, and both Barry's mother and myself have decided that whether they fall out or not will make no difference to us – just let them get on with it.

Part-time nurse, husband an area officer:
[Dan and Michael have been does friends for three years.] He doesn't get upset about it. They seem to have terrific rows. Dan comes in and says 'I'm never going to speak to Michael again', and I gather Michael goes in and says 'I'm never going to speak to Dan Roberts again', and within half an hour they'll be at each other's door saying 'will you come out to play?' so I don't think they really …

Not in paid work, husband a clerical officer:
There's this love–hate relationship … No, she's quite happy. Course, she calls them black one moment,[1] and then they come to the door and they're the best of friends. I'm so used to it new, I just say 'Are we in or are we out? Just tell me where we are, so I know when they come to the door, I can say yes, you're playing, or you're *not* playing, and it doesn't put me in a peculiar position …' It's usually a disagreement that brings about this finish, and then of course just something happens and they're back in again, so I don't bother very much. It doesn't upset her, oh no.

Part-time assembler, husband a lorry driver:
[Des and Andrew have been close friends since they were toddlers.] Well, there are times. Last week they had a bust-up and they didn't speak to each other for three days – but that's a good thing, because as I say they do everything together … My husband says I worry too much, but I don't like them to fall out. You tend to put yourself in their place, but they don't feel how you feel. *I'm* upset thinking *he's* going to be upset about it, but he's not really. They know themselves they're going to get over it.

Taking only the 65% of children who did have best friends, 86% of these children were happy in their friendships, and only 14% got upset about them. Girls were rather more prone to upset than boys: 19% compared with 11%, significant at 0.01. It must be remembered that the mothers are here distinguishing clearly between having quarrels and being upset about them, as we can see from the quotations above. Perhaps being upset over quarrels with friends demands a combination of being person-oriented, which Erik Erikson regards as an intrinsic female quality (Erikson, 1955), and being intro-punitive, self-conscious and lacking in self-confidence, which have often been suggested as characteristics either intrinsic or culturally generated in females. The transcripts tend to support this view.

Typist, husband a lorry driver:
She doesn't make friends very easily, but when she does, if they let her down she can't get over it. She takes it very seriously. A friend's a friend.

Part-time teacher, husband an executive officer:
She's got a best friend, and they fell out this week and she doesn't like that – she's a bit upset. She likes things to stay more on an even keel, and sort of everything in the garden's lovely.

Part-time cleaner, husband an asphalter:
She hasn't had a lot of friends, and this past couple of years she seems to have got one that's permanent, you know, and she's always afraid if they have a little tiff that she'll lose her …

Secretary, husband a media professional:
We have distinct periods. At the moment it's going along very nicely; some time ago it wasn't going so nicely. Jane would be distressed if ... Susan finds that she is able to say something to Jane which upsets her, and Jane is paralysed to think of an answer to Susan back and therefore she'd come home; and we got to a stage where she was crying at night and being distressed about it.

From this last quotation, and from the previous group, we can see that mothers monitor and feel somewhat involved with their children's quarrels, even if their involvement takes the form of a decision *not* to get actively involved. We asked: 'Do you do anything at all about these tiffs and upsets between friends, or do you think they're best left alone to work it out for themselves?' All mothers were asked this question, whether or not the child had a best friend, in order to compare the result with data from the 7-year-old stage. The great majority – 83% – did nothing at all, compared with only 23% who stood aside at 7. For the remaining 17%, intervention was almost always restricted to giving advice of one sort or another, sometimes in collusion with the other child's mother; this compares with 49% who gave advice at 7, and 25% who intervened personally at that age. Few orchestrated their advice as carefully as Jane's mother (see p. 51); both from advice-giving and non-advice-giving mothers, there was a refrain of 'that's life – you have to cope with its ups and downs, however sympathetic I may feel about it'. 'They've got to learn it's not all roses', says Larry's mother (Class III manual), 'they've got to take the rough with the smooth'. 'I did tell him', says Nigel's mother (Class IV), 'it's like this, you meet all these disappointments in life; and his Daddy tells him the same'.

'Aileen seems different when she's been with her ...'

It is one thing to leave children to 'settle their own differences' with their friends; it is quite another to watch friendships flourishing which the mother considers ill-advised or even dangerous. We asked all mothers: 'Are you happy about all his friendships, or do you think some of them have a bad effect on him?' Where they did have reservations or anxieties about any friendship, we asked: 'Have you done anything about that?'

This is in many ways a difficult area to approach. No mother wishes to appear snobbish or intolerant; and she is after all talking about other *children*, who might be considered not entirely responsible for their own undesirability; she is also partly motivated by her recognition, just referred to, that the child has to learn about 'life' – 'he's got to learn to mix with all sorts ... to take people as they come'. This father described how 'other lads' could have a 'bad effect':

The lads he plays with we don't think he should – but then again, he's got to grow up with everyone around him. [What is it about them you don't like?] They argue, and where he goes to school there's an awful lot of stealing, and they swear a lot.

The question of school brings in an additional complication both to the situation faced by the child and to parents' feelings about it. The children of whom parents disapprove at home may have to be encountered day by day at school in a group which is supposed to be cooperative and to engender loyalties. The school system is charged with being fair and impartial to all the children it serves, regardless of circumstance. Parents are compelled to relinquish their children to school; the school in return engages to provide a certain degree of care and supervision, which the parents may however consider inadequate (Newson and Newson, 1984). In one sense, parents are responsible for having placed their children in a situation where they are necessarily involved with others whose value systems are different from those to which their own family subscribes: therefore they can hardly complain if the child forms liaisons within that group. In another sense, they cannot accept responsibility for a school environment in which they had little choice and less control. In so far as the friends who are disapproved of are mainly seen at school rather than in the neighbourhood, there is a strong sense of powerlessness to intervene.

Table 3.1 shows the proportions of mothers who were *not* happy about certain of their children's friendships, leaving aside for the moment why they were unhappy and what they tried to do about it. Overall, a third have this anxiety. Class differences are not straightforward: the trend is complicated by a high degree of anxiety for skilled working-class girls. Overall the trend is not significant, and the difference between middle class and working class arises from this group and from similar anxiety for semi- and unskilled class boys.

In terms of strategies to cope with the situation, both class and sex differences are found in certain areas. The percentages here refer only to the group of mothers who are unhappy about at least one friendship, so they are actual rather than putative strategies. 27% have forbidden the friendship, but this is true of more than three times as many working-class as middle-class mothers: 33% as opposed to 10%. This probably reflects not only more authoritarian attitudes in the working class, but also the seriousness of the situation, as we shall see. This class difference (significant at 0.01) is distributed in terms of other strategies, which therefore do not show class differences. 32% of mothers criticise the friends they are unhappy about, but

TABLE 3.1 Mothers who are unhappy about one or more of their children's friendships

	Social class					Summary		
	I&II %	IIIWC %	III %	IV %	V %	MC %	WC %	Overall popn %
Boys	27	35	31	36	36	31	33	32
Girls	29	21	43	29	30	25	39	35
Both	28	28	37	33	33	28	36	33

Significance: trend n.s. m.class/w.class p = 0.06

Between sexes n.s.

they use this strategy more with girls than with boys (42% compared with 22%, significant at 0.05) – possibly reflecting a greater amenability in girls both to their mothers in general and to verbal persuasion in particular. 20% try to divert the child from his friend by indirect means, and 21% do nothing.

What makes a mother unhappy about the effect her child's friend might have on him? What does undesirability in a friend actually mean? Analysing the content of the transcripts, we can make a rough distinction between the following kinds of reasons given for the mothers' disapproval:

1. Personality of other child in relation to own child.
2. Colour or race prejudice.
3. Social class difference implications.
4. 'Leading astray' in terms of delinquency.
5. 'Leading astray' in terms of sexual precocity.

The discussion will make it clear that these reasons spill over into each other, and therefore it would be misleading to attempt a detailed class/sex analysis, although certain class differences will appear.

1. *Personality* The effect of another child's personality must clearly be gauged in terms of the *balance* created between the two personalities. Tim and Barry (whose arguments are described on p. 49) 'have got such strong will-powers, both of them, that this is what causes the arguments – they each try to outdo the other as far as telling each other, so neither of them get anywhere'. Here the two mothers can agree that the falling-out will 'make no difference to us' because neither child is seen to suffer. Jane's mother (p. 51) shows greater concern, because Jane appears more distressed than Susan. This is not necessarily a case of whether one's own child is being dominated; a mother might (though less often) worry if her child were continually subjugating someone else. One boy's mother is 'for ever on to him' because he behaves in such a 'big-headed' way with his friend; whereas Isla's mother describes Isla as 'a great organiser' who 'organises her friends', but need not feel she is domineering: 'I'm not saying they notice, cause they're organising at the same time!'

There are also two different effects in terms of the *impact* of an undesirable trait and *contagion* of such a trait: for instance, the mother may feel that her child is too often the victim of another child's spitefulness, or she may be afraid that he is learning from his friend to be spiteful as a pair in relation to other children. Some of these anxieties are illustrated below.

Part-time shop assistant, husband a transport manager:
He followed in the shadow of another boy – it really worried me – this child is brilliant, and a very good friend of Noel. Everything Mark did, Noel tried to live up to. Now Noel's not brilliant, he's a good average – Mark's brilliant, and Noel was living in this boy's mind, you see … he was like a god to him

... anyway, we did have to have a little talk to Noel and explain that he must use his own mind.

Not in paid work, husband an engineer:
Well this one she's got now, Linda, she tends to tell Mandy to do things; well Mandy's very easily led, and she does these things. If she doesn't want to do her homework, she says 'we're not doing our homework, are we, Mandy?' and Mandy will say 'No, I'm not doing it' where normally she would – she tends to rule her a little bit, I think.

Assembler, husband a school caretaker:
Well ... one. I think she's a bit babyish for Dot, although she's only six months younger. Dot seems rather old. [Father:] The thing is, it can make Dot more dominant, I think, because she does like to put her thumb down – not in a nasty way, but she likes to have command of the situation.

Hosiery worker, husband a training officer:
Yes, there's one what's got a bad effect on her. She's a very spoilt child, this other girl. She has sort of anything she wants. When Aileen plays with her, she gets that way herself. Aileen seems different when she's been with her.

Part-time secretary, husband a haulage contractor:
Well I've not been happy about the one down the street, to be perfectly honest. She seems to me a bit spiteful, cause she's the only child, you know, and she seems to put her Mum and Dad against one another; and I don't like that, because Tracey sometimes tries it on with us, you know.

State registered nurse, husband an executive officer:
No, it's all right. Well ... I say all right. Except for this 14-year-old. I don't like his influence really. [What do you dislike?] Well I don't know. Roger always seems to end up fighting with somebody when this boy's with them – you know, the older boy tends to egg the younger ones on. And he thinks up things they wouldn't dream of, and they start doing daft things, you know; whereas, when he's not around, everything seems to be peaceful.

2. *Colour/race prejudice* Nottingham has a substantial black population, both Asian and West Indian. A certain amount of race prejudice was encountered, particularly attached to anxieties over school, where immigrant children were frequently perceived as taking up a disproportionate amount of the teachers' time. As one might expect, it was the black immigrant population which was identified here, rather than the longer-established Ukrainian and Polish immigrant community. However, prejudice was much less often expressed in relation to friendships at this age (it was to be a good deal more evident at 16, when sexual implications are an issue). Almost the most frankly prejudiced remark about a child's friend was 'Well, she's Irish – not that that matters' from Mrs O'Grady who had also warned her daughter never to marry an Irishman! More typical were occasional remarks

which ascribed difficulties to the child's colour but which also accepted other black friends.

Cleaner, husband a boilerman:

You see, we've always tried to learn them that coloured children are no different. But there's a family of coloured girls round Yvonne's age that are inclined to feel ... they've got a chip on their shoulder, and so when they're out playing normally, all of a sudden something will blow and ... 'We're coloured'. It upsets both Sally and Yvonne. They come in here one night and I ask them 'What's gone off?' and it's these three girls again – you see, they're carrying the chip – it's not what's been taken *to* them, it's what they're carrying themselves – as much as we try to learn ours, you see. So that they in actual fact are making their own colour bar ... . I've told Yvonne to keep away from them – it's not the colour – it's the attitude. Same as I would tell her to keep away from anyone else with the same attitude. [Does she know other coloured children?] Oh yes. She sits near a coloured boy at school and she thinks he's wonderful. He's always smiling. She'll come home often and tell us about this coloured boy.

3. *Social class difference implications* Obviously one implication of having a friend from a more deprived background might be his subcultural expectations of minor delinquency as a way of life; but in this category we are concerned with social class differences as such, where the mother has no behavioural evidence that her child is being 'led astray'. Leaving delinquency aside then, mothers were almost as likely to be worried about their children associating with 'better-off' children as with children from 'rough' families.

Part-time cleaner, husband a plumber:

This one she has now, her parents are in a different position financially than what we are, and I thought it might be a bad influence, but it hasn't turned out that way. Mine still appreciate what little I can give them. [Did you do anything about it?] No. I left it for a while, and then the girls started going to places I couldn't afford my girls to go to, and so I talked to Tricia and I said 'I don't mind you being friends with her. You can bring her here and you can go to her house, but you mustn't come asking me if you can go, sort of ...' – she goes bowling, ice-skating, things that cost a bit of money which I can't afford. But she understood, she pulled a face at first, but then she understood and it's worked out quite all right.

Part-time barmaid, husband a shop manager:

I can't say recently I've come across any I would want to stop. There was a while ago, she was going round with someone ... I don't know ... a rough family, but you can't always judge them, but I thought it best we broke it off and got other interests ... she never bothered.

'A rough family, but you can't always judge them' – mothers are conscious that they themselves might be judged as lacking in common humanity when they discourage a friendship for no explicit reason. In some ways it was easier to organise such prohibitions when the child was younger and more physical reasons could be adduced for not wanting the other child in the house. While the mother might acknowledge that 'the poor little kid can't help being dirty', she also expected sympathy for the fact that 'when she's gone, your furniture smells, and I have to go through my children's hair'. At 11, her own child is likely to press her for an explanation which she does not wish to give because it is so vague, and based only on a *feeling* that she needs to raise her defences against the influence of an alien subculture with value systems that might threaten her own achievement in socialising her child.

Cycle worker, husband a packer:

Well, I didn't encourage the friendship. I never turned the child away, but I didn't encourage it. If we said 'don't play with her', she'll only want to know why, and I don't want to tell Gracie that. I didn't want the child to feel … she'd not got a very happy home and that.

4. *'Leading astray' in terms of delinquency* Nonetheless, for some parents the situation, although still vague and ill-defined, is very threatening indeed. Mr Robertson, living in an inner-city area, gives the impression of a father at bay against forces that he knows will in the end take over and consume his children.

Machinist, husband a tool grinder:

[Father:] I've stopped her mixing, although I know behind my back at school they've got to mix. And I've told them there's some I don't want her to mix with. If they go against me, I'm not averse to giving them a belt round the ear-hole. You can talk and talk until … well, until you've had enough talking. Give them a belt across the backside, and they'll remember.

As in most cities, there are neighbourhoods in Nottingham, and even individual streets, which have a reputation for supporting a delinquent norm: neighbourhoods for which W.J.H. Sprott[2] coined the term 'delinquescent' to express their gradual absorption into an expected and accepted anti-social pattern. Such patterns are likely to persist and become intensified in a particular street or section, because once there is a group of anti-social families the street quickly begins to look uncared-for, with drifts of litter and much unrepaired damage; fights and uncontrolled noise make life unliveable and drive the remaining 'respectable' families out; and then only those families whose standards are already very low will accept re-housing in the area. In such neighbourhoods, parents who are still trying to socialise their children have their backs against the wall almost literally; they may resort to desperate and ineffective measures like Mr Robertson, or, if they are lucky, get out. For these parents, it is not a matter of 'Are you happy about all his friendships?' – friendship within such an environment is itself perceived as a threat.

Cleaner, husband a maintenance man:
That's why I wanted to get him away. [What were you particularly worried about?] Well, they used to swear a lot, and steal, which … one boy he almost worshipped … he couldn't understand why he was slapped for doing the same thing … [long account of children playing with paraffin, matches and hatchets] …. I couldn't sort of keep him away. If I'd kept him away, it would have made it ten times worse. We just used to tell him he hadn't got to do these sort of things, he knew which was right and which was wrong; and then as soon as we got the opportunity … he would have *gone* the other way if we'd been down there much longer … we just moved in time.

These are the parents who are overwhelmed by sheer numbers of potentially dangerous friends; more often, at this age, delinquency is seen as an issue in just one or two friendships. This can still be a major threat, however, where the child is spending more time out and about, and where the 'bad influence' can be supported by the otherwise desirable qualities of friendliness, admiration, respect and loyalty. Parents recognise that being dared or tempted by friends to steal along with them is difficult to resist; they understand the group pressures that lead children to smoke, swear, insult their elders and wander far afield, in imitation of even one forceful personality. Not many parents in working-class areas have quite the confidence in their child that Mrs Sansom has of Bernard, and indeed it has taken her all of his 11 years to develop this degree of trust in him.

Part-time ward orderly, husband a miner:
Yes, I'm happy about them because, being the leader, Bernard's not going to be led astray by some other lad, which I *would* worry about. He knows right from wrong, I can trust *him* quite well to behave properly so long as he's the leader.

Destructive children who brazenly smoke, steal when they get the chance, are careless with other people's property, and who are insolent to adults and use foul language when they are reprimanded, are commonly deemed to belong to families who are 'a bit rough'. Parents tend to assume that a child known to be delinquent is likely to be backed up by his own parents, or at least to be manifestly out of their control; this is why 'rough families' and delinquent children are associated in their anxieties. They worry that their child might be influenced not only by the criminal propensities of his friend but also by those of the friend's family, or anyway by his parents' assumed tolerance of criminality. They also have in mind that it will be useless to try to negotiate with such parents, and possibly dangerous to complain to them.

Table 3.2 shows differences in mothers whose unhappiness about their children's friendships stems from the fear that the child will be 'led astray'. The proportions given here are expressed as percentages of the 'unhappy about friendship' group. The class pattern existing in that group as a whole affects the significance level, as does the reduced sample number, but nonetheless the differences are fairly striking.

TABLE 3.2 Of the mothers who are 'not happy' about certain of their children's friends, percentages who feel that the child might be 'led astray' by this friend

	Social class					Summary		
	I&II %	IIIWC %	IIIMan %	IV %	V %	MC %	WC %	Overall popn %
Boys	36	32	51	44	50	34	50	45
Girls	4	31	20	13	47	17	21	20
Both	20	31	36	29	48	25	36	33

Significance: trend ↗ ★★   m.class/w.class ★★★★

between sexes ★★★★

The class trend, suggesting an increase in anxiety about the child being led astray as one descends the scale, is significant at 0.02; however, one would expect the difference to be more marked when one compares middle class and working class, since one might assume that the skilled working-class group would be particularly anxious lest their boys be led into delinquency in a general working-class area, and this expectation is borne out by the data: middle-class mothers suffer a good deal less anxiety about their children being led astray by their friends than do working-class mothers (significant at 0.001). There is more than twice as much anxiety about boys compared with girls, although this is not altogether consistent between classes; however, the figures are still striking enough to show significance at the 0.001 level.

The activities into which mothers fear their children might be led nearly all involve stealing, either as the major component or as an implied intention: that is, the first quotation below does not mention stealing as such, but this must be the implication of trying car doors, whether the car or its contents are to be stolen. 'Roaming around at night' and truanting also carry likely possibilities of both stealing and vandalism, and damage to property is frequently mentioned, as is trespass on to property with its similar probable outcomes. The latter would carry rather different implications were this a study of rural rather than urban childhood. Friendship with children already in trouble with the police causes special anxiety, in that it is often feared that the association itself will damage the child's reputation, quite apart from what he might be led to do in such company. Some examples of these anxieties about individual friends (rather than the neighbourhood as a whole) are given below.

Part-time clerk, husband a driver:
There was one at one time I did think so. This boy's younger than him – they've come from Arkwright Street area, and they're a bit rough, you know, he'd do things I didn't approve; you know – they'd be around the pub and he'd be fiddling with car doors. It worried me – he's not a bad boy, but I just think they're left on their own an awful lot.

Not in paid work, ex-husband a labourer:
Well, yes, definitely. There is a boy, and he has been put away now for thieving, and Reg has been playing with him once or twice, you know. It's really worried me in case he's taken him with him. But to be honest I've stopped it, I said 'you're not to play with him'. He's quite sensible and I don't think he would do it, but there's just that fear there all the time – there really is. It has worried me since we came here. There's quite a lot of decent people, but the great majority are the other way.

Not in paid work, husband a crane driver:
He did get in with a crowd – I say a crowd, there was about four of them – and he is easily led, you see, and they got into the Dinner Centre up at the top and quite a lot of damage was done. So we got over that, like, you know, and this man [probation officer] used to come and see Darren, and he only came for about three months instead of the twelve and he'd got quite a good report. But Darren – it was about a fortnight after the police had been, and believe me, his Daddy did thump him – he didn't belt him the first time, but about a fortnight after he were found sitting on the grass verge near the school and apparently two of the same boys had gone in again! Course, they found out, they'd found the knives and forks on these two boys; and I had a few words with the police, like, I said 'Is Darren going to get the blame? Well, we got over that, and as I say, touch wood ... but as I say, they've all gone now, two moved to Clifton, one went up Wells Road, and as I say, he's quite good now. [How did you manage before they went?] Well, we tried to keep *him* away, you know what I mean, we tried to drill it into him not to mix – not cause we were putting all the blame on them, I mean Darren was as bad, like, you know; but we was afraid, like, you know, in case ... because I would say this, I think if he was really enticed, he would go – he *would* do a thing, Darren. But as I say, he's never been any more trouble since.

5. *'Leading astray' in terms of sexual precocity* Although parents are aware that sexual development is more or less imminent in the child, and may already have seen the early outward signs of puberty, they do not yet expect or wish that sexual matters should be an active preoccupation for the child. Many of them know, from experience of their older children, how powerful sexual motivation can be as a distraction from the proper pursuits of a school student; many are afraid of the physical and emotional consequences of their daughters being sexually exploited; and some also express their concern at the notions of sex being given a tawdry or prurient aura by children with whom their child might associate. 'Leading astray' of this kind is not a very frequent active anxiety as expressed by mothers with reference to a particular friend at this age, and hardly compares with anxiety about delinquency; where it does occur, however, it is a powerful one, and clearly what we are seeing here is the beginning of what is to become an increasingly potent

issue as the child gets older. Romantic and potentially sexual relationships at 11 are discussed in Chapter 5.

Not in paid work, husband a charge hand:
I don't like her to go with one particular girl … she's two years older than Thelma, but she's too forward, I mean she's forever trying to get over to the Castle, looking for boys ….

Canteen assistant, husband an engineer:
Well, one, yes. But she don't play with her any more I told her, you know. Best away from her. [What sort of effect was she having?] Well, boys and things like that. Her father'd kill her if he ever finds out. She was one night, 9 o'clock. I thought … I was worried stiff. Found out she went down the shops and was standing there with this girl …. I said 'Stop that game. I didn't have it from any other children.' Cause I had a good girl, that's married now, she's 21, she's a very good girl. [Did you forbid her to see her?] Oh yes, yes, I did.

Nurse, husband a cabinet maker:
One boy in particular I didn't like his friendship with at all, because there was too much sex going on, and I didn't like it because they were making it into something that wasn't clean, and we've always brought them up to look on sex as something normal and natural … he kept bringing home dirty pictures of nude women and pinning them up on his wall … we didn't say it was wrong, we just said 'We'd rather you didn't do that if you don't mind', you know. We had a word with the boy concerned, and we said 'We'd rather you didn't call for Greg', and we did it as discreetly as possible, we said 'We think you should be with boys of your own age – mature boys' … um – that Greg was too young. [How did you deal with Greg's aspect of it?] We just said to Greg 'We don't think that boy's the right playmate for you, would you try and find somebody else?' – he kept saying 'Well I like him.' In the finish we just had to let it go a little bit but keep our eye on him, because Greg was determined he wanted to be with this boy – we didn't like it, but we didn't want to sort of say 'You're *not* going' like that; but we told him we didn't like it, and he doesn't bother with him very much now.

Sharon's mother provides an interesting example of a situation in which the main dangers are clearly sexual, yet the other child herself is not the problem, which is seen to lie with the family of alien values. This particular mother has always expressed doubts about the neighbourhood in which she has to bring up her children, ever since Sharon was a year old; she has not succeeded in leaving it, and since Sharon was 4 her transcripts show a strong sense of powerlessness both in the face of the neighbourhood and indeed in confrontations with her children, especially with Sharon, the eldest.[3] The quotation that follows is somewhat condensed; it seems important to include it as an example of how parents may feel unable to control their children's exposure to what are clearly serious moral and physical dangers if they are trapped in a 'delinquescent' neighbourhood.

Not in paid work, husband a lorry driver:
She's got this friend she's grown up with, you know; she's always up at their house, stays all day when she goes, but they're not like we are; you know, the mother's always out, there's always other men in the house. I do say to her, if there's anyone there, do come home, don't stay. They're always having boozing parties, you know, and they sit, and you know what it's like when there's men half-asleep and half-awake, and I just don't like the idea of her being there. [It's the place rather than the child, is it?] Annette's all right, yes, it's just the place, and the way they live, it's not my way, and Sharon knows it isn't; yet she likes to be there because they're carefree, couldn't-care-less type. I mean, if the kids wanted to build a bonfire in the corner of the room, they'd probably let them get on and do it, you know, whereas I'm just the opposite .... I *have* stopped her from going in the past, but she says 'She's my best friend and I've got nobody else', so she sort of got back with her again .... She came home the other week with a pound; she said 'We've been playing tossing money' – said of course some of the fellows are a bit on the drunk side, and they lost all their money. Annette won a pound and so did Sharon, just tossing coins on the mat. To me, you know, it's not, er ... I just don't like it, especially at that age anyway, I mean men start to notice girls when they begin to develop at that age, don't they? Mind you, I don't think for one minute that they'd ... but I mean you don't know – if a stranger came to the house – you don't know who they are, do you? She says, 'Oh, I'm all right', you know. I just have to leave it to her discretion, that's all, and hope she, you know, finds her way, you know, whatever happens. It will be on her own head, not mine.

It can hardly be said that this mother trusts her child; rather, she treats Sharon with a fatalism that relinquishes her to the outside forces which have been undermining her authority with the child, in her own eyes, for at least seven years.

We have to admit that we originally included these questions because we wanted to know how far mothers were concerned with the mesh between the child's personality and that of his friends, and whether they often felt they needed to take action on this. In this we showed our middle-class bias, for we were not aware that we had in fact devised a question about delinquency here. Piloting the schedule in a middle-class suburb to begin with, our assumptions were fulfilled; but the moment we moved into an inner-city area for the remainder of the pilot stage, we found ourselves firmly propelled by the mention of friends into discussions of delinquency, many pages before we actually asked our questions about 'trouble with neighbours or the police'.

Turning again to the transcripts, we find that a number of mothers expressed a confident trust in the child's good sense and discrimination in his choice of friends.

Teacher, husband a research scientist:
No, I am for children mixing with all kinds, and hope that they will have the sense to select their friends by themselves.

Not in paid work, husband a computer analyst:
No, I think Oriel's friends are very nice friends – I haven't got any worries there at all. I was only thinking the other day when she had a party, all the children she's ever brought here have always been the sort of child I approve of, you know, so I think she's got very good taste in children.

Research worker, husband a lecturer:
Not a really bad effect on her – I mean, one or two of her friends are a little bit silly, but I think she sees their silliness very clearly – in fact she comes home and criticises them for the very thing I would criticise them for.

Not in paid work, husband a clergyman:
No, she hasn't any friends that worry me. Some of them I wonder why she's friends with them, I can't see any reason why she should be. I wouldn't sort of presume to interfere with her friendships, I would let her make her own friendships. After all, after 11 years, if she hasn't got any standards it's a bit late to start trying.

The class occupations represented here are typical of the make-up of the 'trusting' group, and one has to reflect on the luxury of inhabiting an environment which allows mothers both to establish 'standards' with confidence and to do this in a relaxed and unhurried manner. Working-class mothers, tending to have a larger number of children in a smaller house, are physically compelled to release the child to the street society earlier than middle-class mothers; and when he is on the street, they have little control over peer group influences, and in particular cannot easily prevent their child meeting older, bolder children, who may indeed offer the child a certain status in 'mixing with the big lads'. Once the peer group begins to exert this influence, the mother's socialisation attempts may be continually subverted, and her own panic, succeeded by fatalism, must make her efforts less credible to the child. In this we have yet another example of the ways in which the geographical, material and social forces of the subcultural environment make it easier for the middle-class mother to take the calm, consistent, relaxed attitude to child-rearing so beloved by professional advisors. We saw at 1 year how dependent 'relaxed toilet-training' can be upon indoor plumbing and washing-machines (or, alternatively, the outdoor life of a hot climate!). At 4, movement into independent activity at the child's own pace depended on a safe garden. Throughout, it seems evident that accepting attitudes to children's sexual curiosity (and also to breast-feeding) depend on there being enough living-space for the incest taboos (and hence general sexual prudery) *not* to become paramount over other considerations. Later we shall also see that middle-class mothers are much more relaxed in their attitudes to their children's swearing – for the simple reason that their children are not exposed to this in the unremitting way that working-class children are. Attitudes to children's friends are just one touchstone of the difficulties which many working-class mothers still experience in their efforts to 'bring their children up nice'.

Notes

1 'She calls them black' – this is a regional usage and not to be taken literally. 'Call' is used in the sense of 'run down' or 'revile', usually to someone else; cf. 'Well, I don't like to call my mother, but she was a hard mother to me.' 'Black' is used adverbially here to denote an extreme degree, and the sentence as a whole could be translated, 'she totally denigrates them'.

2 Editors' note: W.J.H. Sprott was Professor of Psychology at the University of Nottingham from 1948 to 1964. He was the author of several books about psychology and sociology. We have been unable to identify this particular reference.

3 Sharon's mother is quoted in Newson and Newson, 1968: 409; and 1970 paperback edition: 390.

References

Erikson, E. (1955) 'Sex differences in play construction of twelve-year-old children', in J.M. Tanner and B. Inhelder (eds) *Discussions on Child Development, Vol. III*, London: Tavistock.

Newson, J. and Newson, E. (1968) *Four Years Old in an Urban Community*, London: George Allen & Unwin.

Newson, J. and Newson, E. (1984) 'Parents' perspectives on their children's behaviour at school', in N. Frude and H. Gault (eds) *Disruptive Behaviour in Schools*, London: Wiley.

Tanner, J.M. (1978) *Education and Physical Growth*, London: Hodder and Stoughton.

4

GREAT BUSYNESS

One of the major ways in which children (and indeed people in general) establish their own personal identity both within and apart from their family is by expressing independent interests and preferences in their own chosen activities, and, through the pursuit of these activities, developing their own expertise of knowledge and of skill. The acknowledgement by others of a personal expertise must be one of the most significant of the 'reflected appraisals' which make up the 'self' (Sullivan, 1953). For this reason alone it seemed important to investigate those interests which 'belonged' to the 11-year-old in the sense that his mother identified them as his.

The questions which explored the child's independent activities and interests, and the manner in which they were pursued, were introduced at Q. 71: 'We're interested in the things children do in their spare time. Has N any special interest that takes up a lot of his time?', and they continued through to Q. 89 (see Appendix 1). They were concerned with collections and treasured possessions, creative work in terms of craftwork, writing, drawing, music and drama, special talents and out-of-school training, and autonomy in terms of such interests. These will all be discussed in this chapter, and we shall also look at the activities which the child undertakes as a contribution to the running of the household – housework and other family chores – and at the recreational activities which he shares with his family and which therefore mark his identity as part of that family rather than as a separate person.

'I've more trouble than a little, trying to throw anything out ...'

From as early as 4 years, when a major issue between mother and child was her wish to clear out the more 'rubbishy' parts of his possessions, brought up short by his wish to keep them *all* (Newson and Newson, 1968), through 7 when 73% of children had specific collections and many were still magpies (Newson and Newson 1976), the pleasures of possession for the great majority of our children have been strikingly evident. It is interesting that we appeal to ornithological metaphor to exemplify acquisitiveness, for it seems a particularly human trait. It is also one which is ambiguous in terms of the way people react to it. Most of these mothers would have considerable qualms if they equated their children's acquisitiveness with an attempt at aggrandisement of the self by means of personal wealth; nevertheless, in many societies, including our own, this is clearly one of its functions. A short bout of regular reading of such periodicals as the *TV Times*, which includes many potted biographies of celebrities in its columns, shows how often possessions are seen as a major attribute of the person described, or perhaps major evidence of success: a list of cars owned *normally* figures prominently. Mothers are unlikely to list their children's possessions in such a way; and where they do, the points being made are either that these possessions are valueless in intrinsic terms yet loved by the child, or that despite their value (and evidence of the parent's generosity), the child is not interested in them. Value as actual currency, the traditional role of marbles and cigarette cards, does not receive very much mention in our parent's reports, though one would not expect them to be quite oblivious of this function if it were common. On the other hand, money itself is quite often mentioned, only half-jokingly, both as the subject of collections and as a 'most treasured possession'.

Already at 7 we were beginning to see the aesthetic and intellectual attractions of collecting for some children: the delights of acquiring specialist knowledge, imposing order, system and hierarchy upon mere accumulation, and appreciating different variations within one category. To seek to understand, and gradually succeed in understanding something about the ways in which nature or man creates diversity within a theme, whether in different varieties of lily or different interpretations of how to design such an artefact as a knife, a teapot or a baby's rattle, must be one of the minor but most exquisite pleasures of life, even acknowledging the precedence of exploring symphonic form or the diverse ways of laying oil paint on canvas. At 11, with greater intellectual ability in formal terms as well as more power to follow through initial interests with or without parental support, one would expect this kind of activity to intensify for certain children, as indeed it does.

Research assistant, husband a teacher:
We could do with a house the size of a museum – his main collection is stamps, he really has a marvellous collection, and it is beautifully done; he has three stamp albums, and it amazes me that a child of that age could have done them so well. It's a very serious adult approach to it. He has a Stanley Gibbons catalogue; every stamp is priced; he also keeps a register, and every time he adds a new stamp to any country he adds the numbers on, and he can tell you how many stamps he has got from every country. He knows an awful lot about stamps, and he knows about the countries and the coinage and the language and where these islands are, and he comes up and asks me, 'Do you know where so-and-so is?'. And they're places I've never heard of, and he says, 'Oh go on Mummy, you're joking, come on, tell me where it is' – and I haven't got the vaguest idea where these places are. He collects postcards and

he has them all filed under countries … and one of the main things he spends his money on is postcards of veteran cars, and he's got a scrapbook of these, beautifully done … He also collects packets of sugar – you know, the individual packets of sugar you get in restaurants, he's got these from all over the place from people, including Russia – he's got, oh, about a hundred of these. He also collects all Playhouse programmes, the whole lot, whether he goes to them or not. Stones and pebbles and pieces of rock – coins – everything he does is done, *very well*. They're in little tins, little special tins … etc.

Part-time secretary, husband an accountant:
We have marbles, but they have to be special marbles. I don't know – he'll go on about these marbles with a green inside, but they're not called that, they're called completely different names – he collects these. And then he has football teams of marbles, and each marble has a name, and believe me I've lost Bobby Charlton before today under that sofa. He must have a thousand marbles now, and they've all been collected in these colours, and then they've all got these special names, and then they … etc.

Most children collect in a less systematic way. Stuart has 'boxes of footballers all over the house'; Edwin collects football photographs and 'upstairs most of the wallpaper's football'; Jake's mother 'cannot get into his bedroom for football pictures – inside the door, outside the door, on the walls, everywhere – anything to do with football'; Nick is described as a 'proper hoarder', and has thousands of 'those little cards – footballers and such as that'. Stella has 26 foreign dolls, is writing a project about it for school and has 'just sent away to London for some more information'. Some children seem just to collect 'possessions' – or at least their mothers don't know precisely what categories they collect in but recognise the collector's urge in them.

Not in paid work, husband a train driver:
He *cares* very intensely about everything, you know. He's the type of child that has possessions. He's got things that are really of no importance; he's got an old case stuck under his bed, and it's got a collection of little possessions, nobody else is allowed to go near it – tins and things. He cares – oh, if one of the other children go up in his bedroom and he finds out, he really gets worked up about it.

Part-time factory hand, husband a labourer:
Books. Every book she can afford from W.H. Smith's. 'I love that bookshop', she says. She spends all day when she goes to town. I know where I could find her if I wanted her all right.

Not in paid work, husband a postman:
Oh my word – I couldn't say she collects stamps or anything nice to put out in books, but she collects the most horrible little oddments – everything, even cuttings of material that should be thrown out. Boxes upon boxes – any wool I leave lying around disappears suddenly, and I find them in these boxes.

TABLE 4.1 Children who have specific 'collections'

	Social class					Summary		
	I&II	IIIWC	IIIMan	IV	V	M.class	W.class	Overall popn
	%	%	%	%	%	%	%	%
Boys	77	77	65	73	54	77	65	68
Girls	49	69	44	40	35	58	42	47
All	63	73	54	56	45	68	54	58

Significance: overall trend ↘ ★★★★   m.class/w.class ★★★★
Non-linear feature p = 0.03
boys vs girls ★★★★

58% of children have collections of one sort or another, pursued with this degree of enthusiasm. Both social class and sex differences can be seen in Table 4.1. In all social classes boys are considerably more likely than girls to have collections. Collections decrease as we descend the social class scale, but there is a non-linear trend mainly because of a heavy increase in collecting in Class III white collar; however, this increase is entirely among white-collar girls.

Those 42% who do not collect have either no specific interest in any one thing, or no persistence. One child collects 'different things at different times – depends what crops up at school', but we did not count this as a collection in our terms; another 'might start, but a couple of days later he loses interest'; another is 'not bothered about keeping things'.

Things that the child might go to some lengths to preserve, even in an extreme situation, seemed of interest in telling us about the child's sentiments and attachments, other than human or animal attachments. The question asked was: 'What do you think is his most treasured possession – if there was a fire, what would he grab first?' The initial answer was often 'the baby' or 'the cat', but live creatures were ruled out. Mothers thought very hard about this question, and indeed it does have the same perennial fascination as the old challenge of 'What would you take to a desert island?' or 'What would you jettison from a hot-air balloon?'. The very reason for its fascination is that, if oneself is the subject, one is forced to examine one's more personal and intimate values as opposed to market values; and if making the decision for another, one acknowledges oneself to be making a judgement about *his* most intimate loves, not about replacement costs. Indeed, if one does make a decision based either on market value, or on lack of preference, one thereby makes a judgement about a much deeper aspect of the personality: as one mother said, 'I don't think she'd grab anything, cause I don't think she's got any feelings'; and another, 'His money, I think. He's terribly stingy – he has plenty of money. He'll go without anything if he can hug his money to his heart.'

We cannot of course be sure that the mothers are correct in what they judge to be the child's most treasured possession. However, the fact that they saw it as a serious question and took time to answer it suggests that they drew carefully on the evidence as they perceived it. Sometimes, in fact, they distinguished between what the child would actually admit to loving and what she would in the event probably grab.

Not in paid work, husband a machine operator:
She doesn't like anyone to know she's still got an old teddy, but as I say, 'Older people like a teddy bear.' But – 'Oh, don't let people know!' She'd be red as a beetroot if she thought you knew. Still talks to him. Saturday she went to London and stayed the night at her Aunty's. So last night when she went upstairs Ted was supposed to say 'You're a nice one, not coming home Saturday night' – 'Oh well, you didn't mind for once.' I could hear her, you know. They were having this little conversation. She always takes him on holiday; her father said, 'Now look, you'll be 12 this year, have we got to pack him again?' – 'Um, well, perhaps I'll have to hide him in a cupboard when we get there, but', she said, 'I'd be very worried if he was left at home.'

29% of mothers overall could not decide firmly on any treasured possession, either because the child seemed to value many things equally or because he valued none. Leo's mother felt that 'possessions aren't really important to him', Lindsay's mother said, 'I don't think she ever thinks of anything as a possession', and Paddy's mother was stumped, 'Now that is hard to say – I don't know – I don't think he'd grab anything – as long as he got out, that'd be it – he wouldn't bother about nothing as long as he got out!' However, there is a class trend (★★★★) such that children decrease in their likelihood of having a known treasured possession as we descend through the working class: 49% of Class V mothers cannot name such a possession. Middle-class children do not increase in treasured possession in a commensurate way, however, and in fact Class I and II girls oppose the trend: 31% are not known to have one particular treasure. Overall, while there is a through-class trend, there is no significant middle-class/ working-class *difference*: nor is there a significant sex difference in whether a treasured possession is identified.

This leaves a majority even in Class V, and 71% overall, whose single most treasured possession can be named with some confidence. What are these possessions, and what patterns can be seen in the kinds of objects treasured? The seven most popular items, with the number of times chosen in brackets, are: dolls (79), teddies or other soft toys (77), books (44), money (42), football or football kit (36), bicycle (26) and special items of clothing (21). No other single item reaches more than 20. Mechanical equipment such as radio tape recorder, record player, camera, microscope and typewriter reach 46 between them, jewellery reaches 15 (all girls) and soldiers or toy guns 15 (all boys). Other less popular items are pop-star and football pictures, fishing gear, watch, musical instrument, stamp collections, self-made models and competitive trophies, each scoring between 10 and 20.

Part-time nursing auxiliary, husband a sales manager:
I should say it's a doll, she's had it for years. She calls it Andrew, and not only is this Andrew loved by her but I think everyone round here. It's dropping to bits, but I think she's … it's been like a little brother or sister to her. Sometimes it's a girl, but it's always called Andrew!

Not in paid work, husband a representative:
This! [produced a battered Tiger Tim]. I was going to hide him before you came. He'll bring him down every morning, puts him on his chair – and I used to make a habit of taking it upstairs and putting it on the bed – he'd come home at lunchtime and go straight up and bring him down. I've called him Tatty Tiger, and we're really hurt, we cried, we're so fond of him!

Part-time checker, husband a setter operator:
Her maxi-coat – this she bought herself; I said she couldn't have one, but that kiddy she does at various times have quite a lot of money given her, and she saved every penny up and she asked if she could have one, and what could I do? I still don't know if I've done the right thing, I didn't want her to have one.

Not in paid work, husband a sales manager:
I'd say the little teddy bear that belonged to our first baby that we lost, she loves that teddy. I would say him, definitely

Not in paid work, husband an accounts clerk:
The Beanos! [comics]. I really think that's – she thinks more of the Beanos than anything, yes, I do, because you know we've tried to throw them out, I mean a pile – she puts them under her bed in a box, and they're piled all over the floor and I'm always on to her about them, but she will *not* get rid of them. I don't know why, because once you've read a comic, you've read it, haven't you, really? But she does love her Beano.

Not in paid work, husband a clerk:
We've bought him a bush hat, you know, one of those from the army and navy surplus stores, and he's really tickled with this – he's been out playing with it, and he has it at the side of his bed. The first night, I went upstairs, it was really funny, he'd got it on in bed …

Not in paid work, husband a bus driver:
Our Robert. [Apart from humans, is there anything she owns that she'd grab?] No, they've got no toys at all.

Not in paid work, ex–husband a labourer:
The cat. [Well, not counting animals – anything else?] No, because he just destroys anything else he gets.

The most interesting pattern to be found here is in terms of sex differences. While girls do not differ from boys in whether they have a treasured possession, their preferences cluster far more on a few items, whereas boys have a greater spread of choices. Boys and girls also differ considerably in their choices. Thus, taking the six most popular items given, the first three (dolls, teddies and other soft toys, books) are the three most popular items chosen for girls: 71 votes for dolls, 58 for soft toys and 24 for books. The items in fourth, fifth and sixth places (money, football gear and bicycle) are the three most popular items for boys: football gear comes first (35), money second (26) and bikes third (26). 19 boys treasured soft toys, 20 books and eight dolls (all of them Action Men!). 16 girls would grab their money (one in the form of Green Shield stamps!) only three their bike, and one's treasured possession was her football gear. Girls and boys were equally fond of clothes items (often some kind of uniform); but if we had included football gear (which usually includes the football) under clothes, boys would have turned out the peacocks.

Significance levels of differences between boys and girls for the six most popular items overall are: dolls, football kit, bike (★★★★), teddy or other soft toy (★★★), books, money – not significant. Only three of the items show significant class trends. Bicycles as a treasured possession show a steady decrease as we descend the class scale (★★★★): that this is not *just* due to their expensiveness is shown by the fact that there is no such trend for expensive gadgetry such as tape recorders and typewriters; however, ownership itself is class-related (p. 91). Football kit shows a non-linear trend (★) – at its lowest in Class I and II (where however the only girl is found), it immediately peaks in the two Class IIIs and declines through IV to V. For teddies and soft toys there is a steady class trend decreasing at the lower end (★★★). This is of interest in relation to earlier findings on 'cuddlies' and social class. At 4 years, there was a significant class trend in attachments both to soft toys and to cloth cuddlies (defined by the child *insisting* on this particular one at bedtime), both being more popular further up the class scale; this class trend was matched by thumb-sucking, often in concert with cuddling, and reversed by dummy sucking, a more popular habit both at 1 and at 4 years further down the scale (Newson, Newson and Mahalski, 1982). Thumb-sucking tends to persist longer than dummy sucking, as we found by 7; and the persistence of social class trends in attachment to soft toys over the years is still more striking.

It should also be noted that if we consider incidence of these items as a percentage of the whole sample, including those who do not have a treasured possession, 21% of all girls most treasure a doll, 16% of girls treasure a soft toy (5% of all boys), and 13% of all boys treasure football kit. Since these are all considered to be their *most* treasured possession, these results, particularly in their polarisation by sex, seem quite important in telling us something about the sentiments and identifications of girls and boys of 11.

'She'll sit at a thing, she won't be beaten. She likes to conquer things ...'

One of our questions which probed the child's 'general personality' was 'When he has to amuse himself, is he a busy sort of person, or does he easily get bored?' 67% of children are now rated by their mothers as 'busy', and there are no significant class or sex differences. Apart from maintaining their collections, what are they busy *at*?

This is a time when a child, if he wishes, can be creative in ways that result in artefacts which both he and others will be pleased with; that is, while earlier the objects he produced were mostly judged as 'very good *for his age*' (child art being perhaps a special case, however), now many children can produce wearable small garments, usable gadgets, and presents which do not need a sentimental eye for their appreciation.

Part-time cleaner, husband a bus conductor:
He does embroidery – he's a lovely embroiderer, and he wants to learn to knit and crochet – but he embroiders ever such nice things. He's made ducks all in felt, and he's made a rabbit for baby, and he's embroidered fish on the squares. He likes machining as well – he can use a proper one – he's going to be a tailor, I think. I've learnt him French knitting.

Teacher, husband a scientific officer:
He's very keen on doing things with his hands – constructing models – he plans these things for hours before he actually does anything – he doesn't just get a piece of wood and get on with it – he must draw it first, and measure it, and plan it very carefully – plans them first and then makes them, and they work ... he constructed a model of some sort of pump with pistons out of paper which he glued together, cut and so on, and the thing worked – obviously you couldn't put water in because it was made of paper, but it did work.

Research worker, husband a lecturer:
The most interesting thing she's made was with her cousin – they started it at Christmas and finished it at Easter. This was a tremendously complicated board game based on Puffin books – they're both tremendous Puffin Club fans. This board game involved – er – throwing the dice and you go to the library and get your book and then go on ... the things that happen on this board are all to do with the people in the Puffin books – having a ride in Auntie Robbo's car and going to have tea with the Princess and the Goblin – it was a most elaborate thing, very nice, I must say I was very impressed. I'm always being impressed by Clare, and by the things she and her friends between them produce. They did this in such detail, and they sent it off to the Puffin Club just as a present; and they had the most marvellous letter back, saying this was just about the best present they'd ever had, and they were trying to work out whether they could produce it commercially for Christmas – it was going to be a bit expensive to produce they thought, but they were trying to work out some way of getting round this – we haven't

heard yet … This is the sort of thing – they start by saying, oh, let's make up a game, and they do something which is quite fantastically good, you know – you can only gasp!

31% of children are regarded by their mothers as 'unusually good with their hands'; class and sex differences are not significant. Obviously, we cannot know whether all mothers (or all classes) have the same reference point for this judgement, but presumably we can suppose that these children are at least showing a sustained interest in working with their hands, and getting results which are satisfactory enough to gain praise and keep them going. 58% of all children do at least one of the activities involving carpentry, sewing, knitting and crochet, and 'tinkering with mechanical things'. 64% are said to make models, or drawings, and 23% make presents for people. There is no class difference for carpentry, sewing etc., but there is for models, drawings and presents: in these children are more active further up the class scale. 'Models and drawings' show a class range from 73% to 57% (★★★) and 'presents' a range from 33% to 9% (★★★★). Boys are more active than girls in 'models and drawings' (76%:53%) but less active in carpentry etc. (40%:76%) and in making presents (13%:33%) – all these differences (★★★★).

Another likely creative activity for children of this age involves writing down their thoughts in various forms. We asked whether the child wrote stories in his own time (that is, not at school): whether he wrote letters 'for the fun of it' (thank-you letters being excluded); and whether he kept a diary or any sort of notebook at home. Stories and letters were coded as to whether these were written often, sometimes or never. Examples of these activities or their absence are described below.

State registered nurse, husband an executive officer:

He's always writing – writing stories – he writes loads of stories. Good ones too. He makes books of stories, and he reads them to Edward. Horrible things they are sometimes – about snake-pits and things. [Letters?] Yes, yes, he does. People say to me, you know, 'I've had a lovely letter from Roger'. He just posts them off and doesn't tell me, you know. And phone-calls – terrible! [Who does he phone?] Radio Nottingham. He's won three prizes on there. And people keep saying 'I heard your son on the wireless'.

Not in paid work, husband a nylon warper:

She's always cutting up and making folders and writing stories. She collects leaves, presses them, writes out what they are – finds out in the book what tree they belong to. Beetles, how they're formed, things like that, you know. Then she likes story-writing – writes lots of stories. She never gets tired of the insects and the story-writing, never seems to get tired of all that – cutting paper and that, make a cover for it.

Teacher, husband a professional engineer:

She writes to anyone who sends her a card – they get an *epistle* back!

Research worker, husband a lecturer:

Rather grown-up notebooks – like for instance when she was teaching Susan to read, she kept a notebook about the principles of teaching reading – what she thought were useful things to remember about teaching reading and what things worked. She was terribly down on me because I came in on this and tried to explain something to Susan – she thought this was not important to explain at this stage. She's very like that – she's terribly sort of … it's a funny mixture of an intellectualising and a very down-to-earth practical thing – she tells me things on principle which have come straight out of the practical situation. And these are the things she writes down.

Not in paid work, husband a scaffolder:

He's got a lot of books on boxing, and he'll copy from them and illustrate it, and football he's started on now. He loves to sit and write about it, most nights he does.

Not in paid work, husband a train driver:

He had difficulty learning to read and he finds writing hard work, you know. He's fairly neat in his writing, but it's a task to him handling words; you know, he can speak, and his head's full of ideas, but it's the hard slog of putting it into words and getting it down on paper …

Not in paid work, husband a window cleaner:

[Letters?] Not for the fun of it. But he wants to write a letter to me husband's sister, but, er – he'd need a lot of help there, so he'd have to wait till we could help him. He often says 'I want to write to Auntie Edith'. I says, 'When we get time to help you with your spelling, you can write one.'

Not in paid work, husband a lorry driver:

[Does she write poems at home as well as at school?] No, she don't write owt at home, does she Jim? They write letters to one another when it's holidays – 'Dear Kath, are you my friend?' – 'Yes I am, Elaine' – that type of thing.

Part-time secretary, husband a miner:

He starts, but he's not a great writer at all – you're hard pushed to make him write at all.

These quotations illustrate a very wide range of commitment and ability in action, and considerable class and sex differences can be seen. 19% of all children write stories often at home, but girls are more likely to do so than boys (27%:11% ★★★★). A steady class trend moves from 27% in Class I and II to 5% in Class V (★★★). Looking at children who never write stories, these are in the majority over the total sample – 53%. This goes up to 69% for boys and down to 37% for girls. Apart from Class V, the social classes all hover around the 50% mark, but in Class V 74% never write stories, rising to 87% for Class V boys. These class and sex differences are highly significant (★★★★).

Letter-writing for fun is very much a minority habit; only 3% do it *often* and 76% not at all. Even with such small numbers, a class trend (★★) is found, with 10% of Class I and II girls *often* writing letters (sex difference ★★★).

Diaries and notebooks retain the class differences shown by stories but lose the sex difference. 14% keep diaries or notebooks, rising to 29% in Class V (★★★★). The lack of sex differences seems to be due to the inclusion of notebooks, many of which are concerned with football and trains; in fact, it is interesting that the large number of these cannot reverse the sex composition.

Because the topic of independent activities was introduced in an open-ended way, other interests and hobbies were also mentioned by parents. Excluding for the moment organised activities such as choir etc., sports teams, clubs and uniformed associations, which we shall come to shortly, these divided roughly into non-organised sports and miscellaneous hobbies. 41% of children had sports interests aside from any which were organised or school-based, but far more boys than girls (57%:24% ★★★★). Sport was more popular further up the social scale (★), with a relatively sharp drop at Class V (29%). Girls compensate by their other interests: while 36% of all children have some 'miscellaneous' hobby, this applies to 25% of boys and 46% of girls (★★★★).

This miscellaneous group is itself of interest just because the activities concerned do not fall into obvious categories. Several children, for instance, have put on a whole series of entertainments which have no adult organisation.

Part-time cleaner, husband a lorry driver:

They have concerts up in the garage when it's holidays. A gang of kids. And they have coffee mornings, things like that. They put a notice on the front gate – 'Coffee etcetera'. And she pinches my coffee and biscuits. [Who comes to the coffee mornings?] Oh, anybody. They pay for it … I don't know what they bought with the money. Made about 30p, didn't they? Cost 'em more than that for the biscuits. They didn't make a profit.

Some children, however, have every intention of making a profit, and some succeed. Some of these use school as one of their bases, but school is not involved in the organisation. Where the children are a group moving between school and neighbourhood, school being merely one of their venues, we have counted this as independent activity.

Part-time nursing auxiliary, husband a sales manager:

There's four or five of them always together. [Is this a secret society?] Oh no – they do a lot of things together – like they had collecting for the Lord Mayor's Kidney Fund, you know, they used to make cakes and sell them, each took so many, that sort of thing. Oh, they sent a cheque to the Lord Mayor. [This group organised it themselves did they?] Oh yes. And Jillian and another two little girls all walked to as far as Bramcote Lido on a sponsored walk and got quite a bit, and presented it to the Kidney Fund. They're always getting up to some sort of thing – they do little plays. They take old clothes from home ... we never hear them, of course, they're done to the other children during wet playtime.

Other children develop special foci for their activities. Marcia cooks 'whole dinners, Yorkshire pudding and all' for her family, and also cooks for her blind grandmother. Naomi is 'happiest when she's taking other people's babies out' and will confidently manage three small children at once; Curtis was mainly interested in fishing, but this has developed into a consuming love of snails which he watches and breeds; and another child is 'not bothered about toys' but 'with fishing net and a jam jar he'd never be unhappy!' Moira spends a lot of time tending the grave of the bird that belonged to her dead grandmother, keeping fresh flowers on it and changing the design of shells weekly, and she also regularly visits old people although it depresses her to do so: both these activities have been kept up for more than a year. Roger operated 'all the time' on his teddy bear which is now conveniently stuffed with tissue paper; this boy has since gone on to train as a nurse.

State registered nurse, husband an executive officer:
He has Edward now as the anaesthetist, but now we've got machines all drawn on the wall as well, and all the air flows and oxygen tanks. He's getting more – how shall I say? – professional now. Before it was just imagination, but now he buys bottles of Dettol with his pocket money. He's got these gas machines he's made. He has notices pinned up outside with 'Surgery' and 'Anaesthetist', all spelt properly too! And 'Roger Manton' and 'Do not enter', and he's got the gases written up on the wall ... Everything's got to be real for Roger, you can't have any makeshift!

'She'll go out and she'll achieve things ...'

For Roger, his real-world interests must perforce for the moment remain in fantasy play, despite the real Dettol, but there is a considerable group (54%) of children who, partly because their increased mobility allows them to, are now looking outside their own homes for activities that might gain greater real-world significance by being part of a wider system or organisation. In this discussion we are including out-of-school lessons and training; obviously these could be an almost private activity between child and teacher, but in practice it seems unusual, and indeed difficult, for children taking lessons not to become involved in working for public 'grades' and 'medals'.

Table 4.2 gives a summary of the kinds of community-based out-of-school activities in which 11-year-olds are involved. Percentages refer to a random sample of the group named at the top of the column: middle class, working class or whole 11-year population. Significance levels refer to the class difference.

TABLE 4.2 Community-based out-of-school activities

Activities (not mutually exclusive)	M.class %	W.class %	All (random) %	Significance
'Cultural': acting, orchestra, choir	12	2	5	★★★★
Sport: swimming, football, athletics etc.	24	22	23	n.s.
Uniformed: Scouts, Guides, Boys' Brigade etc.	34	18	22	★★★★
Sunday school and related (not youth club)	18	12	13	<0.06
Youth club (some church-organised)	7	13	11	<0.06
Other miscellaneous (not lessons/ coaching)	5	6	5	n.s.
None of the above	36	50	46	★★★
Out-of-school lessons, coaching, training (not necessarily paid for):				
Music	18	4	8	★★★★
Dancing	9	9	9	n.s.
Sport	16	10	12	p = 0.06
Other lessons	9	3	4	★★★★
Examinations already taken in above	17	8	11	★★★★
Competitions already entered in above (excluding team events)	9	4	5	★★

Significant sex differences, boys:girls – Sunday School 10%:16% ★★; dancing 1%:17% ★★★★; examinations 5%:16% ★★★★; otherwise non-significant.

With the exception of youth clubs, where the working-class membership outnumbers the middle-class, there is a clear class trend in whether children take part in organised community-based activities of any kind, middle-class children apparently receiving more encouragement to participate in this way. Boys and girls polarise to certain individual activities, dancing being preferred by girls, and *team* sports by boys: that is to say, within the 'sport' category in the first half of the table, for the great majority of boys this means football, a *necessarily* team activity; whereas girls prefer skating, with a little horse riding – basically an individual performance, though they may be performing for a team. The 'miscellaneous' group also conceals membership of dancing clubs, sometimes specialised (old-time, disco and so on), mainly by girls. Clearly, boys are more likely to be involved in competitive team activities, though boys and girls are equally likely to compete individually; while girls are three times as likely to be working to reach a standard demanded by music grades and dancing medals.

Some of these children are already very much experts in their chosen activity, and indeed are spending much of their time moving among experts, including adults.

Part-time machinist, husband an asphalt mixer:
If it's dancing or anything she really does know about, she likes to be in charge and she'll tell them what to do. She's that type of girl. Two years ago, they won the Derbyshire dancing festival; and they were in the Nationals for two years and always just one point off it. This particular year they won it; and April saw one of the older girls, 18 years old, who was in a bit of a predicament over a movement, and April said, 'Oh, it's not like that – you do it like this.' And the coach naturally approached her, and said 'Well, can you do it?' So naturally she dived at the chance of dancing with the 18-year-old, and they got into third place with her dancing. She danced for two teams – her own team and the 18-year-olds.

Not in paid work, husband a hosiery mechanic:
He belongs to a football club; Wednesday night, Sunday morning, and he plays for them Sunday afternoon. He plays for West Nottingham and he's in the squad of Nottingham Boys. We did have a directive from school saying that schoolboy players couldn't join a club, but we didn't take Bartholomew out because he's so interested and he's signed a contract. It doesn't interfere with his playing for school.

For some of these 'expert' children, the parental back-up required is formidable. This is much less marked in football, where active support is team-based rather than parent-based; but dancers, swimmers and often skaters would find it extremely difficult to reach competitive heights without an exceptional investment of time and money by their parents. For instance, James, who is a junior swimming champion for his county (no longer Nottinghamshire), has to train every day, because, as his mother says, 'he has reached the pitch where he is physically crucified if he misses a day', and this involves one or other of his parents driving him several miles to the pool each evening and back as well as to competitive weekend events – not surprisingly, they have themselves become expert coaches, but the fact that their daughter also rides competitively has made massive inroads into the spare time of this profession couple. Dawn's parents, in Class IV, are equally stretched by Dawn's competitive ballroom dancing; not only does she need ferrying and chaperoning for both evening coaching and weekend events, but yards of tulle and sequins have to be sewn for the frequent changes of dance dress demanded.

What is interesting about these highly focused families is that, far from conforming to the stereotype of the pushing parent achieving vicarious success through the exploitation of their children, these parents give the impression of not knowing quite what hit them; often the whole thing started in an almost accidental way. For instance, Dawn's mother encouraged Dawn to learn dancing out of her own chronic lack of confidence: 'I really didn't want her to go in competitions, I wanted her to go just to be able to dance, and when she gets a teenager she won't be left out – that's all I wanted really'; while Stuart's successful career as a boxer (cups and trophies all over the living-room) started 'because he always used to be coming in with children hitting him, and crying, so my husband enrolled him in this boxing club'.

All of the activities mentioned in this section necessarily involve the child leaving his home-and-school environment and moving further afield, often well away from his own neighbourhood. This is still an active source of anxiety for their parents. Middle-class parents are clearly much better able to resolve such anxieties, being better equipped with cars and other resources to provide both chaperonage and checks on their children's safety, and this must clearly be one factor in the class difference we have seen; in addition, of course, there is also the question of whether parents value the child's outside activity enough to allow it to override their anxieties if they cannot resolve them. Parents' worries about the dangers of being 'out and about' are certainly relevant to children's independence of activity, then; but we shall leave this discussion until Chapter 5.

'Well I do like her to wash the pots, but I don't think she's took a fancy to it …'

We turn now from the various activities that children choose both inside and outside the home, in order to focus on those which might be required of them as a contribution towards the running of the household. Here again, what we take for granted as members of a Western society is crucial; in talking about required contributions we are not talking about the child working for gain in order to make a financial contribution. Yet we would only have to change time, place or both to find that kind of contribution assumed in an 11-year-old; indeed, at 7 years we quoted extensively from the Report of the Commission on Children's Employment of 1834, which found that 'almost all the children of the labouring classes' in the Nottingham, Leicester and Derby districts were employed in lace-making or hosiery, and that 'in general, regular employment commences between seven and eight; the great majority of the children having begun to work before they are nine years old' (Newson and Newson, 1976: 222). Typical work for children over 7 involved serving several different workshops situated far apart, many of which would certainly entail a journey (always on foot, often in the dark) of more than half an hour (see Table 5.2), and the Commission also found that children *normally* worked the same hours as adults, 12 or more hours being the usual period (Children's Employment Commission, 1843). In our own time, we do not have to go outside Europe to find subcultural groups where children of 11 are expected, though illegally, to contribute to the labour force of certain manufacturing trades, their labour being sold to ensure their families' subsistence; while in many parts of the world large proportions of children expect to find much of their own subsistence, either through paid employment or by varied forms of hustling.

Although 34% of our 11-year-olds occasionally earn money and a further 31% regularly do so, they are not expected to contribute this towards the household expenses; the worst that may happen is that their parents will feel relieved of any need to provide pocket money. However, their increased competence in all areas does mean that their help with household chores could be a realistic benefit, rather than the mere symbol of willingness that it tended to be at 7. Particularly where both parents are working, sharing of domestic tasks might seem almost a necessity. However, while most children will occasionally 'take a fancy' to doing a little housework, if only for its novelty value, the real usefulness of such a role (as opposed to the warm glow in response to an occasional grand gesture by the child) lies in its regular dependability. For this reason, the question was framed: 'What jobs do you *expect* him to do for you now – I mean without being paid?' Jobs were coded into four categories: 'help at mealtimes' (table-laying, washing-up, drying-up); 'light indoor housework' (tidying, vacuum cleaning, dusting, bed-making); miscellaneous dirty and outdoor jobs (gardening, sweeping yard, window- or car-cleaning, mending fires, potato-peeling, shoe-cleaning, bin-emptying etc.); and 'running errands', mainly to the shops. The categories listed seldom include real cooking or major chores such as washing and ironing; these are occasionally done by particularly domesticated children (mainly girls), or as an occasional 'fancy', but they are not expected.

Table 4.3 shows these different task categories in relation to boys and girls; we have included middle class and working class summaries only, since class differences are not significant.

The most obvious finding from this table is that by 11 years the pattern of children's involvement in housework depends upon their sex: more girls are involved in various kinds of light housework, whereas more boys are expected to do outdoor jobs and to run errands.

From the transcripts it is clear that parents rarely make heavy demands in this area; and in many instances children are only expected to offer self-help such as

TABLE 4.3 Children's expected participation in household chores

Task category	Sex	M.class		W.class	All random	Sex difference significance
		%		%	%	
Help at mealtimes	Boys	41		40	40	★★★★
	Girls	61		64	63	
	Both	51	n.s.	52	51	
Light indoor housework	Boys	21		19	19	★★★★
	Girls	47		43	44	
	Both	34	n.s.	31	32	
Dirty/outdoor jobs	Boys	41		35	36	★★★★
	Girls	11		7	8	
	Both	26	n.s.	21	22	
Running errands	Boys	32		41	39	★★★★
	Girls	17		22	21	
	Both	25	n.s.	32	30	

tidying their rooms, putting away their own toys or clean clothes, looking after their own pets and making the occasional cup of tea when asked. Table 4.3 does not show unambiguously that girls are expected to do more than boys, because it does not take into account the frequency with which demands are made and acceded to; in particular, it is not easy to compare tasks which recur daily or more, such as table-laying, bed-making or washing-up, with less frequent tasks such as weeding or car-washing. However, inspection will show that those tasks expected of girls do tend to be the most frequently recurrent ones. If in fact we divide the children into those who at best make only a token contribution, and those who have regular jobs including those who do several jobs daily, there is no doubt that girls are expected to do more in this area than boys: regular jobs are expected of 54% of girls compared with 40% of boys (★★★★). Of course, if boys spend more time 'out and about' than girls, they will be in a better position to avoid housework; and obviously they may find it in their interest to pick up any stereotypes they may encounter about what is 'men's work' and 'women's work': 'other boys don't have to do it!' is a protest that it may be difficult for the mother to check on. However, enough mothers themselves foster such stereotypes to make it easy for many boys to be 'off out' without suffering many pangs of conscience.

> **Part-time dinner-lady, husband a storeman:**
> Well, I think with him having two sisters – they're usually the ones that do the washing-up and other jobs – he's a bit slap-happy if he's doing a job …
>
> **Part-time presser, husband a cable-jointer:**
> Well, boys – none. I mean, girls, they don't mind doing domestic things, but for boys I don't think it's …
>
> **Taxi driver, husband a window cleaner:**
> A boy doesn't do much.
>
> **Part-time kitchen assistant, husband an electrical engineer:**
> It's left to them to keep their bedroom tidy. And he does go shopping for me. He's often asked me if he can wash the pots and set the table – but that I think is a girl's job, and that is left to Jenny.
>
> **Part-time machine operator, husband a press operator:**
> Well, I do like her to wash pots, but I don't think she's took a fancy to it. I think that's one of the nasty jobs. I like her to do a bit of housework, even if she doesn't do it properly. I mean, I think she ought to show a bit of interest, cause I mean females have to don't they?

Equally significant, of course, is the *special* pride of some mothers in boys who do help, or who help *when they're in the mood*: 'When he wants to be, he can be one of the best lads you could ever wish for'; or, indeed, the defensiveness of mothers who encourage their boys to help. Again, what mothers take for granted, and what they do not, is crucial.

Not in paid work, husband a store departmental manager:
He's helpful, he – it probably doesn't seem right for a boy, but – he enjoys washing the pots, wiping the pots, or anything in the house he doesn't mind doing, he enjoys it. He's even started asking if he can do some ironing – probably because the two other boys always press their own trousers – the eldest boy, apart from his underwear, does insist on doing all his own ironing. I think a boy *should* be able to do housework, I think also a man should know how to do simple cookery. [Do they get this from your husband?] Well, they might. He doesn't mind doing these things. I look at it from this point of view – I don't know whether you would agree with it – but when they marry and have children, if the wife or mother is ill, these children are still being looked after.

The implication of these figures, of course, is that more than half the children do very little for the household at all. If we take this analysis further, to look at *how many* different jobs are expected, we find that 10% do absolutely nothing, while 15% do three or more; on these extremes the sex differences disappear. However, interestingly enough we now find a class difference in that children who take on several regular jobs in the home are more common as we go up the social scale, while those who do nothing at all increase as we move down the scale: thus families with the lowest incomes in fact make less effective use of their children as a potential source of domestic help, while those who are more likely to have paid help also expect more help from their children (★★★).

One might expect more use of children's help by mothers at work, and this in fact is true: 61% of children whose mothers are at work full-time give at least modest help, compared with 47% of children whose mothers work part-time and only 43% of non-working mothers (★★★).

Mothers quite often explained their low housework expectations of the child in terms of expecting a lot of him at school: that school was his 'job' – and indeed, this was a point of view that we had already encountered when the children were 7.

Not in paid work, husband a printer:
Well, he don't do a lot of jobs. Well, I don't expect them to, not when they're at school, because he don't have long when he comes home. He might do an errand at night, but not often. But as regards jobs around the house, I do them. He'll wash the pots on Saturday.

Not in paid work, husband a garage owner:
I don't expect them to do a lot. I sort of consider if he gets his homework done, the job he's supposed to do, I think that's enough at this age.

To test whether this reason was in fact rationally applied, it seemed worthwhile to look at the relationship both between housework and educational aspirations, and between housework and homework. No evidence was found that children whose mothers expected them to stay at school until they were 18 were either more or less involved with household chores at this age. However, there is a striking relationship between housework expectations and whether the child has homework at the junior school (it should be emphasised here that homework is not usual at the junior stage, and in fact only 12% of our children were given this). But in this minority group, more children were also expected to participate regularly in household chores: 68%, compared to 45% of those who had no homework (★★★★).

'I try and make the effort to take them ... There again, the money problem, you know'

To complete this discussion on children's activities, we will look at some of those that children follow not just within the home but as part of an active family group; and this topic will form an introduction to the more central theme of communication and family cohesiveness with which we shall be occupied in the next chapter.

The questions on family activities followed those more intimate ones on mother/child and father/child relationships which we shall explore shortly. They were introduced:

Q. 132 What about the things you might do together as a family (if three or more children) − or several of you together? − for instance, do you ever manage a family outing to the seaside, or into the country?

This was followed by additional prompts to cover going to a film together, to a theatre, museums, stately homes, going swimming or for a picnic, and 'any other sort of outing or entertainment'. Mothers were also asked whether the family read aloud or sang together, or sat down and played a card game or board game together; whether the children would get up a family concert or play, and whether they ever organised 'a little jumble sale or some sort of fair among themselves'. These last two questions were included on the basis that these events required an audience and customers, and that sales and fairs within the family needed a certain amount of cooperation from the adults; it was found possible to code answers on this basis. Since the possibilities for families with financial resources are fairly obvious, we have chosen here to illustrate the theme with two long quotations from families who are feeling the financial pinch.

Part-time waitress, husband a lorry driver (seven children in the family):

Oh yes, definitely. We go camping, you know, we've got a tent and everything, and week-ends − work permitting of course − pack up Saturday afternoon till Sunday night in the summer − yes, we go to the sea, and we go out every afternoon if we don't go camping − Clumber Park or Colwick Woods, sometimes just down by the river, but we always go out. [Stately homes?] No. We can't – it's just the expense, with the lot of us, so we stick to places where we can go and have a good romp and we don't have to dress them up, we can go in old jeans and sweaters, and they can have the time of their lives. [Museums at all?] Two or three times – we went to the Castle a couple of times last year. Wollaton Hall, we go there, but there again, it's free you know. We do go round, but not because we particularly like museums, but it's there and it's something to do. We don't go to the theatre; sometimes we go to films, not very often, but if there's something they'd particularly like to see, I try and make the effort to take them – perhaps three or four times a year, that's all. There again, the money problem, you know – it just can't be done all the while. [Any other …?] Well, they swim, I don't go because I can't swim, I stay at home with [the baby], but Terry takes them swimming. [Read aloud, sing?] Oh yes, yes, you ought to hear this place sometimes. Singing and reading, yes – we're very fond of reading, all of us. [Who reads?] It depends who's elected at the time – June [11], she's a very very good reader and she loves to read out loud, sometimes it's me, sometimes it's one of the boys, you know. [What do you read?] Fiction – Black Beauty, Little Women, Heidi. Tom – we bought him a set of animal encyclopaedias, he'll often sit and read us facts and figures out of there. I've always encouraged reading because I love it myself, I'm a great reader, I read anything – my mother always said I'd read a sugar bag if there was nothing else, you know – I encourage them to read, I buy them books, and we read anything to hand – they're all in the library, so of course they get a pretty good range of books. [Board games, card games?] Oh yes, we're great games fans. We've got practically everything you can think of – Monopoly, Mousetrap – June has a great big compendium of games, she had that last Christmas. Oh yes, we're a great fun-and-games family.

Not in paid work, husband a crane driver (six children in the family):

When they're off school and that, I take them out, like. We pack up – all the children, you know. We've been down Trent Bridge to the paddling pool, and to Carrington Lido, in the summertime. [Picnic?] No – we used to, when we was nearer my friend, like – they'd got a big van. We used to go fishing, us and their family – used to cook chickens on a Saturday night, you know, and take the bread as it was, and take the butter as it was, and pop and we used to go about 7 o'clock on a Sunday morning, and come back p'raps 8 o'clock at night, you know. And we used to enjoy it. But of course he's parted with the van, you see … my husband's after another one, so we can go out a bit, like … We went away for a month last year – it was my husband's foreman's caravan. It was after I had baby, you see. It was marvellous – Mablethorpe – and we can have it again this year. We had quite a lot of rain, like. Course, Mester didn't come, cause he was at work, but he used to come at weekends and bring my money and stay for the weekend – it was nice.

TABLE 4.4 Families involved together in spare-time activities

Activity 'as a family'	M.class %	W.class %	Overall popn %	Boy/Girl significance	M.cl vs W.cl significance
Outings: country, stately homes etc.	96	83	86	n.s.	★★★★
Outings: spectator sports, swimming, fishing etc.	54	34	40	n.s.	★★★★
Outings: other specified	41	31	34	n.s.	★★★
Cinema, theatre	65	43	49	n.s.	★★★★
Reading aloud	20	16	17	n.s.	n.s. (trend ★★★)
Singing, playing instruments	47	46	46	n.s.	n.s.
Board/card games	82	81	81	n.s.	n.s.
Family concert	9	4	6	★ girls more	★ (trend ★★★★)
Getting up a play	16	10	12	★★★★ girls more	★ (trend ★★)
Jumble sale/fête	16	15	15	★★★ girls more	

Table 4.4 shows proportions of families who are involved together in these various activities. These results are given here to record sex and social class patterns for each activity separately; the same data eventually contribute to an index of family cohesiveness in relation to the particular child of the sample, by including features of family communication which may be special to him or to her (see Tables 6.2 and 6.3).

As one might expect from data mainly concerning whole families rather than individual children, sex differences are not significant for any activities which tend to be dependent on parent initiatives; however, they are for the last three activities, where the 'target' child may well be largely responsible for getting the activity going, and parents take the role of facilitators rather than initiators. It is notable that all the activities which involve going out of the home, and usually out of the neighbourhood, are strongly social-class affiliated; undoubtedly expense must play some part here. It is interesting that reading aloud does not show a stronger class difference; small numbers make it difficult to show a working-class/middle-class difference, but there is a reasonably substantial trend (from 21% to 8%).

Overall, whatever the reasons for lower working-class participation in the facilities offered by the community and by the world at large, these results, in terms of any individual child's experience, add up to a narrowing of horizons for the working-class child compared with those born into middle-class homes. At the lower end of the scale, this may mean massive cultural deprivation. As we pointed out when the children were 7, sharing *with parents* in what the wider world has to offer is likely to be a crucial experience in resolving the child's various identification processes.[1] At 7, as at 11, children at the lower end of the scale can, in many different aspects of their everyday life, be seen to be at risk; once again, it is the *persistence* of such patterns which must concern us.

Note

1 See Newson and Newson (1977) Chapters 3, 4 and 6 for a detailed discussion of this topic. However, the argument is offered in a much more succinct form in E. Newson (1982).

References

Children's Employment Commission. (1843) *Second Report of the Commissioners on Trades and Manufactures*, Irish University Press Series of British Parliamentary Papers, facsimile reproduction, Shannon: IUP, 1968.

Newson, E. (1982) 'Child, parent, school and culture; issues in identification', in M. Braham (ed.) *Aspects of Education*, Chichester: Wiley.

Newson, J. and Newson, E. (1968) *Four Years Old in an Urban Community*, London: George Allen & Unwin.

Newson, J. and Newson, E. (1976) *Seven Years Old in the Home Environment*, London: George Allen & Unwin.

Newson, J. and Newson, E., with Barnes, P. (1977) *Perspectives on School at Seven Years Old*, London: George Allen & Unwin.

Newson, J., Newson, E. and Mahalski, P. (1982) 'Persistent infant comfort habits and their sequelae at 11 and 16 years', *Journal of Child Psychology and Psychiatry*, 23 (4): 421–36.

Sullivan, H.S. (1953) *The Interpersonal Theory of Psychiatry*, New York: W.W. Norton.

5

RISK, ANXIETY AND FRANKNESS AS CHILDREN GROW UP

The approach of the two watersheds of puberty and transfer to secondary education inevitably signals to parents a diminishing of their own control, as the child comes under new pressures, new influences and new temptations. The degree of chaperonage they exerted at 7, they know will no longer be feasible; freed from that chaperonage, they are aware that the child has the opportunity of engaging in behaviour, or acquiring knowledge, that it was formerly within their power to suppress if they wished. This chapter looks at parents' attitudes to these issues, firstly in relation to the child's mobility, secondly in terms of sexual awareness.

'I was worried, imagining all sorts, cause you read such a lot, you never know ...'

When these children were 7, we saw that there were a number of hazards about which their mothers were fearful while the children were not under their own or the school's supervision. These were, in order of priority, 'strangers', traffic, and dangerous places such as railway embankments and deep water.

At 11, these same hazards are still very much in mothers' minds; and often their fears are exacerbated because it no longer seems reasonable, with an older child, simply to prevent the child experiencing such hazards by keeping him within beck and call or by insisting on an adult companion. Parents are conscious that the children do have to grow up and face these dangers alone at some time. Timothy's mother says 'You feel as though you've got to let them do these things, although you worry when they've gone'; Neill's mother says 'You've got to – the longer you leave it, the less self-reliant he will be', though she admits to 'hanging out of the window watching the bus stop' when Neill goes to Woolworth's; and Isobel's mother worries about Isobel being out on her bike, but says 'I thought I'd just have to stop worrying.' The question is when to allow more freedom and how to ensure a child's safety: most mothers clearly think you can't with any certainty, and that the best one can hope for at this age is to make the children a better risk. In one way parents are impelled into cutting the leading reins now, because secondary school is in sight, and will almost always involve a longer journey on which the child will not usually wish to be seen to be under chaperonage. At the same time, the school journey, which is clearly regarded as predictable in route and duration, and leading from one sanctuary to another, is felt to be a rather different matter from allowing the child out on an open-ended trip to town or to a distant park.[1]

Following questions about how far and for how long children were allowed to go out on their own, which we will look at shortly, we asked mothers:

90. How do you feel about children going off to places alone – does it worry you at all? (In what way?)

From this question we were able to judge what worry was uppermost in the mother's mind. 86% of all mothers said they *were* inclined to worry whenever their children were out on their own; girls' mothers were more inclined to worry than those of boys (92% compared with 80%, ★★★★). This sex difference reflects the fact that at this age, as at 7, the most commonly expressed anxiety was that the child would be harmed by some other person; this also tended to be the most forcefully expressed anxiety where several were mentioned. Sexual molestation was the major concern here, and, as one might expect, it was much more often expressed in relation to girls, although mothers frequently made the point that boys, too, needed to be on their guard. A less frequent, but still substantial worry, particularly in relation to boys, was attacks by other children or adolescents. For 53% of mothers, then, the main fear was 'people', but this rose to 66% of girls' mothers compared with 42% of boys' mothers (★★★★).

Part-time machinist, husband a cook:
Yes, yes, I am bit anxious about them [Felicity and older brother], and it's only with things as they are today. I mean, I drum it into them, don't talk to strangers and all this business, but if anybody talks nicely to Felicity, I've still got a sneaky feeling that they could persuade her. I don't know whether I'm right or not, but if anyone's, you know, really nice, I've still got my doubts whether she'd say no and run away, much as we've tried to drum it into them.

Part-time surveyor, husband a quantity surveyor:
Yes it does, young children. I'm afraid it's probably just society as it is today – the things one reads in the newspapers about boys being set on, I mean this had happened to Jamie, locally – you get all types. I know they've got to go out and meet people, but they can do this when they're older. When I read of boys setting on to young boys for no reason apart from bullying, I feel, right, they're better off here for a while. I mean it's usually a group. Just by the bridge here – he was going to the shops with a friend on a bicycle, and these

boys got them off their bicycles and gave them a jolly good hit. So when this is happening just locally, it isn't your own children you can't trust, it's just that you wonder what *is* going to happen.

Fear of traffic was rather more often expressed by boys' mothers: rightly so in view of actual accident statistics in Nottingham up to age 11, although once girls start going to secondary school their accident rate rises markedly. 21% of boys' mothers were mainly afraid of traffic, compared with 14% of girls' (★★). Fear of deep water, cliffs etc., were not on their own of great importance, and we coded these among situations in which the child wouldn't be able to cope, including getting lost; boys were only slightly more numerous than girls here (18%:13%, not significant).

> **Part-time worker in the family business, husband a wholesaler:**
> I can't say it doesn't worry me – I think it does – well, obviously it does. Neill's responsible, but he's impulsive. Now I could be quite certain that Martin [older brother] would use the zebra crossing, but I couldn't be that certain with Neill. This is the thing that worries me – I think he's quite sensible, but I think he'd have unguarded moments.

What strategies, then, do parents employ to protect their children? Obviously one possibility is to keep them in, to restrict their movements or hedge them about with rules. Another is to chaperone them personally wherever they go. Thirdly, children can be heavily warned of the dangers and hazards. Fourthly, tactics and training can be offered them.

Most parents have been concerned to teach traffic sense since their children were at infant school and earlier, and schools too back up this aim; though research suggests that formal road drill has not been very successful in teaching children to deal with real road conditions (Grayson and Howarth, 1982). Cycling proficiency is formally taught in many cities – perhaps especially in Nottingham, where it is supported by the influential cycle industry. Parents are appreciative of this facility, though they sometimes feel pressured into having given more freedom than they wish to a child who has manifestly 'passed his proficiency'. A particular problem for modern children is that travelling round town by bus or car may be a very poor way of getting to know how the different roads connect on foot, such are the convolutions of one-way systems in most city centres; a few mothers who particularly distrust their child's power to cope in town, or whose child himself lacks confidence, allow him to lead them round to prove that he can find his way. It is less easy to give the child actual strategies for dealing with the sexual molester, though some mothers do feel they must go beyond mere warnings.

> **Packer, husband a pipe-layer:**
> I've always told him, if he's coming from school and anyone tries to stop him or take him into a car, just pretend that the first gate he comes to is his house,

and walk in and go to the front door, and tell the person there *why* you've rung the bell.

Clerk, husband a clerk:
We've explained that she must never get into a car or let anyone entice her – that if there was any reason that she was wanted and I couldn't get there myself to fetch her, and I'd got to send a message, I'd send something belonging to me.

Typist, husband a shop manager:
I've told Joanne that if she's ever caught by anybody, a harmful method of defence is to lift her knee and kick him where it'll hurt most in a man, that's the only way you can sort of … I think children should be taught ju-jitsu, but then you see you're going to defeat your object in a generation's time, because this person will already *know* ju-jitsu.

Warnings are, inevitably, repeatedly given, to the extent that some parents are aware that they may have overloaded the circuit. There are of course specific and real difficulties in warning children sensitively about sexual dangers, particularly if the actual sexual nature of the danger is to be explicitly referred to. For this reason, we shall return to what precisely parents say to their children about this in the final section of this chapter.

Constant chaperoning is clearly impracticable in large families unless the children are rather limited in the range of their independent activities; nor is it easy without transport, or if the mother does not drive. However, some mothers are conscious that they have so far managed to bypass the child's demand to get out and about on his own, by prolonging chaperonage in a rather habitual way. Mark is a youngest child with grown-up siblings.

Research assistant, husband a teacher:
Well, yes, it does worry me. But you know what it is, with the car, they just never do go, do they? It does worry me, yes, but I have never had to consider it with Mark, because he's just never been anywhere alone – it *would* worry me.

The restrictions put on children's independent mobility are partly a matter of negotiation, of course, and there are some mothers who need put few restrictions on the child because he has no wish to be geographically adventurous – a few are even wondering whether they ought to be encouraging the child to take more risks! Others, like Max's mother, feel that 'it's not a question of how far he's *allowed* to go, it's how far he goes!' Given that both mother's and child's wishes are involved in what the child finally does, it seemed worth probing both what he was allowed to do and what his geographical range actually was; thus the index of chaperonage that results from these questions partly rather than wholly reflects each person's attitude, but should accurately indicate the outcome, i.e. the degree to which the child in fact remains under chaperonage. The index is made up of data on use of buses, where children may go, and how long their journeys take; in addition we sought information on use of cycles, but could not include this in the index because of variation in ownership of these. We also asked about independent train journeys, which would have been difficult to include in the index because of their expensiveness, but which turned out to be almost non-existent anyway.

> Does he ever go on a bus on his own? (Coded: school only/other/none).

60% of all children go alone on buses on journeys other than to school; additionally 6% go to school only. Boys are slightly more likely than girls to take bus-rides other than to school (65%:56% *), but there are no class differences.

> Would you let him go into town on his own – to the big Woolworth's, say? Or – to Boots in the Victoria Centre, say? (The destination was chosen according to where the child lived, to ensure that the child would need to negotiate the city centre to get there.)

49% of children overall may do this; there are both class and sex differences. The class trend (****) runs from 63% in Class I and II down to 41% in Class V. 60% of boys may make this journey, compared with 39% of girls ****), rising to 68% of Class I and II boys and falling to only 24% of Class V girls. On evidence elsewhere in the interview, one would suppose shopping trips like this would be much more attractive to girls than to boys, so the restriction is especially striking in view of the motivation.

> Would you let him go to Wollaton Park/Trent Bridge Embankment by himself? (Depending on where the child lived, the 'park' specified was chosen to entail a cross-town journey to get there. Both these places have attractive recreational facilities, both have the danger of water, but neither has a *particularly* bad name for prowlers.)

Parks, however probably because they offer more opportunity than crowded places for attacks to take place unwitnessed, are considered suspect. Only 18% of children were allowed to undertake this expedition. There was no significant class trend, although middle-class parents as a whole were very slightly less restrictive than working-class as a whole (*); class differences were more manifest for boys than for girls, probably showing that parents were agreed that parks as such were dangerous places for girls. The sex difference remained marked: boys were three times as likely as girls to be allowed this journey (27%:9% ****).

We also asked whether the child would be allowed to go with other children of his own age or only with a responsible older person. Clearly other children are some sort of protection; however, mothers are aware that sometimes one child will abandon another if trouble brews up, and also that groups of children can lead each other into dangerous situations (particularly of the 'daring' variety) which would be shunned by a child on his own. On balance, then, although peer group companionship extends those allowed to make this expedition by a further 30%, there is still a majority restriction to older companions-in-charge only (52% – boys 43%, girls 60% ★★★★).

> (Referring to longest journey undertaken by child alone) Does that mean a journey of more than half an hour on his own?

The striking finding here is not in terms of class or sex differences (which are not significant), but in the shortness of journeys undertaken by 11-year-olds generally. The longest journey alone for 65% of children takes less than half an hour. 'About half an hour' is the duration for another 11%, and only 24% ever undertake a journey lasting more than half an hour on their own.

> Has he got a bicycle? How far is he allowed to go on it? Do you have any rules about which roads he can go on? Is he ever allowed to ride it after dark?

Ownership of bicycles, as one might expect, is closely class-related; it is also, less predictably, sex-related (Table 5.1).

Paradoxically, when one considers what bicycles are supposed to be for, ownership of a cycle does not automatically guarantee geographical mobility; nor, indeed, does it ensure that one can actually ride it to the local shops. Our findings support Roger Hart's in the United States, that 'cycling range lags behind the extent of the children's pedestrian range' (Hart, 1979).[2] Like one nervous mother who encouraged her husband and son in small-dinghy sea-sailing because at least they were then not cliff-climbing, some mothers relax their rules about keeping one's possessions in good repair because at least a broken bicycle is not being ridden.

TABLE 5.1 Children who own bicycles at 11

	Social class					Summary		
	I&II	IIIWC	IIIMan	IV	V	M.class	W.class	All (random)
	%	%	%	%	%	%	%	%
Boys	85	70	50	54	34	78	49	57
Girls	67	51	47	39	22	59	43	47
Both	75	60	49	47	28	68	46	52

Significance: class trend ↘ ★★★★   m.class vs w.class ★★★★
between sexes ★★★★

Not in paid work, husband an engineer:
Well, it's broken at the moment, and we're reluctant to get it mended because goodness knows whether she'd go on the roads – we don't really agree with her going on the road on a bike.

Part-time librarian, husband an insurance clerk:
If I can help it, he's not allowed to get it out of the garage! He's just passed his proficiency test, and until now he's only been allowed on the pavements. If I let him out on the road now, which I can see he's going to put pressure on to do, I will not let him go on that main road, on the bus route. I'll still insist he goes in the immediate vicinity of the house on the road – if at all.

Part-time worker in family business, husband a wholesaler:
He's only allowed to go around locally. I don't let him go any distance, and quite frankly I discourage this as much as possible. Why we ever bought them in the first place I don't know.

65% of children who own cycles are not allowed to use them on main roads, and there are no class differences. However, girls are less trusted than boys – 72% of cycle-owning girls are forbidden main roads, compared with 58% of boys (★★★★).

The index of chaperonage is made up of scores derived as shown in Table 5.2, which also shows the results discussed in this section (excluding use of bicycles and trains) in terms of this index.

The index is particularly interesting in terms of comparison with a similar attempt to measure chaperonage at 7 years. At that time we were able to base the index on far more questions because there was in fact much more variety of restrictions considered appropriate for children of 7; at the same time, most of the restrictions then operated within the child's own neighbourhood – for the child to move outside his neighbourhood at all was not at issue, and those who did this were to that extent considered out of control. The index at 7 referred to whether the child was fetched from school, whether he had to report home before playing out, and whether there was an adult there to meet him; whether the child was allowed friends in to play, and whether he played on the street or not; how easily he could be found when wanted; whether rules were enforced about reporting back before moving from one friend's house to another, and about how far he might go; and whether he was allowed to go anywhere such as the cinema, swimming baths, or recreation ground alone (Newson and Newson, 1976, Chapter 3).

On this basis it was clear that, as we descended the class scale, 7-year-olds were increasingly likely to be 'off on their own' and out of adult supervision (★★★), and this was seen as a significant way in which class affiliation had an effect upon the influence capable of being exerted by parents at 7, as well as upon the kinds of activities encouraged in the child – the more academically-oriented activities tending to take place within an adult–home orbit rather than away from it. At 11, the position is different in the sense that many of the more intellectually and otherwise 'stretching' opportunities now open to the child are community-based

TABLE 5.2 An index of chaperonage at 11 years

Scoring system

Based on:		Reply	Score
Q. 84	Bus on his own?	Never	2
		School only	1
		Elsewhere	0
Q. 85	Into town on his own?	No	1
		Yes	0
Q. 86	Through town to park/ embankment?	Only with older person	2
		With same-age person	1
		Alone	0
Q. 88	Maximum journey time	Less than ½ hour	2
		About ½ hour	1
		More than ½ hour	0

Note: Score range 0–7.

	Social class					Summary		
	I&II	IIIWC	IIIMan	IV	V	M.class	W.class	All (random)
	%	%	%	%	%	%	%	%
Low scorers (0,1,2)								
Boys	39	35	37	31	31	37	37	36
Girls	26	21	20	26	17	24	21	22
Both	33	28	29	29	24	31	28	29

Significance: class trend. n.s   Boys vs girls ★★★★

	I&II	IIIWC	IIIMan	IV	V	M.class	W.class	All (random)
High scorers (6,7)								
Boys	21	26	21	28	33	23	24	24
Girls	24	30	38	41	41	27	39	36
Both	22	28	30	35	37	25	31	30

Significance: class trend ↗ ★★★   Boys vs girls ★★★

and take place in organised groups. It is at this point, then, that middle-class parents are relaxing their restrictions on mobility, despite their undoubted anxieties about it, because they now find the advantages convincing: that is, the child's greater freedom is paralleled by (justified by?) an influx of 'worthwhile' community activities. Not only are class differences negligible for low scorers on chaperonage, but for high scorers the class trend is actually reversed compared with the situation at 7.

It must be remembered, of course, that further up the social scale parents have much more choice both in having the means to ferry their children around and the resources to monitor and moderate whatever freedoms they allow. For instance, a child may well be allowed to go under his own steam to a certain place, but be expected to phone back home in order to be collected by car when his activities are completed. Clearly in such a case his activities are under some long-distance supervision: he will have to be seen to be in the approved place at the approved time, and the period away from his parents is itself likely to be shorter; equally clearly, this is dependent on ownership of both car and telephone, and monitoring becomes increasingly feasible with a second car and a mother for whom chauffeuring is seen as one of her roles. As so often happens in any anthropological study, the most interesting insights come from listening to people taking things for granted.

> **Not in paid work, husband a telephone technician:**
> [Father:] We don't mind as long as we know he's been there before and he knows his way back and he's going to visit someone, and we kind of let them know he's going then, so he's got a limited time of freedom. [Mother:] And he knows how to use the phone, so he phones up and lets me know where he is and if he's stranded, so one of us could pick him up.

It is sometimes suggested, one suspects with a sentimentality motivated by guilt, that working-class children are compensated for their lack of facilities by the richness and variety of their street culture. Imagine, thinks the middle-class myth-maker, the wild freedom of roaming the historic streets of London instead of being confined by the middle-class blandness of Dulwich or Winchmore Hill! The restrictions placed on these working-class children show a rather different picture; and this is supported by Colin Ward, who in his study of children in cities (Ward, 1978) describes children living in Southwark who had never crossed the Thames.

The persisting sex difference is as interesting as the changing class findings. At 7 we found girls more closely chaperoned than boys, even within the neighbourhood, at every point on the class scale (★★★). At that time we suggested that chaperonage might contribute strongly to the personality differences between boys and girls that have been repeatedly found in other studies as well as our own: that boys tend to be thrusting, aggressive, active and 'thing-oriented' (Erikson, 1955), while girls tend to be nurturant, amenable, sedentary and 'person-oriented'. We are not suggesting that these differences are entirely environmentally induced, and indeed we would strongly question whether marked personality differences between boys and girls could be induced, within a climate of person-responsive child-rearing, unless there were already sex-linked genetic patterns which were hospitable to the differential treatments offered to girls and boys. But differential treatment must build on and exaggerate such genetic patterns, and differentials lasting persistently and consistently over the years are likely to be especially potent.

'They held hands going to swimming one day ...'

We saw in Chapter 3 that for only 1% of our children was an opposite-sex child identified as their 'best friend'. This may of course lie partly in the mother's perception of what is appropriate in a 'best friendship'; but a difference between 1% and 64% can hardly be wholly attributable to a distorted perception of the reality, and must at the very least be supported by the children's overt behaviour. However, because puberty had actually arrived for some children, and was seen as imminent by most mothers, we thought it pertinent to ask both about proto-sexual relationships at this stage, and about mothers' expectances of these.

The conventional developmental account of the emergence of the sexual relationships is that from about 7 years old – when, as we saw in earlier studies, sex-linked attitudes and interests have already polarised fairly sharply – until puberty, there is a so-called latency period. This term is, of course, borrowed from Freudian theory, which assumes an earlier period of sexually motivated attachment which ends with the resolution of Oedipal conflict and gives place to latency period. (Our own view on the psychoanalytic formulation is that early 'sexual' attachment could be more properly described as 'passionate' attachment, and that the ascription of a sexual component is an 'adultomorphism', the result of the adult observer's equation of passion and sex.) The implication of the latency period, whether in psychoanalytic or developmental terms, is that cross-sex friendships during this time will be platonic until the hormonal changes of puberty trigger a sexual awakening.

Clearly one has to ask whether the strong identification of boys with boys and girls with girls, even in the co-educational setting of ordinary primary schools, is a phenomenon which is induced into children, explicitly and implicitly, by the attitudes of teachers and parents. Among most adults, the tendency to form sex-role stereotypes remains very strong, even where the adult also has a rational or political reaction against this. Richardson (1976) found that mothers who consciously identified themselves as subscribing to the ideals of the Women's Movement still found themselves compelled by sex-role considerations in their dealings with their own young children. From the moment of birth, the new baby's primary identity is in terms of 'girl child' or 'boy child', and this ascription of sex, *with all its cultural gender implications*, rapidly becomes fixed in parental perceptions; but there is now evidence from a number of studies that sex differences in the first two years are sufficient to support and reinforce sex-differentiated perceptions on the part of parents. However, it is also true that in cases where sex has from a genetic standpoint been incorrectly ascribed, these perceptions are reversible only with the greatest of difficulty and indeed trauma. Whether one implicates genetic or environmental forces, then (or whether, as seems most credible in relation to the evidence, one assumes genetic states which are differentially hospitable to environmental sex-role expectations as historically defined), one must doubt whether it would be possible to create a situation in which the interests and attitudes of primary school children, and hence their friendship patterns, were *not* polarised according to sex.

Polarisation in interests is not, of course, the same thing as sexual latency; it cannot be seriously suggested, for instance, that sexual activity is wholly dependent upon shared interests other than a joint interest in sexual activity itself. In many ways, in fact, ordinary boys and girls diverge still more sharply in adolescence so far as a-sexual interests are concerned, but cross-sex relationships then become paramount because of the superior motive force of sexual attraction, which does not, as in friendship, require mutual interests to sustain it, in the short run at least.

However, it may also be true that existing sex differences in interests between 7 and 11 may be not only sustained by a sexual latency which makes contact between sexes unnecessary, but also encouraged by adults – just because adults both are aware of the power of sexual motivation and have ideas about when that motivation should become activated. That is, parents and teachers may reinforce the belief that little boys and girls are not sexually attracted to one another before puberty, out of an underlying fear that, unless this belief is firmly maintained, the children might all too easily be drawn into premature sexual experimentation. That possibility is in fact obliquely referred to when some parents of children as young as 7 make facetious references to 'his girlfriend', 'her little boyfriend' rather than using the non-specific term 'friend'; interestingly enough, working-class parents are much more likely to make this joking innuendo, and it is they who are also more likely to object vigorously, and indeed punish, when the children do show frankly sexual interest in each other. Whether the children are examining each other under the guise of 'playing doctors' (a game often explicitly forbidden by working-class mothers) or whether sexual romping is involved, the criterion for concern seems to be the amount of one-to-one concentration: mothers are much more tolerant of the gangs of little boys who sometimes sweep through the school playground, tweaking up the skirt of every little girl, to their pleasurable alarm and scorn; and these male sorties do seem to have more in common with the scatological jokes and competitive 'peeing up the wall' that convulse male groups in both infant and junior school.

By 11, as befits children who are now the elders and betters in the primary school hierarchy, an idealistic and romantic element tends to enter conscious friendships between boy and girl. Both the growth spurt preceding puberty and the actual changes of puberty tend to begin in girls earlier (by 24 and 9 months respectively) than in boys (Tanner, 1978) and it would seem reasonable to expect a romantic awakening in girls before boys – especially as sex stereotyping would predict greater romantic interest among girls anyway. However, this is not particularly evident from these mothers' observation. 22% of boys and 20% of girls have some kind of romantic attachment, as defined by the question 'Has the question of girlfriends/boyfriends come up at all yet – I mean, is there anyone N feels a a bit romantic about?' Half the girls' attachments and three-quarters of the boys' attachments are reciprocated by the other child.

Secretary, husband a policeman:
Oh yes – there is – John. He took her skating on Saturday afternoon, and he uses his brother's aftershave, but he doesn't shave yet!

Not in paid work, husband a policeman:
Yes – she's had a Christmas card ever since she was 7 from this particular boy, and she's started to go all blushy now … Daddy said 'Let me have a look at it', and he chased her upstairs, and she came down, and she was all aglow because she'd had a card.

Kitchen helper, husband a winder:
Oh yes – I've been told who the wife is going to be, but I haven't been introduced yet.

Travel agent, husband a representative:
I think they hold hands; and I heard him saying to Harry the other day that Maureen didn't like to be shown up in public – saying why he wasn't going to kiss her!

Not in paid work, husband a professional engineer:
[Father:] He has girl friends but we don't really know much about them. He's got a girl friend on holiday – the farm we go to – they've got a daughter of his own age who he's quite keen on. [Mother:] He spends all his money on her. [Do they kiss and hold hands?] [Mother:] Oh yes. They go round together and go in the hayloft and … you know … kiss and so on. [Father:] *Do* they? I didn't know that!

This was not the only interview in which this kind of information was revealed by one member of the family to another, and it was clear that there must be more romantic attachments than were known about by the mother.

Part-time dinner-lady, husband a stonemason:
Oh, he's always on about girls. [Sister: Linda Beggs!] Yes, there's one, Linda Beggs. [Sister: She's my best friend.] [Does Linda feel the same way?] No, I don't think so. [Sister: Yes she does.] Oh! Oh!! [Sister: She won't tell him, but she keeps saying 'I like your Harvey' and she wants to go out with him.] [Do they hold hands, and kiss?] Not to my knowledge. [Sister: Sometimes they do. Coming home from the swimming baths.] Oh! The truth will out!

Some accounts illustrated the child's readiness to think in these terms rather than his ability, or even motivation, to sustain such an attachment.

Not in paid work, husband a sprayer:
Yes! He went round with his hat – we all put money in to buy her a box of chocolates, and then after three days he says, 'Huh! I bought her a box of chocolates and now she's gone off with somebody else! But *I'm* not bothered.' And we never heard any more about it.

Not in paid work, ex-husband a second-hand dealer:
He's got engaged once at school! Engaged, and she went home with a ring on –
I don't know where he'd got the flaming ring from, I'm sure! Then he said
'She gave me the engagement ring back. She saw me kissing another girl!'

Some children are apparently not thinking in romantic terms at all; many boys,
at least, display a definite aversion, though this may of course conceal more private thoughts. Seamus has 'no time for girls at all, they're all cissies as far as he's
concerned'. Both Mrs Arnfield's sons 'would be appalled at the idea of *looking* at
a girl, never mind kissing one'. To Larry, 'girls are totally unnecessary – he thinks
it's bad enough having one for a sister!' Girls feel romantic about Lloyd: 'there are
often two or three at the gate, but he doesn't want anything to do with them'. The
transcripts, like the larger proportion of boys whose affections are reciprocated by
girls, suggest that rather fewer girls are so positively against romance: one is Eleanor,
who 'speaks with the utmost contempt' of boys; and 'when Chrissie was 5, she used
to say Hello to the boys – now she hates them!'

The heightened awareness of self-image which we noted in Chapter 2 is certainly linked for some children with an awareness of the opposite sex as an audience, even where there is as yet no particular attachment.

Clerk, husband a clerk:
No, *but* – if he sees some girls, or knows some girls are coming here, he'll go
and wash his face and do his hair, which is *very* unusual!

Not in paid work, husband a quarry worker:
Well, I wouldn't say romantic. There's a young lad who comes on a bicycle, he
cycles round and round and round, his name's Terry. Well, she talks at the gate to
him. Course, she has the tendency to look smart when he's around, you see, and
this was about three weeks ago, but he doesn't come often now, so that's gone.
The other day I asked her to fetch things off the line – and two young lads were
sitting on the shed at the bottom of the garden, and there she was brushing her
hair. And I said, 'Go on, Bernice, it's raining.' She said, 'I will in a minute.' Her hair
had to be done, and she went down and pretended to pick something up off the
path – but it was really because they were on the shed, because I watched her.

All in all, only a very few mothers are seeing the writing on the wall in the urgent
sense of perceiving the beginning of sexual, as opposed to romantic, activity at this
age. Those who do are not very happy about it. Mrs Glint has older daughters, one
of whom has already brought her 'trouble' in the form of an illegitimate grandchild,
and both in this transcript and elsewhere it is clear that she is almost resigned to
Marilynda 'going the same way': for her the writing was, literally, on the pavement.

Part-time waitress, husband a printer:
I don't know – I haven't a clue. I didn't know till yesterday that she was
interested in boys, until I went to the shops and scrawled on the pavement in

chalk was 'Marilynda Glint loves … somebody' and I thought, 'My goodness me, what's going off here?' Yet I can't say anything, because when we were that age, we were the same – we used to sit in the classroom and write little love-notes and pass them all over the classroom. I mean, we've experienced it ourselves, so we know – it's a phase every child goes through. But as I say, it is a bit worrying, especially when they start periods and things like that. With Yvonne and Gabriella, I was too embarrassed to talk about anything like that, because I had a mother that was very narrow-minded, and I had to find out a lot of things for myself. I'm still very ignorant of a lot of things of the facts of life. Going out to work has broadened my mind a lot – I meet people, and I hear things, and things like that, and I know more now than I ever knew when I was younger, and I've had to learn, sort of, my way. These children today, it's taught them at school, it's taught them on the television, it's in books, it's in papers – I mean, Marilynda comes out sometimes with things that really shock me. And I think to myself, well, it's the trend today, there's nothing I can do about it. But just let's hope that they know what they're doing, and I always says to Marilynda, 'Well, you know right from wrong, and if you do wrong then you know you've got to take the consequences.' I says, 'I can't say no more.' Cause I think if a child's going to do wrong behind your back, it'll do it. I mean, my husband used to demand them being in at a certain time, but if they're going to do wrong, they'll do it before nine o'clock – or after nine o'clock – they can do it any time of the day. I said 'That doesn't mean a thing really.' [Do you think she'd tell you (about romantic attachments)?] She hadn't, no. My daughter's opening my eyes. [Would you expect … at 11?] Oh yes; definite. Let's face it, today it's nothing, you see them at the [teacher training] College and all over the place. I mean, it's done so much in the open now, that there's nothing really … as I say, no matter how you fetch a child up, they go their own road. They've got a mind of their own today, and you or no-one can alter it. And as I said to my husband, I think it's four years since I shed a tear, because I stopped shedding tears a long time ago over children. It's a fact, that – as my mother says, 'They make your arms ache when they're babies and your heart break when they get older.' It's a true fact, that is.

Angela's mother describes herself as 'come-day, go-day' (i.e. easy-going), but she 'goes mad' on this particular issue.

Not in paid work, husband a plasterer:
Oh crikey, yes, somebody – they keep calling her Mrs somebody-or-other, when she goes down Grassfield Road now – I can't remember his name – I ought to do and all, cause they're always on about him. I know she's a bit of a lad-mad, cause if … even a man … you know, a man probably even somewhere round *my* age comes on [television] and he's got a nice face, she'll say 'Ooh, *he's* all right, Mam – look!' I say, 'hey, how old do you think you are?' you know, and I go mad.

'In this day and age one never knows ...'

We were interested to know to what extent parents expected children to 'be interested in each other in this sort of way (kissing etc.) at 11', and when, indeed, they would expect such an interest to start. The salient finding was that parents were not at all certain about the validity of their expectations; that is, they were mainly aware of an *expectation of being surprised* – that the times were changing and predictions could not so confidently be made. Some mothers accepted this uncertainty, others were clearly very anxious about it.

> **Part-time civil servant, husband a lecturer:**
> Well, they seem so much more advanced these days, you know, really. I wouldn't really disapprove too much [at 11], I don't think. I mean, you know, I feel you've got to be so much more broad-minded these days, really.

> **Part-time barmaid, husband a leather worker:**
> Well, then again, it depends on what the society's doing at the time, I mean to me things are far more brought to the fore at the moment – I don't know whether it's me that's old-fashioned, I mean you see it yourself and you think you've got to expect it. But I wouldn't like to think he was doing much like that much before 16.

> **Part-time machine demonstrator, husband a glazier:**
> I do [expect it now], and that's why I talk to her. I had a thorough talk to her, and she knows how far she can go. It's not like when we was children.

> **Part-time computer operator, husband a power worker:**
> I wouldn't *expect* it ... I suppose in a way I'd be quite horrified if I thought ... but I mean they're much older in their mind, aren't they? I suppose it's going to start when they get to senior school. To be quite honest, it frightens the life out of both of us ... I believe in sex education in school, but you know, the way things are ...

> **Not in paid work, husband a professional engineer (same parents as on p. 97):**
> [Mother:] Yes, I do [expect it now]. Yes. [Father:] You do, I don't, curiously enough. I'm surprised, you know. [Mother:] I kissed people when I was 11. [Father:] I think I sort of belong to the tradition where boys hate girls till they're all of 16. I'm always highly amazed by all our children's early attachments.

The question was therefore answered as a sort of amalgam of hopes, fears and expectations, and for this reason the figures must be treated with caution. It is interesting that, among the group who expect this kind of interest to start by the age of 11, boys' and girls' mothers do not differ: 23% of each have this expectation, nor are there significant class differences. A further 16% expect this interest to start between 12 and 13 years, and here class differences are negligible so far as boys are concerned; however, for girls this is the modal age for middle-class mothers to expect such an interest to begin (Class I and II 35%, Class III WC 26%), and the least expected age for Class V mothers (7%). 14 years is the expected age for 28% (negligible class differences except that Class V mothers choose this as the modal expected age for their girls (41%)). 15 years is the expected age for a further 15%, with no class or sex differences. Finally, 10% do not expect this interest until 16–17 years, and 3% later than that; the only class group in which a substantial number expect such interests to be delayed until 16-plus is, oddly enough, Class V mothers of boys (21%).

The main overall class and sex differences can be seen by looking at a combined table showing those mothers who expect an active interest in kissing and holding hands to begin at or before 13 years. Table 5.3 shows these. It will be seen that the class trend shown mainly derives from the girls' data. It is perhaps surprising that middle-class mothers have greater expectations of early sexual/romantic interest than working-class mothers in view of the fact that there is a clear class difference in measures such as age at birth of first child (for this sample, 24% of Class I and II mothers were 21 or less compared with 53% in Class V). However, there are certainly some working-class mothers who regret their own early start, or at least hope their daughters will 'play the field' rather longer than they did, instead of 'getting tied hand and foot with babies'; there are also many who hope that their children will reach a higher standard of education than themselves, and who see early sexual interest as incompatible with this.

Part-time waitress, husband a printer:
Well, I hope not, not yet. I know at 14 and 15 you expect it a bit; but Mandy's 13 now, she's got pin-ups but not actually having a boyfriend. I'm hoping that will be another couple of years, and I'm hoping they'll all be like that, because if they get [interested] young … they've *no* chance, have they? They'd be talking about getting married before they've had any life. I'm talking from experience, I got married young myself. I won't say I've regretted it, but I won't say it's good!

TABLE 5.3 Mothers who expect active romantic interest at age 13 or under

	Social class					Summary		
	I&II	IIIWC	IIIMan	IV	V	M.class	W.class	Overall popn
	%	%	%	%	%	%	%	%
Boys	46	44	31	43	33	45	34	37
Girls	51	44	43	38	20	48	40	42
Both	48	44	37	40	27	46	37	39

Significance: class trend ★★★   m.class vs w.class ★
between sexes n.s.

Not in paid work, husband a textile worker:
I'm slightly old-fashioned myself. I think if they do get on to this boyfriend lark and start slipping out at night, it affects their schooling and they can't do both. It emotionally upsets them; and I've said 'there's plenty of time for that later on'.

At the same time, it would be unwise to go along with these mothers in assuming that they as a generation were slower to develop sexual and romantic interests than their own children, even though this is their impression. It is true that the transcripts repeatedly emphasise this belief: 'If they're 11 now, it's like when we was 14'; 'They're more advanced than what we were'; 'It's how things are these days'; 'They're growing up so quickly in comparison to how we grew up, I don't altogether agree with it, it's something we've just got to accept.' Statistics for abortions and first pregnancies under the age of 15 give credence to such beliefs (Francome, 1983),[3] yet these tell us little about the onset of sexual interest. What is more certain is the greater availability to 11-year-olds of sexual information, sexual titillation and sexual example via the media. Clearly we should have taken more trouble to ask parents to think back to their own childhood and try to date their own early interests more precisely; for some did have second thoughts about their own first reaction to 'the day and age', which perhaps should make us cautious.

Nursing aide, husband a joiner:
If you'd asked me that before her [eleventh] birthday party, I'd have said no, but I'll admit at first it shook me a little bit. I didn't expect it really. [When would you have expected it?] About 13, I think – [pause] – though when it did happen, I looked back ... er ... to my school years, and thought, 'I wasn't ...' – and then I thought, well, I *was*! I remember a boy I really liked ... so!

Research worker, husband a lecturer:
I should be rather sorry if it happened at this age – um – I think inevitably they talk romantically about each other, because the grown-ups do. I don't personally do it at all, you know, I don't talk about girlfriends and boyfriends; but they are surrounded by talk about girlfriends and boyfriends – other grown-ups I find *do* talk in these terms. I don't like it, I wish they didn't – I can't stop it because they are grown-ups who are rather close. [Later:] Thinking about this boyfriend thing – I'm not sure why I said what I did, it seems a bit prissy, remembering myself at that age. I definitely had a boyfriend at 9, and we certainly kissed – public show! – and we were regarded as engaged by the other children, though I remember thinking that this was not going to be permanent. And I got seriously engaged in a romantic way when I was 11. So my misgivings seem a bit nonsensical, on second thoughts ... I think what I mean is that I don't want grown-ups to push children into these situations; I want her to find her own way in her own time, and I feel a bit puritan about the way adults seem to indulge themselves at the child's expense with these, sort of, titillating references ...

We would suggest that middle-class mothers' greater willingness to contemplate the beginnings of sexual interest at 13 or less is the result of a number of factors. We have consistently shown more prudish attitudes in working-class mothers over ten years of child-rearing, and this, combined with the more authoritarian style of working-class mothers, could lead some of them to feel that they 'certainly wouldn't expect that' *and would therefore not countenance it*; in the same way as some had been shocked at the idea of a 4-year-old being interested in where babies came from:

> I think if she *did* ask me, I'd be really shocked, a child of that age, thinking she'd been mixing in the wrong company while she's been out playing. I should go round wanting to know where she'd got that kind of talk from. I mean, at 4 years old, I don't think they ought to have anything like that. I'd tell her, from the hospital.
>
> *Newson and Newson, 1968: 379*

Conversely, middle-class mothers may, as part of their democratic style, more comfortably adopt a determination to be tolerant to the child 'finding her own way' and to be adaptable to the child's status as a representative of 'this day and age'. But, finally, this seems another example of the phenomenon which we described in Chapter 3 in relation to tolerance of undesirable friends; that middle-class mothers can afford to be more tolerant of threatening situations *because they have a better chance than working-class mothers of retaining some measure of control*. The confidence that this gives them, at least at this stage, pervades their communicational patterns with the child. In the final section of this chapter we will look at mothers' willingness to give the 11-year-old information involving various kinds of sexual content. In the chapter that follows, we shall look at communication more generally.

'I don't think she knows, but I know I never told my mum that I knew, so whether she knows or not. I don't know ...'

The discussion of death, religion and events in the news, which will concern us in Chapter 6, seems for the majority of mothers something which happens in response to the individual child: they wait for the topic to come up, and take it as it comes. The topic of sex is somewhat different in a number of ways. In a sense, death and religion *need not* be deliberately discussed by parents who have no particular faith that they feel should be imparted; whereas all parents are agreed that there will come a time when *someone* will have to give the child information about sex. Secondly, while parents may feel at a loss to answer questions about death and religion, they rarely feel embarrassed to do so; whereas questions about sex encounter taboos and inhibitions which often have to do with feelings that lie too deep to be under parents' control. Thus, although most mothers theoretically would wish to answer children's questions about sex as they arise, to suit the child's age, they differ very much in the ages at which they think information *can* suitably be given; in addition, the way some react to questions clearly may discourage the child from asking any more, so that by the age at which they are prepared to answer more candidly he has already sought his information elsewhere. Very few mothers *want* their children to pick up their knowledge in the street or playground, yet even this prospect may not overcome their inhibition: Adrian's mother, for instance (Class IV), says that she wants Adrian 'to find out the nice way [about intercourse]' – she is grateful to the school for the comprehensive 'mothercraft lessons' her daughter has had at 13, but knows Adrian is likely to be 'told it wrong' by the 'roughnecks in the playground' before that age.

'Telling about sex' clearly has a number of different stages, which are preceded by attitudes to modesty and genital play before there is any question of 'telling'; we have discussed these early influences and stages, including the prevalence of 'little fairy-stories', in some detail elsewhere (Newson and Newson, 1968, Chapter 10). At every age-stage in this longitudinal study, questions have been included which explored mothers' attitudes on these topics. For simplicity, we divided the things mothers 'tell' into the following broad stages, which might be expected to occur roughly in this order:

1. The 'basic fact': babies come from their mummy's tummy.
2. How they got in there, i.e. the father's role in terms of intercourse.
3. The fact that girls and women menstruate.
4. The possibility of contraception and its implications.

What we did not know when we planned this scheme was that for many mothers there was another stage between stages 1 and 2, namely *where babies get out*: a substantial group were prepared to tell the child about 'mummy's tummy', but were not at the same point prepared to elaborate, which must have puzzled many practically-minded 4-year-olds. This is an example of how the researcher may only know after the event what questions *should* have been asked. As we shall see shortly, the *implication* of contraception was another area which was not explored until we were already halfway through fieldwork at 11.

The 'basic fact' We first asked about this at 4 years, dividing the answers into 'he knows already', 'not yet, but would tell if asked' and 'wouldn't tell yet'. For those children who did not know this fact at 4, we asked again at 7; and for those still remaining in ignorance, we asked once again at 11. Table 5.4 summarises these findings; presumably children whose mothers have not told them by 11 have actually learned from elsewhere that babies come from their mother's tummy.

Mothers' dependence on the child not asking, even where they have said they are willing to tell him if he does, can be clearly seen by comparing 'would tell if asked at 4' with 'didn't know by 7'. If all the mothers who said they would tell if asked at 4 had actually done so during the next three years, the line of ignorance at 7 would read 12%, 27%, 55%, 47%, 75%, even leaving aside the mothers who would not tell at 4 but might have thought 5 or 6 a suitable time. We noted at 4 that many of the mothers who said they would tell if asked would have much preferred not to be asked, and this appears to be the case – only in Class V have mothers told more

TABLE 5.4 Age of telling children the two reproductive facts: 'baby's from mother's tummy' and 'how father put it there'

	Social class					Summary		
	I&II	IIIWC	IIIMan	IV	V	M.class	W.class	Overall popn
	%	%	%	%	%	%	%	%
'Mummy's tummy'								
Already knows at 4 (trend ↘ ★★★★)	44	26	15	14	15	35	15	20
Would tell if asked at 4 (trend ↘ ★★★★)	44	47	30	39	10	45	30	34
Doesn't know, won't tell at 4 (trend ↗ ★★★★)	12	27	55	47	75	19	56	46
Still didn't know by 7 years (trend ↗ ★★★★)	31	35	62	56	69	33	61	54
Still not told by 11 (trend ↗ ★★★)	5	5	11	6	19	5	11	9
'Father's part'								
Knows at 11 (trend ↘ ★★★★)	47	35	22	29	23	41	23	28
No, but would tell if asked at 11 (trend n.s.)	42	42	49	41	41	42	47	45
Wouldn't tell yet (trend ↗ ★★★★)	11	23	29	30	36	17	30	27

by 7 than they promised to at 4, and probably because so very few would accept the child's question at 4 in the first place.

If there are still mothers who have managed to avoid telling the child by 11 where a baby grows, we can hardly be surprised that there are many more who jib at talking about intercourse. One feature which often precipitated mothers into talking about pregnancy was the increasing number of documentary television programmes featuring birth, either of animals or of humans, which brought the forbidden topic into their living-room before they had time to switch off. Intercourse seldom appears on the screen in this kind of explicit way, and the 'jumping in and out of bed' in television plays (which was often deplored, and for other reasons than wishing to keep the *fact* of intercourse from the child) does not necessarily inform the child, who already knows that some men and women, notably his parents, share beds.

There is a marked similarity in the middle-class figures for telling about babies at 4 and about intercourse at 11; each seems to represent a similar watershed. Working-class mothers show much less resistance at 11 than they did at 4, but still nearly a third of them hold out, firmly; the major shift is in Class V mothers' willingness to tell if asked, but it is clear from the transcripts that many 'would tell' mothers now hope the school will get to the child first.

> **Part-time hospital orderly, husband a miner:**
> They've just had it at school. He did ask me, and I said 'I'd rather you asked your Daddy about it', and he did do; but he said 'Come to me when you're a bit older.' But in the meantime they've learnt it at school, so that's saved that one.

Menstruation 6% of the girls had already started menstruation. Mothers on the whole expect to explain in advance to girls that this will be happening, and those few whose daughters had been taken by surprise (as indeed were their mothers) felt somewhat guilty about it. 75% of the girls who had not yet menstruated already knew that it would happen, though mothers are not necessarily very good at explaining the process. A further 17% were intending to explain in the near future. However, 8% felt that it was easier to explain once their daughter had experienced her first period, and this was what they intended to do. This attitude was heavily weighted by social class: no Class I and II mothers intended to wait so long, while 13% of Class V mothers believed in waiting (trend ★★★, m.class vs w.class ★★★★).

> **Not in paid work, husband a tyre fitter:**
> I should imagine with Mavis, if she did start [her period], she'd start crying, because she's frightened of blood. I mean, I'd just pet her up and explain things to her. I won't tell her before, I think it would frighten her.

With boys, of course, there is much less urgency in that the mother is broadening her son's knowledge rather than preparing him for an inevitable event. Only 21% of boys had been told about periods, and the mothers of a further 28% were prepared to tell them as soon as the subject came up. 42% of boys were felt to be too young to tell, and in this group well over half the mothers would hide sanitary towels or tampons in order to avoid embarrassing questions.

> **Not in paid work, husband a machine operator:**
> Funny you should say that, because I went shopping one day, and if the kiddies are there and I've got Tampax, I always unpack the bag and then put the Tampax bag in a paper bag inside the shopping bag until I go upstairs. But Adrian wanted something out of the bag, and he just left them in the open on the kitchen cabinet. He says to Stephanie [older sister], 'I don't know what they are, they're not toffees and they're not biscuits.' And Stephanie told me. I says, 'Who's took them out?' – she says, 'Adrian, but he doesn't know what they are.' I do try and keep them away from him.

Again there is a clear class difference: 63% of middle-class mothers have told or would tell their boys about menstruation at 11, compared with 44% working-class

(****), and this drops to 25% in Class V (trend ***). All these figures on menstruation, incidentally, show the percentages actually obtained, although about 5% of children were omitted because the question was not asked owing to the child's listening presence.

Contraception It seemed unlikely that parents were discussing mechanical means of contraception at this age, but the much more widely aired topic of oral contraception made it seem reasonable to introduce this theme by asking: 'Of course, there's been a lot of talk on television about the "Pill" lately – has he asked any questions about that?', and to go on to discuss what the mother had or would say to the child about this. In fact it proved difficult to categorise these data in a meaningful way; a great many children were familiar with the notion of 'the Pill', but the question of just what it meant to them was not easy to gauge invariably from mothers' answers, and we realised that we should have been more detailed and precise in our phrasing of the questions. In a sense we were hoist with our own petard: as one mother said 'She takes it for granted – course, you can talk about the Pill where you can't talk about other methods – it's socially acceptable'; but this also meant that one mother after another would say something as vague as 'She knows people take it so as not to have babies', which does not really get at the issues of contraception very clearly, especially where pills are also taken so as not to have headaches, indigestion and so on.

Rather late in the day, we started asking additional probe questions, which however were necessarily subtle and rather complicated, and not always fully understood. The simplest way of asking what we wanted to know was: 'He knows you take it so as not to have any more babies; but suppose he said to you, "All right, if you don't want to have babies, why do you do this thing with my Dad?" – would you be prepared to tell him that people have intercourse because they like it, not just to have babies?' Sometimes it took quite a lot of discussion to get this point across. What was interesting, however, was that this was clearly a new thought for the majority of mothers of whom we asked these additional questions. It caused both amusement and horror – the hypothetical question posed by the child was felt to be a 'facer' which they would have great difficulty in answering, very few mothers had foreseen the possibility of being asked this, and indeed almost no children had actually asked it. Most could not in fact imagine their child asking this at 11, but those who were used to free-ranging discussions in this area could not understand why their children had not seen this implication of the Pill, let alone why they themselves had not seen the need to make it explicit in this connection. Probably the reason does lie in the Pill's very simplicity and ease of use – perhaps children would feel they did need explanations of why their mothers felt it worthwhile to undertake the more tedious forms of contraception.

The question of how to get across to children both the facts of sex and reproduction, and the human relationships which go along with these facts, is one which has exercised sex educationists for a long time. A number of the informative books available for children now start with the loving relationship and the wish to be physically close, and go on from there to tell how sometimes a baby is conceived as a result of this particular kind of closeness. The problem is that this is not where children's questions start. In an intact family, their parents' relationship is likely to be a taken-for-granted thing which to them has nothing to do with the scientific question 'where does a baby come from?' It is then all too easy for parents, 'meeting the child's questions as they arise' as they are advised to do, completely to forget to include the fact of love-making as not only a part of baby-making, but something which was there before the wish for babies and will survive that wish. If some inkling of this understanding is left out of the early stages of 'telling', it may be difficult to put back because the child finds it strange suddenly to apply such knowledge to his own familiar parents. Erica's mother, a science teacher who is professionally involved with sex education, replied to the question 'Suppose she asked why have intercourse if you don't want babies?':

> Certainly this question hasn't cropped up as yet. I should have to explain it to her. Urn – it's a thing I find much easier to do with other people's children than my own. Er – I don't really know why this should be. You see – I have to give lessons on this, and I find it very easy to be completely objective with other people's children. But when it comes to my own children ... I think you can imagine other people doing this thing, but not your own parents.

Perhaps this is the difficulty – that sexual matters cannot be 'completely objective' among human beings, and yet parents often try to make sex education so. They are then dependent on the child to put back the humanity and subjectivity with his questions; and not enough children are by that time relaxed enough to ask what they need to know: 'She said, "Mum, do you like sexual intercourse then? Is it nice?" So I said "Oh yes. Quite pleasant." So she said, "Oh, good".'

'You've got to disillusion them, but you don't want to destroy them ...'

The communication task which most universally caused mothers anxiety was how to warn children effectively of the dangers of sexual molestation while neither 'frightening them out of their minds' nor giving them a wholly negative view of sex. The difficulties are indeed very real, for such warnings oppose the mother's other intentions in child-rearing. In particular, mothers want their children to be friendly, polite and forthcoming to other adults, and they value innocence and a trusting nature; it goes against the grain to tell children: 'Never trust anybody but Mummy and Daddy.' Most parents in fact mitigate such a warning by limiting it to 'strangers'; yet this itself is unsatisfactory, both because they would also like their children to be able to relate easily to strangers, and because a child is in fact statistically speaking, more at risk from familiar adults.

Part-time machinist, husband a cook:
It's a shame really, when you think about it, nowadays, because it teaches children not to be friendly, doesn't it – I mean, that's what makes people more cold and they don't want to speak to strangers – I mean, now, you've only got to look at a person and you don't know if they're going to cut your throat. It's a terrible situation when you think about it – I mean, you want children to be friendly. You see all these old age pensioners and old people, that years ago always *were* friendly, and they want to speak to people, and your children don't know whether to speak to them or not.

Part-time typist, husband a warehouseman:
It's awkward, because *I* speak to people I've not known. Janine has said 'Who was that?' and I've said 'I don't know' – 'I thought you told me not to speak to strangers!' I say 'Well, I'm big enough to look after myself – you're not.' It's awkward though to set them an example being pleasant and at the same time not do it yourself.

Not in paid work, husband a professional engineer:
They've had the standard warnings – and I've also told them that these people could look awfully like a next-door neighbour, a policeman, things like that. That's where I find it intensely difficult to tell them to be careful. They do know about men who are sort of interested in little boys, but I haven't actually told them the intimate things. But if they asked, I would.

But how to 'tell them the intimate things'? As Ross's mother says, 'I feel it's very difficult to explain sex as something wrong in one instance and then try to put it something rosy in the next.' It is bad enough to have to warn one's child that 'there are men about who might attack children and even kill them', and nearly half the mothers feel that they can go no further than this (which indeed is obvious to the child from the most superficial attention to television news); yet almost all mothers worry that this will not protect the child against the soft approach.

Part-time typist, husband an assistant manager:
I don't know what some of the perverts will get up to, so it's no use my saying they'll do this or that, because ten to one he'd do something different, and Jim would think, well, this must be OK. So we've said let no-one put their hands on you at all.

We asked: 'Have you explained *why* it can be dangerous to go off with someone or get in someone's car? ... Would you explain anything about sexual danger, or do you think it's better not to mention that?' The sex angle had already been discussed with 17% of children, and here there were no significant class or sex differences; a further 35% were waiting for an opportunity to discuss the sexual danger, and 48% thought it better not do so. Sex and class differences do appear here and are shown in Table 5.5.

TABLE 5.5 Children whose mothers felt it best not to discuss the sexual nature of molestation

	Social class					Summary		
	I&II	IIIWC	IIIMan	IV	V	M.class	W.class	Overall Popn
	%	%	%	%	%	%	%	%
Boys	43	44	57	55	70	44	58	54
Girls	42	38	45	40	43	40	44	43
Both	43	41	51	47	57	42	51	48

Significance: trend ↗ ★★★ m.class/w.class ★
boys vs girls ★★★

One point which has to be made, and which is substantiated by this table, is that although (as one might expect from our other findings on sexual information-giving) mothers further down the class scale are less willing to discuss the sexual nature of molestation, the potential danger of *not* telling does in fact exert a heavy influence on them. For this reason, there are mothers who would not be discussing sexual matters at all with their children were it not that they are impelled into this by the need to warn; it therefore seems likely that some children learn *first and mainly* about the negative aspects of sex and its frightening connotations.

Looking at the ways in which mothers put these warnings across to their children, it is difficult to categorise them. Often it is clear that mothers are trying to make the same points, but do so in utterly differently ways by virtue of the manner of making them. It would therefore be meaningless to categorise according to the message given to the child, which lies partly in the factual content but equally in the words used and the context in which they are spoken. We shall therefore merely illustrate this below, deliberately choosing representative mothers who are not particularly idiosyncratic, without attempting any further analysis.

Part-time worker in family business, husband a wholesaler:

I've tried to put it over to Neill that no other person but us is entitled to cuddle him or touch him or love him in any way that he doesn't want them to, and certainly no stranger is entitled to touch him in any way at all, this must *not* happen – that there *are* dangers, without trying to make a horror story of it if he didn't want us to touch him, that he's entitled to say no – that his body is his own property and it's very precious – it's *his* to do as he wishes as he gets older – we've tried to protect him in this way. Whether we've done the right thing … I'm hoping I have.

Butchery assistant, husband a driver:

I've said a man would take you down a country lane, take down your knickers and play with your privates, and you might not be able to have children at all when you grow up.

Research assistant, husband a teacher:
He has asked me what 'sexual assault' means. I did tell him that it was a forced intercourse, and he knows what intercourse means, and I think that was as far it went. [Did he just accept this, or was he upset by the idea?] No, he wasn't at all upset with the idea, because I think it was such a very remote thing from him. I said, well, instead of having intercourse because you love somebody, somebody forced you to do it, and it wasn't pleasant and could hurt you and so forth.

Part-time factory-hand, husband a gear-setter:
I've tried to explain all this to her – not how babies are made, but how it *could* be done. You've got to really. When she started to be unwell [i.e. menstruate], it didn't bother her a bit, and I thought to myself, oh well, I'd better explain that if a man touches her down there with his particular organ, that this is how babies are made, and he'd spoil her for life – I said 'You shouldn't do that sort of thing unless you are in love'; but that's all I've said to her, and she said 'Oh shut up, I know all about that.'

Not in paid work, husband a clergyman:
If the subject comes up on the television or on the radio, we usually make it a talking point. Let them all talk about it and think, not really what happened to the child, but *why* she went, and how the person persuaded her to go. Let them think it out for themselves. And also, I think, by not pulling any punches about what did happen to those children, not trying to gloss over it.

Part-time machinist, husband a building foreman:
I've always told them the men are ill – it's illness inside their head. I've said *they* can't help it, so it's *you* got to look after yourself. But when I feel as if I've told them enough to be careful, then I stop, I don't like to go right into it.

Not in paid work, husband a nylon warper:
I have told all the others. When she gets inquisitive, I'll tell the truth. But I think at 11, just turning 11 – I don't want to spoil it, her mind, do you know what I mean? I think if you tell a child horrifying details, it's going to build something up in their mind and they're never going to trust it, are they? I want them to learn the good side of it – the family life. But if they ask you things, naturally I explain it.

Factory worker, husband a manual worker:
Well, I've had to tell Elsie in a roughish way, because as I say, I had trouble with Janet. So as Elsie was getting a bit older she knew what was surrounding her, like ... I've told her that *some* boys – I haven't said every boy – that *some* boys want a girl for rude things, you know. So I've told her in a roughish way – she has asked questions, and I've tried my best to tell her.

The question remains, of course, how far the way in which children learn about sexual matters may have a lasting effect upon them for good or ill. There is much anecdotal evidence to suggest that it is not easy to shed early inculcations of disgust or guilt; but do we really know even this, let alone the protective effects of more sensitive introductions? All that is certain is that mothers generally think this *is* a significant area of communication, whether or not they shy away from it. The difficulties of addressing such an enquiry would be daunting; nonetheless, since this is likely to be one of those areas in which the more impersonal school contribution cannot quite compensate, the answers would surely be worth having.

Notes

1 In 1981, a Midlands child was sexually attacked by an intruder inside a school cloakroom. When local mothers were interviewed for media coverage following this, what was repeatedly expressed was the sense of shock and outrage that *an assumed sanctuary* had been violated; this clearly marked for most of them a traumatic loss of confidence.

2 Roger Hart, in his detailed and subtle study of children's environmental explorations in a New England town, found that boys revealed 'considerably more ambiguity over their descriptions of parental range limitations than girls', and thinks this was 'because their mothers more readily "turn a blind eye" to the breaking of range restrictions'. If the latter is true, as seems likely, then boy–girl differences in range may be in effect still greater than mothers' reports on restrictions suggest – especially when this factor is added to girls' greater amenability and the fact that they are more in touch with their mothers in terms of communication (Table 6.5).

3 Births and abortions to mothers under 16, taken together, numbered 3.1 thousand in 1970 and 4.9 thousand in 1979; the increase was in number of abortions, not in actual births. Pregnancies in teenage girls of 16–19 decreased overall during the same period, presumably because of more effective birth control in the older group.

References

Erikson, E. (1955) 'Sex differences in play construction of twelve-year-old children', in J.M. Tanner and B. Inhelder (eds) *Discussions on Child Development, Vol. III*, London: Tavistock.

Francome, C. (1983) 'Unwanted pregnancies amongst teenagers', *Journal of Biosocial Science*, 15: 139.

Grayson, G.B. and Howarth, C.I. (1982) 'Evaluating pedestrian safety programmes', in A.J. Chapman (ed.) *Pedestrian Accidents*, Chichester: Wiley.

Hart, R. (1979) *Children's Experience of Place*, New York: Irvington Publications, distributed by Halsted Press/Wiley.

Newson, J. and Newson, E. (1968) *Four Years Old in an Urban Community*, London: George Allen & Unwin.

Newson, J. and Newson, E. (1976) *Seven Years Old in the Home Environment*, London: George Allen & Unwin.

Richardson, D. (1976) Unpublished Master's thesis, University of Nottingham.

Tanner, J.M. (1978) *Education and Physical Growth*, London: Hodder and Stoughton.

Ward, C. (1978) *The Child in the City*, London: Architectural Press.

6

UNCERTAINTY AND INCOMPLETE ANSWERS

In this chapter we shall concern ourselves with a number of aspects of communication between parents and 11-year-old children. It is of course the acknowledged business of parents to communicate directly or indirectly with their children: that is to say, there was no mother in our sample who did not think that there was an imperative on parents to socialise their children (however that concept might be interpreted), nor were there any who did not believe that this entailed *getting through* to the child by one means or another. The differences between parents' socialisation styles lie in the means they employ to get their message over (words, physical sanctions, example, or most usually a variable mixture of these), in the principles that inform their intentions, and in the nature of the messages themselves, both explicit and implicit.

Thus the kind of communication for which every parent accepts parental responsibility is that which concerns the mediation of discipline and control – if we can use those two harsh-sounding words in, for the moment, a neutral fashion. Parents are less universally agreed about their responsibility for communication in other areas of daily life; yet the patterns a child experiences of inquiry, debate, casual chat, anecdote, affectionate gesture and response, statement of opinion and belief, expressions of desire and fantasy, jokes, teasing, evasions, threats, sulks, blackmail, guile and downright lies, cannot fail to affect his perception of his parents' disciplinary attempts, and eventually to make up the matrix within which he will come to define his own identity. The aspects of communication that we shall examine in this chapter are those which are *not* directly concerned with parental discipline, though for some parents disciplinary issues are not far away; and we shall leave the ways in which parents try to exert control until the chapter that follows.

In tackling the question of communication, then, we chose once again to adopt a 'multi-faceted' approach – that is, to return to this issue at many different points throughout the interview in order to gauge the degree of communication within several different areas. For instance, as we have already mentioned, mothers were asked about their role in helping the child through 'tiffs and upsets between friends' (Q. 26), and in undesirable friendships. They were asked whether they did anything about teasing, and whether they themselves teased (Qs 33–7); about conversations in response to the child's anxieties, and over issues such as religion, death and world events (Qs 50–6). We explored their warnings and explanations about sexual molestation (Qs 91–4); mediation through difficulties with teachers (Qs 106–10); expression of affection and tenderness (Qs 123–4); shared interests and 'grown-up' discussion (Qs 126–31); censorship or discussion of televised material (Qs 139–42); sex information (Qs 143–6); and censorship of books or magazines (Qs 147–8). This approach sidesteps the difficulties which arise when an interviewer hammers away persistently at one child-rearing dimension, so that the mother becomes uncomfortably aware that it is her communication, or child-centredness (or whatever), that is under the microscope.[1] The multi-faceted approach allows the focus to remain on the topic-area under discussion – school, friendships, family life and so on – while gaining detailed knowledge, almost incidentally, of these central dimensions of child-rearing; so that, in this particular case, we had a fair understanding of the climate of communication in terms of the areas mentioned above before we started on the direct questions about conflict, argument and sanctions which make up the darker side of the communication issue. In particular, we also asked about ways in which mothers valued the child's presence, this seeming basic to the communication process; and this is where we shall start this discussion.

'I try not to be biased, but he's got such a lovely character ...'

How much pleasure do mothers get out of having the 11-year-old child around, and what kinds of things contribute to that pleasure? This topic came up indirectly in the answers to the last item in the 'school' section, and in effect formed an excellent introduction to the section on 'family and interaction': 'If you could choose, and it wasn't a question of money, would you like N to go to boarding school? What do you think of boarding school for children of this age?' Only 16% of parents would have accepted such an offer, despite the fact that most parents mentioned at least some advantage in boarding school. The plus factors of such schools were seen as discipline, organisation, independence for the child, social polish and better education – a Class III manual mother said that 'if Fay was outstandingly clever and I knew she was going to make a politician, that'd be different'; however, middle-class mothers in particular were less sure that they did offer a better education. Mothers were in fact agreed that 'family life' was the major deficit in boarding schools, and the great majority felt that any advantage they could think of (and some could think of none) would be outweighed by their children becoming strangers, distortion of natural emotional development, and loss of active parental influence; a Class II mother who had been to boarding school herself was sure that 'you never get the same relationship again', and a mother actively involved in voluntary work, her husband a journalist, pointed out that 'it is after all a time when they're developing quite rapidly, it's a shame to have someone else mould your child for you'. Some parents who could think of no advantages used words like 'unnatural' (Class II), 'not human' (Class II), 'snob idea' (Class IV), 'grim' (Class V), and agreed with Henry's mother (Class IV): 'I don't know where people's heart is, to send a child to boarding school.' There was also a strong feeling throughout the sample that this was a 'shedding of responsibility' (Class I mother) or 'only to get rid of them, sort of thing' (Class IV mother).

Interestingly, there are no significant class differences in whether mothers would have liked their child to go to boarding school; throughout the 84% who would not, there ran the refrain of, at best, 'it might be all right for other people's children, but not for mine' – and in some comments a kind of pity could be detected for parents who, it was almost said, didn't know any better.

Not in paid work, husband a policeman:
I don't like the idea of shoving them off – I don't know, I suppose if you'd got plenty of money you'd move in different circles, but no, not for mine.

Part-time cleaner, husband a bricklayer:
Well, I should imagine it would be a good thing if you've got the money to do it straight away, you'd be hardened to it then; but I think it's an odd question for such people as us, because I think I'd be lost without mine now.

Not in paid work, husband a clerk:
Oh, I suppose they're good for certain children, you know. They bring them out, I should think, but I wouldn't like mine to go. [Do you mean for certain kinds of personality?] Yes – I suppose. It seems as if you're trying to get rid of them to me, sending them away to boarding school. I don't think our class of people usually do, anyway. [Well, that's why I said 'if it's not a question of money' – do you think it's a good *idea*?] No – I don't think so. [Would you say it still seems like getting rid of them, even if you're talking about another class of people?] Well, it does to me, yes. I think that's why they send 'em, to tell you the truth. Just, like, to get them out of the way. I always say I want to get mine out of the way, but I don't think I'd want 'em to go really. You say things like that, don't you, when you're annoyed and they act on your nerves, but you don't mean it.

Not in paid work, husband a manager:
I think if you have children they're your responsibility, if you're going to send them to boarding school you might just as well shove them off out. It's like having a child on loan, isn't it? I mean, I know sometimes they're a bit of a problem and they get on your nerves, but that's a part of having a child, isn't it? You've got to go through all the troubles *and* its joys, and share in all the rest of it.

In short, mothers like having 11-year-old children around, even those whom they have already described as 'difficult' or 'wearing'. It seemed worth repeating the question we asked at both 4 and 7 years:

Q. 122 Can you tell me now about how you and N get on together – is there any
special thing about him that gives you a lot of pleasure?

This is perhaps a more taxing question, demanding that the mother identify some
positive thing, rather than simply express her general love in a 'wouldn't be without
him' sense. Both at 4 and at 7, we noted that many mothers found it a conversation-
stopper, although all but a handful could answer it after some thought. At 11, there is
an increase in parents who can think of *nothing* specific which gives them pleasure:
8% overall fail to discover anything, even given time. There is a difference between
middle class and working class (middle class less than 3%, working class 10% ★★★)
and a highly significant class trend (★★★★): 15% of Class V mothers of boys can think
of nothing about their sons to give them pleasure. A further 1% takes pleasure in the
child's obedience, but mainly for its rarity value!

> **Not in paid work, husband a bookmaker:**
> No, no, I really don't know – I'd miss him, I'd possibly miss if he was gone
> a long time. But to be quite honest he drives me mad, I wish he'd hurry up
> and grow up, go his own way. It's not a nice thing to say – I mean if anything
> happened to him I'd be heartbroken – but at the moment I'm relieved when
> he's round at Grandma's, such peace and quiet. Because he runs the roost, he
> really does.

> **Not in paid work, husband a road cleaner:**
> Um. Well, as I say, this last year he's altered so much that you can't put your
> finger on *anything* really, that can really please you. When I do feel really
> proud and pleased is when he is really behaving himself and he's *not* being
> big-headed and bossy. You know, when I feel as if I could plonk him outside
> and say 'Well, this is my son' sort of thing, you know!

It is perhaps an indication of the very personal quality of mothers' 'pleasure in
the child' that only 4% could not name what would be the child's best quality *as
judged by an outsider* and that for 78% of mothers the aspect in which they took
special pleasure was *different* from what they thought an outsider would choose. It
did in fact prove possible to make a rough categorisation of the features in children identified as giving mothers most pleasure. The most important feature was
the child's ability to offer companionship and rapport (26%), closely followed
by his being thoughtful for others and affectionate (22%). In comparison, other
features were nowhere; they comprised entertainment value (4%), appearance (3%),
achievement (3%) and independence (2%), while other idiosyncratic features made
up 30% of answers. There was a surprising homogeneity in the way answers fell
into these categories: the only middle class/working class difference was in the
valuing of achievement (★★★), middle-class valuing of achievement in *girls* (8%)
accounting for this. Similarly, boy/girl differences just reached significance on only
two features: achievement (girls more overall ★) and thoughtfulness/affectionate

behaviour (more valued in boys ★, especially middle-class boys). Given that these are the only sex differences, albeit on very small category numbers, one must wonder whether the special pleasure these mothers derive from achievement in girls and affection-giving in boys stems from some element of surprise in finding it there.

So far as affection is concerned, this is justified by a sex difference (★★★★) in children's willingness to show affection spontaneously to their parents. We asked whether the child showed his affection to people, 'or is he a bit bashful about it nowadays?', and whether he would give either parent 'a hug or a kiss without being asked for it'. Although 56% of children overall still spontaneously demonstrate their affection, this rises to 66% in girls and falls to 46% in boys, with minimal class differences. If the rest of the children are divided into those who are affectionate but shy and those who are definitely reserved, the sex difference is again marked in the extreme category, 27% of boys being 'definitely reserved' compared with 16% of girls.

When the children were 7, we were interested to know whether mothers' expression of affection to their children was beginning to be limited by feelings that the children were getting too old for this; we found at that time that this was clearly a minority view, 87% showing spontaneous affection, with no class differences (Newson and Newson, 1976, Chapter 8). By 11, however, the position has changed; mothers are becoming much more inhibited in the show of affection, and this is especially so further down the social class scale. In fact, whereas at 7 such inhibition was more commonly reported among children than among mothers, so that we had to conclude that there were 'not enough cuddly children to go round', at 11 the mothers have dropped below the children in their ability or willingness to show affection. The question asked, following those on the child's show of affection, was 'What about you – do you find it easy to show him you love him?', with a probe question, 'Do you use pet-names like "darling" or "love" or "sweetheart" when you're talking to him?' 42% found the show of affection easy, rising to 51% in both Class I and II and Class III WC, and falling to 30% in Class V (class trend ★★★★). Sex differences were not significant. Most of the remaining mothers fell into the category of 'somewhat reserved' (41% overall), and only 16% identified themselves as *definitely* reserved.

Not in paid work, husband a painter:
Oh, I tell her a million times a day – can't help it!

Not in paid work, husband a road cleaner:
Oh, I would – but he won't let you. I often put my arm round him. [Re kiss and cuddle at bedtime along with other children:] He says 'No'. I say 'Oh, come on, you do – now where do you want it?', laughing like that, but he won't let you give him one … I say 'Here's a big kiss for Douglas', and he says 'Oh horrible thing, fancy doing that' – you know, he laughs over it – but at the same time I feel hurt deep down that he'll not let you show affection for him.

Not in paid work, ex-husband a labourer:

I wouldn't say that I find it particularly easy. I do because I know that he needs it, but – I dunno – I think you find it a little harder as they get older, I don't know why.

Part-time factory-hand, husband labourer:

No – er – I think it's with having more than one child round the house [she has seven], you don't tend to have, er, a lot of time for paying any particular what-d'you-call-it to one child, you know. I think it's quite a few years since I really hugged any of them. They just take it for granted I love them all, and that's it.

Not in paid work, husband a printer:

No – not with boys, I don't think I can. I've always got that feeling I shouldn't like him to be soft. I like boys to grow up with men – to be a man, sort of thing.

Part-time factory hand, husband a gear-setter:

No, I'm not affectionate myself – I can't bear to see it when you get these kids cuddling and everything – oh! – they've got to stand on their own feet. I just don't believe in being sloppy with them.

Not in paid work, husband an unemployed labourer:

No, no, I can't, I'm very reserved in my feelings. I couldn't show it – it's very hard for me to show it – he has to take it for granted. [Pet names?] I think we're not that kind of a family for pet names, I never have been able to, and they're the same. They must get it from me, like I got it from my parents – cause my father was a very hard man, and my mother was never open with us, like I said. It's passed on – and I suppose he'll pass it on to his children, don't you think so?

As we have pointed out elsewhere (Newson, 1978), there are a number of behaviours in childhood which carry a certain amount of cultural disapproval as the child grows older, but which mothers are indulgent about within the home on the understanding that the child will no longer display them in public. Examples are dummy and bottle-sucking, fantasising, little girls fighting, tantrums and 'cheek'. The consequence is that parents tend to assume that the norm is less indulgent than it is, since these are essentially private behaviours; while psychologists and anthropologists cannot rely on observation in these areas, but must find ways of asking people (in a non-threatening manner!) what they actually do. Thus, when hugs and kisses cease to be easily observable, which seems to happen at the junior school stage, we cannot know, except by asking, whether these have ended altogether or merely become private, nor at what point private behaviour does become non-existent behaviour, nor whether there are subcultural differences involved. One concern at 7 was to throw light on two opposing stereotypes that had frequently been raised in public discussion: that of 'working-class warmth' on the one hand, and that of 'working-class emotional deprivation' on the other. In terms of the affection shown explicitly to children, we are now in a position to make fairly confident statements. At 7, although the mother's affection is less obviously displayed in public (partly in response to the child's own self-consciousness), a massive majority of mothers do cuddle, hug and kiss their children in private, and this kind of warmth and tenderness is common to mothers in general throughout the social strata. Somewhere during the junior school years, the 'taboo on tenderness' begins to be felt with greater force, to the extent that it invades the privacy of the home, and mothers are particularly vulnerable to this as we descend the social scale; so that, by 11, half our middle-class mothers and more than two-thirds of Class V mothers are no longer able to show the spontaneous affection, by word or gesture, that was so normal at 7.

How important this emotional distancing is, for good or ill, in the child's total development remains for the moment a question. How it is answered is likely to depend partly on the interweaving of several other dimensions in the child's life. For instance, at 7 we suggested that 'child-centredness' was another way in which the child learned about his own value, and saw that the index measuring this was quite independent of the display of affection, and was highly subject to class-affiliated attitudes. 'Family cohesiveness' and 'communication' are indices which, at 11, may lead us closer to understanding how far explicit affection is backed up or extended to establish the child's strength of identity in other ways.

'... and you think to yourself, if we hadn't have sat talking, I wouldn't have got to know that ...'

The quotation which heads this section would do very well as the motto for the whole of this long-term study, emblazoned perhaps over our door or on our filing-cabinets. In the course of being a good listener (which is a highly active occupation), the interviewer is of course aware that some mothers are extremely fluent communicators in their own right, others are naturally reticent, hesitant or inarticulate, and others again seem long out of practice at expressing their feelings, yet seize the opportunity with such eagerness that the interview may last four or five hours. Even with inarticulate or very shy mothers, however, it is very rare indeed to have a conversation which proceeds by monosyllables; and one major reason is that the two women start off with one enormous advantage: a shared interest in this particular child. Because the interviewer's interest is genuine, she will almost certainly gain a ready response from the mother, whose interest is not only genuine but proprietorial – even when, perhaps especially when, the mother is aware that she is unused to contemplating her child's personality in so conscious a way:

> **Part-time dinner-lady, ex-husband a skilled manual worker:**
> It's only when you sit down like I am doing now and talking, that you really discover your children. I must admit, up to now – I *do* have a lot of time for

them, I idolise them – I'd just die without them – but you don't seem to study them as much as you should do. It's times like this when you … you're finding out about them.

In the same way, a shared interest between child and parent will tend to stimulate conversation between them, at the very least because one wants information which the other has or because both have opinions which they wish to express. There are of course exceptions; like Vance's Dad, who 'as long as it's sport, then he'll sit hours with him watching sport, but to have a conversation with him – no'. More often, however, shared interests do act as a focus for conversation, and are often given as a reason for increase in conversation with one parent rather than the other.

We therefore probed not only how much the child talked to father and to mother separately, as well as together, but what they talked about, in what depth, and how far they shared activities *as couples*, i.e. father–child and mother–child. The results are particularly interesting for their gender polarisation, but also for class patterns. 56% of all children share some activity with their mother, and there are no class differences; however, in all social classes, girls are much more likely to do so than boys (girls 71%, boys 42% ★★★★). 53% of children share an activity with their father, and boys are more likely to do so than girls (boys 63%, girls 44% ★★★★); however, this time there is a clear class trend running from 63% (boys and girls combined) in Class I and II down to 40% in Class V (★★★★), while manual and non-manual Classes III close ranks at 55%.

In asking whether child and parent discussed 'serious, grown-up things at all', we had in mind sustained discussion which would allow the exchange to reach some degree of subtlety, range or depth; clearly this did not have to be in academic or political terms – it might equally be on human relationships or indeed on sport. In the event, it proved not too difficult to rate father–child pairs and mother–child pairs each on a three-point scale: 'much conversation including serious', 'much casual conversation' and 'little conversation'. Table 6.1 shows a social class analysis of these findings. Sex differences reach significance only among father–child pairs; boys' and girls' results have therefore been combined in the first part of the table. Only the extreme points of the scale are shown here; the middle point, 'much casual conversation', is residual to these figures.

It seems clear from these findings that children of both sexes are rather dependent on their mothers for conversation, and this is even true at the upper end of the social scale despite the heavy increase here. On the other hand, boys for once are at a linguistic advantage over girls by virtue of their fathers making more effort to talk to them, although at the lower end of the scale this really only improves their score on *casual* conversations.

Overall, however, what must depress anyone who values conversation as a major educational influence in learning about life in general is the massive social class trend away from conversation *of any sort* at the lower end of the scale. Obviously we must be concerned at a drop in 'serious conversation with mother' from 62% at one end to 14% at the other; but the fact that a quarter of working-class 11-year-old children

TABLE 6.1 Range and depth of children's conversations with mother and father

	Social class					Summary		
	I&II %	IIIWC %	IIIMan %	IV %	V %	M.class %	W.class %	Overall popn %
Conversation with mother								
Much (includes serious)	62	41	31	37	14	52	30	36
	Significance: class trend ★★★★					m.class vs w.class ★★★★		
Little conversation	11	15	24	27	37	13	26	22
	Significance: class trend ★★★★					m.class vs w. class ★★★★		
Conversation with father								
Much (includes serious)								
Boys	45	35	17	18	8	40	16	23
Girls	38	20	12	15	9	29	12	17
Both	41	27	14	16	9	35	14	20
	Significance: class trend ↘ ★★★★					m.class vs w.class ★★★★		
	boys vs girls P = 0.07							
Little conversation								
Boys	18	19	33	31	49	19	34	30
Girls	21	31	47	43	57	26	47	42
Both	20	25	40	37	53	22	41	36
	Significance: Class trend ↗ ★★★★					m.class vs w.class ★★★★		
	boys vs girls ★★★							
Little conversation with either parent								
Both	5	9	16	19	33	7	18	15
	Significance: class trend ↗ ★★★★					m.class vs w.class ★★★★		
	boys vs girls n.s.							

(over a third of Class V children) do not even have much casual conversation with their mothers represents a severe deprivation – especially when this is not compensated for by their fathers to any great extent, as the findings in the last line show.

What factors contribute to these findings? Certainly the child himself, his personality, interests and style of activity, must be seen as one (although this begs the question of what forces made him the way he is).

Teacher, husband a scientific officer:
You have no option but to talk to Jeremy, because he talks to you and he expects an answer.

Shop assistant, husband a manager:
No, we don't talk at all – that's the whole trouble – Norman doesn't talk, you can't get to know him at all. The TV goes straight on after tea, and that's it for the night – he doesn't treat a home as somewhere to talk or anything like that.

Often there is a recognisable *family* style into which the child, unlike Norman, fits comfortably.

Working in her husband's newsagent business:
Well, anything to do with selling businesses and buying houses we always discuss with them, and they always come with us to look at things. We work as a family, not individuals.

Not in paid work, husband a miner (deputy):
[Father:] We never stop talking in this house – we're all the time talking. We perhaps talk a lot of rubbish, but there's other things involved, all kinds of things – any subject – if on TV he sees a subject on a children's home, you know, we'll start talking about it. All kinds of things – we're that much involved in things. We do a lot of arguing … like I say, we'll very often fall out in the process, but as you fall out with any of our children there's no animosity afterwards. As fast as we fall out, we're right again – we're all the same.

Part-time bakery assistant, husband a driver:
We don't talk a lot actually, I think it's the day and age, and you seem as if you never have time for nothing.

Certainly there are some mothers who are so weighed down by the cares of the family that they seem to get past talking; and equally fathers who are exhausted by the time they meet their children.

Not in paid work, husband a jointer:
Sometimes by the time she comes home from school I'm in such a raging temper, I'd hit anybody, I'm at war with the world. I suppose it depends on

how many kiddies you've got – if you've only got two, you're more tolerant, I suppose, than six, it makes a difference. [So there aren't a lot of conversations?] I'm usually busy doing other things, you know … [Father?] Well, I suppose if the television wasn't on and he wasn't at work, there'd be more time.

Not in paid work, husband a seven-day-week stoker:
No – mind you, his Daddy, if he's at home he's sleeping – he's hard working, on long shifts, and I think he's more tired than not interested.

On the basis that larger families are more exhausting, as well as needing more time if each child is to receive a comparable amount of individual attention, we analysed the category 'little conversation with either parent' in terms of family size. There is a difference overall, 11% of small families (1–3 children) falling in this group compared with 18% of large families (4 or more children) (★★). However, this difference only applies to working-class families, where 13% of small and 22% of large families are in the 'little conversation with either' group (★); middle-class families divide equally.

Fathers' own styles and personalities can also make a difference. Below are four quite different examples, each of which seems to typify a recurrent personality group. The first, in marked contrast to his highly articulate wife, is an outstanding example of the 'strong silent' type – yet he certainly does have a listening and sup- portive presence (interviewer's repeated experience), and he is actively involved in this silently supportive way in his family's joint activities (see the quotation on p. 82).

Part-time waitress, husband a lorry driver:
Not a lot with her Daddy. Marlon isn't a talker; he's a listener, not a talker. He doesn't say an awful lot at any time. I couldn't honestly say they sit down and share heart-to-heart confabs, you know, or anything like that, because he's just not that type of man.

The second father is involved with his children mainly in a jokey, play way: this father was classified as having 'much casual' conversation.

Part-time assembler, husband a lorry driver:
Well – they talk, fight and play. He's got a marvellous Dad really. He brings him- self to their level. They don't really discuss serious things, but he's a lad's dad.

The third confirms this important point that fathers in many ways may be deeply caring and tender without doing much talking to their children.

Not in paid work, husband a semi-skilled mine-worker:
No, he doesn't really talk to any of them much. He's very quiet. The only time he's noisy [sic] really is when they're ill. And he's all over them then, he

spends hours with them – that's the only time. As long as they're all right and everything and he knows they're well, he doesn't really bother with them; but let them be ill or anything, and he's got more patience than I've got then – he'd sit up with them and everything.

The fourth is very much a non-participant father.

Part-time cleaner, husband a labourer:
Well, it's a bit difficult, because my husband's a good man, but he's not got a lot of time for his children. I know I really shouldn't say that, but – I couldn't answer your question, because Father doesn't listen a lot.

While families and individuals may find that talking comes naturally and easily to them as part of their way of life, so that talking to the child is simply an unforced extension of their personalities and 'the way things are', there is also for many parents a strong sense of the value of conversation and of an imperative to make time for it. The mother above is conscious of saying something derogatory: others may deliberately make an effort, if effort it is, or may be self-critical at having fallen short.

Part-time dinner-lady, husband an electrician:
Yes, we talk, I mean I'm interested – I take an interest in his football – we discuss it and talk about it. [Was this something you were interested in before, or do you show interest just because of the boys?] Well, you haven't much option. You have to follow it up and be able to discuss it with them, you know. I think it makes a difference when you know your football the same as they do. I think it helps a lot.

Not in paid work, husband a professional engineer:
[Father:] Well, I've always criticised myself as a parent, cause I've always felt that I've failed miserably to take – er – I don't *play* with my children a lot really. I don't ignore them … [Mother:] He does play with them – he doesn't take them to football matches, cricket matches and things. You do talk to them. [Father:] Oh yes, of course I *talk* to them. [Mother:] You don't sit behind your paper or watch television all night and don't say a word. We always talk a lot. [Father:] No, but I don't particularly sit down … I don't *go out of my way* to talk to him particularly. We talk about things, but it's not because I've *set out* to – I sometimes think he starts rather more conversations than I do. [Mother:] The thing is, there's a lot of us, and we all talk together. When you actually get one on his own – like you go somewhere with Matt – you come back amazed. [Father:] Yes, that's absolutely true. One of the frightful things about a family this size [four children] is that everybody talks, nobody listens, and you never get … there's so much noise that anything like a sustained conversation is virtually impossible, and I think if he ever tried

to talk to me about anything serious, there'd be all sorts of chiding from his eldest brother. So it's only when you get any one of them on their own that you suddenly realise what totally different characters they are to what they are collectively. That's it. So if you take one of them out on their own, you get a running commentary and conversation, things you never normally get. But you don't get much opportunity to do that, because when one says 'I'll come with you', the other one, who had no intention of coming with you until the other one did, will then decide to come too. The problem in this house is sheer lack of privacy. *We* complain that we have no privacy together at all, do we, Laura? And individually *they* get no privacy.

Before looking at some of the content of 'serious' conversations, together with the ways mothers approach serious issues which might cause anxiety to both the child and themselves, we can now draw together some of the information presented here and in the last chapter in order to establish an index of 'family cohesion'. This index is designed to reflect the child's participation in activities involving children and parents together. Table 6.2 shows how the index is made up, and an analysis of high and low scorers on this measure is given in Table 6.3.

The items brought together in this index clearly reflect a mixture of both attitudinal and situational factors that are associated with social class. We have already seen from the quotations in this section that frequent and sustained conversations can partly depend on lack of physical exhaustion and on privacy, both of which are probably, on balance, harder to find lower down the social scale; but that they also have to do with parents' attitude to the value of discussion (a somewhat education-oriented view). More important, probably, they reflect parents' readiness to treat the child as someone with opinions and ideas of his own which are to be respected similarly to those of adults in the family; and at this point, two related and class-affiliated dimensions enter the equation: democratic versus authoritarian principles and child-centredness. Other items in the index which cost nothing in themselves to undertake (reading together, singing and dramatic activities) may still thrive on situational support such as a reasonably comfortable living-room, and perhaps the stimulus of having owned books or been in a theatre; while they also reflect an easier identification of middle-class people with pleasures derived from literature or the arts. Most of the remaining items need to be interpreted in the light of the fact that going on family outings or sharing a hobby are likely to demand financial resources which the larger families in less skilled occupations may not be able to command – although, as we saw on pp. 82–3, determination may partly compensate for limited resources.

Nonetheless, however much one may appreciate the difficulties which face families further down the class scale, and empathise with the attitudes associated with such problems, from the standpoint *of the child* we have to see a low score on family cohesion as reflecting a damaging degree of deprivation. We live in a society in which following leisure pursuits together with members of one's own family is the *expected* norm, continually promoted as such in that part of television most familiar

TABLE 6.2 An index of family cohesion

Contributing items	Criterion	Score	% in random sample
Conversation (Qs 126–8)	Little with one, much casual with other	0	15
	Much casual with both	1	21
	Much casual with both other	2	23
	Serious with one, less with other	3	25
	Serious conversation with both parents	4	16
Child shares some activity with parent (Qs 129–30)	No	0	24
	Yes, with father only	1	
	Yes, with father only	1	
	Yes, at least one with each	2	34
Family reads aloud together (Q. 133)	Never	0	84
	At least sometimes	1	16
Family sings together (Q. 133)	No	0	54
	Yes	1	46
Family plays board/ card games together (Q. 134)	No, or only 2 people/or children	0	19
	Yes – game involves min. 3 people and includes a parent	1	81
Family concert/ play/jumble sale/ fair/fête (Qs 135–6)	No	0	74
	Yes – organised by children, but some parental participation	1	26
Family outings (Q. 132)	Cumulative score, maximum 4, as follows:		
	Cinema, theatre	1	49
	Seaside, country, stately homes	1	86
	Sporting events, swimming	1	40
	Other specified outing	1	34

Note: Possible score range 0–14 points; actual score range 0–14 points.

TABLE 6.3 Analysis of high and low scorers on family cohesion index

	Social class					Summary		
	I&II	IIIWC	IIIMan	IV	V	M.class	W.class	Overall popn
	%	%	%	%	%	%	%	%
High scorers (9 or more)	48	44	27	25	12	46	25	31
	Significance: class trend ↘ ****					m.class/w.class ****		
Low scorers (5 or less)	10	16	31	38	58	13	35	29
	Significance: class trend ↗ ****					m.class/w.class ****		

Note: Results for boys and girls are so consistently close within each social class that they have been combined here.

to children, the commercial breaks (and it is pertinent that commercial television is particularly likely to be watched by working-class children). Those who cannot count on such experiences as a natural right must be regarded as underprivileged in comparison with other children of their age.

And here perhaps we should take note of a difficulty which assails those who work in the emotive area of social class differences. Because one is aware of the advantages which certain child-rearing attitudes confer upon children – child-centredness and lack of 'bamboozlement' (Newson, 1982) being notable examples – these attitudes themselves begin to acquire a moral value or aura; they are not only seen as a 'good thing' for the children, but as a virtue that one would like one's friends to have – and thence, a moral attribute *which it would be insulting to suggest they lacked*. And there's the rub: social researchers do work on terms of friendship with families in every walk of life, who indeed become intimate friends in the sense that they willingly share their private feelings, and on successive occasions, when they have no necessity or pressure to do so. It is the business of social researchers to empathise very closely with these families, and to suspend any moral judgement (which would indeed impede an effective empathy and hence understanding). At the point of analysing the data which they bring home from these warm and not-so-brief encounters, however, the *identification in parents of attitudes which are in effect disadvantageous to the child* puts the researcher in the personally painful role of insulting (behind their backs) her friends. It is then perhaps not surprising if, like one such worker, the researcher is trapped into making essentially sentimental and value-laden statements about deprived and depriving mothers such as 'these mothers *deserve* to be called child-centred'!

Our own view is that the consequences are too grave for us to allow this to become a moral issue about good versus bad mothers. Deprived and depriving mothers have deprived and depriving lifestyles; any compensation which we can make to their children has to start at that point, which includes convincing mothers that they have competences that could be of value to their children, and making it possible for them to use them. No amount of sympathy for their difficulties will avail their children unless we are also prepared to look closely and clear-eyed at the damage which was never a part of their child-rearing intentions.

'I watch her, and I think, "I wonder what you're thinking". If only I could get in there to sort it out and help her along, you know ...'

Competence in communication is a two-edged weapon. Children of 11 are not only better able to express themselves than when they were younger; they are also more capable of covering up their feelings and withholding information which they don't want their parents to share. Because they are also more self-conscious and more socially empathic, they may realise that certain disclosures will have social repercussions, even though they may not be sure what those repercussions will be. At this point, then, a few parents may begin to feel that their child is becoming a stranger to them; and although most have no wish to know every secret, and accept that 'at this age she'll start having things that she *doesn't* want to tell me', they also know that the reticent child may be suffering from needless anxieties, or anxieties which at least the mother could comfort and put into perspective: as one mother said despairingly after recounting such an episode, 'Why she hadn't come and told me ...! – Three months of agony needn't have gone on at all.'

Thus, when we asked 'Do you feel that you know about most of his thoughts and fears, or do you think there's quite a lot he keeps to himself?' we tapped a source of anxiety in mothers as much as in children; and those who were reasonably sure of having an open communication line to their child knew themselves to be fortunate.

> **Not in paid work, husband a dyer:**
> I think there's quite a lot Naomi keeps to herself unless we're on our own and we start talking – then she'll often slip little things out as she hasn't mentioned before you know; and you think to yourself, if we hadn't have sat talking I wouldn't have got to know that.

> **Research worker, husband a lecturer:**
> I think in the end I know – I mean, to the extent that she kept the 'grey woman' to herself for about three weeks [serious anxiety fantasy compounded by group hysteria at school]. I knew there was *something* brewing, but I think she can't keep it in – because she's so interested and she knows that if she wants to discuss a relationship or feelings or fears or anything of this sort I *will* discuss it – so she wouldn't keep it to herself for long because she'd want to have a discussion and find things out about it.

Part-time mender, husband a foreman:
He's a worrier, but you don't really know what's worrying him until he can't sleep, and then – I go up, you know, and sit and have a talk to him, and he'll sort it out then, but he won't tell you straight away. He's a bit like his Dad in that respect – they, *keep* things. How can I put it? You know if somebody upsets me, I say my piece and I'm done, kind of thing. They don't – they keep it and keep it, and then a little thing'll blow 'em sky high. Barry seems inclined that road. His Dad's the same, like his grandpa was the same.

Not in paid work, husband an unemployed labourer:
There must be quite a lot I don't know about him. Well, only the other week we was going over Trent Bridge, and he told me he used to be scared of going across there, looking at the water. Well, I never knew that, you see. But I don't see how you can ever know everything about a person, I mean a grown-up even – how can you know everything that passes through people's minds? It's only a little thing, a brain, but all that knowledge, all those thoughts – I often think about that, you know.

Not in paid work, husband a foreman:
No, I don't think I know much about him at all really. He's a closed book as far as I'm concerned.

58% of mothers thought they did know about 'most of' the child's thoughts and fears, but a substantial minority of 40% felt they did not; the remaining 2% did not know how to answer. Class differences did not reach significance. The fact that a mother might know about a particular current fear did not necessarily make her feel that she knew about most of them. 32% of children were regarded by their mothers as 'a bit of a worrier' in general terms; and 52% were known to have specific fears or worries. There was a modest but steady increase in these further up the social scale (class trend ★★), which probably reflects the increase in serious conversations rather than actual incidence of fears. Similarly, 52% must be a conservative estimate of children who have specific fears.

Of the anxieties mentioned in reply to the question 'Has he any fears or worries, as far as you know?', the most common ones were connected with school (Newson and Newson, 1984).[2] 14% of all children (especially boys) had worries about school serious enough to be identified at this point – that is to say, other minor anxieties were elicited during the later discussion about school, but 14% have some school affair seen as 'his fear'. 11% of all children were afraid of the dark, and 10% were worried about death. Other things known to cause anxiety in at least 5% of all children (each) were their own medical problems, their parents' problems (other than death), specific animals, and being alone. 13% were worried about idiosyncratic things.

The importance of the point made above, that these percentages refer to whatever the mother identified as the child's *major* fear, can be seen when we look at the prompt questions which followed this general one. We asked about the child's reaction to certain topics which we felt *might* have been anxiety-producing – death, the news, and aspects of religion. Both 'death' and 'the news' produced add-itional accounts of anxiety in the child, but religion did not. We also reminded the mother of anything which she had reported the child as being afraid of at the age of 7, and asked whether he was still afraid of this; 20% of all children had fears persisting from 7 to 11 years, girls being rather more subject than boys to persisting fears (★★).

Death and 'something in the news' come closest, perhaps, to the reality-based fears of adults generally, and there was certainly evidence that some children were now watching news programmes with a sense of their relevance to themselves – some more so than their mothers.

> **Part-time typist, husband a warehouseman:**
> She's scared about the fighting – the war in Belfast. Actually, she shows far more interest in that than I do, because I *very* seldom sit down and watch it; and then in the *Post* there's all murders. Well, I think you can get so used to a thing that it doesn't have any effect, and unless it personally concerns me … I'm more bothered who's won the first division championship, I turn to the back page, but she's very interested in general news, like. She can tell me what I should probably tell *her*.

14% of children are frightened by news programmes; class differences do not reach significance, but almost twice as many girls are frightened as boys. This is probably explained by two of the main sources of fear: news of the murders of children, who tend to be girls, and programmes showing fighting in Ireland and elsewhere, which perhaps are too like the fictional war programmes that boys are otherwise enjoying. The third kind of news which disturbs children most concerns famine and refugees, particularly where children are shown as victims.

> **Part-time shop assistant, husband a manager:**
> I think when he sees things on the television, say to do with Ireland; he don't say a lot – but this is when he asks if there's going to be another war.

> **Canteen assistant, husband a boilermaker:**
> When this girl got murdered not long ago. Anything like that I switch off straight away. I say, 'Well, she might have got run over or something.' She says, 'No, Mum, somebody killed her', she says, 'poor child, how did she feel?' She feels for them she does, oh yes, yes, she does.

> **Part-time leaner, husband an asphalter:**
> Starving children – famine – she's very troubled about that. Thinks it's ter-rible. I do avoid letting her see these things if it's … but they've got to know about these things. The only trouble is, I'll have tears rolling down my cheeks, and she'll look at me and join me.

We can see in the last two quotations the dilemma for parents: they do not wish their children to suffer anxiety, yet these *are* real disasters and there is a limit to how far someone growing up into a world like this can or should be shielded from its truths. Other mothers express this very explicitly.

Part-time nurse, husband a teacher:
At one stage we did stop putting the news on, because there were so many depressing incidents that I think perhaps, for a child – they begin to think this is life, everything is either violent or sad. [Do you think it's better to shield children from this sort of thing?] Not from everything – I think some of the things which have been happening in Northern Ireland and some of the things in Africa – not shield them altogether, but it's difficult to know where to draw the line. [Were you afraid it would upset her, or was it because you didn't like her seeing violence?] Both – um – I think it did upset her, and I don't think it's good for children to have a steady diet of violence.

Ross's mother is almost sorry that he is *not* disturbed:

I suppose in a way he just feels that his home is so secure, it's so much his world, that nothing could touch him, and therefore – although he knows it goes on, all the violence and so on, and he will be interested and he will make a comment about it – it's in a different world, it's not his world. I sometimes think I ought to make him realise; but then again, I think it'll come to them quick enough – therefore it's very difficult to keep worrying about things like that, you know – and as long as they're happy.

Sam worries in bed about starving children, and his mother feels 'a bit torn' about exposing him to such programmes, but that 'you can't cushion a child indefinitely where things are factual'. Death is an ultimate fact which mothers themselves know they have to face, and which some have already faced or are already anxious about; as Lewis's mother said, 'It's me that's frightened of dying – oh lord, yes!' Children of this age tend, as one might expect, to be afraid of their parents dying, rather than themselves: 'I try to tell her she mustn't worry, but she'll say "I love you and I need you!"' Usually worries about death seemed to mothers to have been triggered by some event of relevance in the family or neighbourhood: a grandparent or (worse) an aunt or someone of the mother's generation had died, or the mother herself had been in hospital: 'Inevitably', said Clare's mother, 'you think, well, my mother isn't quite as invulnerable as I thought she was.' In several cases it was a *second* hospital visit by the mother, often for something trivial and unconnected with the first visit, which had evoked in the child a fear of his mother dying, and one can understand the child's reasoning: 'she said she was going to hospital to be made better, and I thought she *was* and now she's going again so she must be really ill'. Children of divorced parents seem particularly vulnerable;

not only are they not sure what will happen if they lose the parent they live with, but they have already experienced in some measure a breaking-up of their known world. For all children, their consciousness that adults do have secrets and do try to protect a child from bad news makes their uncertainty greater: one mother, in her awareness of this, deliberately allowed her daughter to overhear her talking confidently to an *adult* friend about her impending operation, in order to back up her direct explanations, while others allowed their children to work through a series of contingency plans.

> **Secretary, husband a media professional:**
> Me dying; – very much in at the moment. When we were divorced I think she was very aware that I was the only one left for her, and if I'm a bit late and she doesn't know where I am … and unfortunately once I went to the hospital for a check-up and they said 'stay in for a day', they happened to have a bed free, and I regretted very very much that I hadn't told her I was going for this check-up. I didn't want to bother her, but the way it happened it bothered her more. She thought it was something very serious … and now she'll say 'Well, what if you get killed?' And I tell her 'Well, I take much more care on the roads because I know I'm responsible for the three of you; but if I did die, you have had enough care to be able to cope with the rest of your life. You'd be sad, but you'd still live and you'd still eat and you'd still meet people.' And she'll say 'Would I have to go and live with Daddy?' And I'll say, 'Not necessarily. You could live with Grandma and Grandpa.' And she'll say, 'But what if they weren't there?' I have friend the same age as myself, and they are legal guardians of the children; and I've more or less said 'It won't happen; but this is what would happen if it did.'

Some children by this age, of course, have already had to cope with the reality of parental death, either actual or imminent. Mary's mother feels that she and Mary clung together after her husband's death because Mary is her only girl – 'You don't get this with boys, do you? – not so much, anyway.' Geraldine's father is very ill: 'She fears the future for him – there I think it goes very deep, deeper than I think I somehow realise she seems to have come to terms with it except that my husband's only got to lurch once more than usual – he falls easily – and I see her whiten a bit round the mouth.' Reg's mother is disabled with a progressive spinal condition, and has tried to prepare Reg to meet her death with her own religious strength: 'I said to Reg, "Now if I die …" but he brushes it aside: "Don't say that, I don't want to know – don't talk about things like that. Please don't." And I says, "Why – what fear have you got when I say these things?" So he says "It makes me feel that it's definitely going to happen" – he doesn't like you to talk of death at all.' Whatever the wonders of modern medicine, some children's parents do still die, by disease or through accident, before the child can possibly be prepared for such an event; and on the evidence of our transcripts, each time this happens to one family, other children see in that fatherless or motherless child a grim reminder that their own parents are not immortal, however much loved and needed. In the same way we have since found that the death of one of our 16-year-olds started shock-waves that we picked up among young people in our sample who did not even know him. It may well be, as Illich (1975) suggests, that in the midst of a violent and dangerous world we have entered into a collusion with the medical profession to treat death as vanquished, with the consequence that it is unfaceable: yet perhaps this is better for children generally than the recurrent house-guest our forefathers knew?

Religion, while not the consolation for children it once was (if children's literature is to be believed), also does not seem to be the source of fear so often described in autobiographies of childhood; or at any rate, only 1% of mothers of 11-year-olds were aware of this, even when prompted. We asked first, however, whether religion was something that interested the child, leaving the question of anxiety until after the mother's answer. 36% of children were positively interested in religion at this age, more children being interested further up the class scale (range 46% down to 29% ★★★). Girls were slightly but consistently more numerous than boys in every social class (★). A feature of mothers' accounts of their children's interest was a strong feeling of equality in the value of adults' and children's opinions; a suggestion that nobody could *know* the answers in this area, therefore the child's view was equally to be respected. Among our parents, there are of course some who do believe, as an article of their sect's faith, that they *know*; for the present, perhaps fortunately for the family's harmony, these children were not challenging their beliefs.

Part-time telephonist, husband a school caretaker:
He's an atheist at the moment – the last time you came he was very religious. He's changed completely and he disproves everything at the moment. There was a thing in the paper about 'was God an astronaut', and he read right through the whole lot and that was his proof. Of course, he goes on about science, evolution, that type of thing, and I think he's worked it out from that really.

Research worker, husband a lecturer:
She's interested, but I think the main *fascination* has passed, because they had a lot of discussion about this three years ago – she got very interested in God and religion, and came to a very rational conclusion that although she could see it was very nice to believe in God, she couldn't see the point – this was her rational decision at the end of it – Ben [14] is a much more emotional atheist than she is. I think she sees it as all 'opiate of the masses'. I think she rather thinks of it as I think of the Catholic Church, I can see the delightful aspect of believing this, but for me, no.

Part-time kitchen assistant, husband a cotton winder:
There's one thing that's worrying him – he hasn't been baptised, and he keeps asking about it. I say to him 'I didn't have you baptised because I thought

you'd wait and see if you wanted to go to church – it's quite easy for you to be done even at 11, or later.'

Not in paid work, ex-husband a labourer:
Well actually he hasn't been christened yet, and I said to the vicar to get him christened now. But Reg won't – he used to go to Sunday school, but he won't now. And I seem to push him a little bit, but no matter how much I push him on that point, you can't force him. He doesn't want to be christened – and I said, 'If you're not christened, you don't go to heaven.' And he said, 'This is rubbish, Mum.' He said, 'That's old-fashioned, everyone goes to heaven, unless you're bad and you go to hell.' He seems to think there's no point in being christened, but I can't see his point of view. I'm trying to fathom it out, but I haven't quite come round to his way of thinking yet.

Home worker, husband a progress chaser:
Well, tonight at our meeting in front of 130 people he'll stand up and give a Bible reading. He'll do it and enjoy it – put expression and everything into it. We've been training him to do it … students of the Bible – that's the first aim of life, and we put that first, you know, we train our children to put these things first in their life. Well, we would like him to be a door-to-door preacher, or Pioneer, as we call them. It's not for us to make the decision – it's up to the child himself, because you can't make a child do what he's not happy in. The child would have to make his decision on your guidance, so what happens in the future and what decision he makes waits to be seen.

Part-time nurse, husband an area officer:
I don't think he worries, to me he seems quite confident – that's not the right word – he has, shall I say, a very simple faith. It's quite an eye-opener to me, quite a lesson to me. He says prayers every night, and he's the one who will not miss them and not miss reading his Bible, and his prayers are, you know, quite searching. I realise I underestimate my son very often.

Not in paid work, husband a school caretaker:
We used to have family prayers and that – well I found with the little ones it was just a bore, you know; and now when we talk about religion we talk about him talking to God as he talks to anyone, do you understand what I mean? And Ivan is very much with this, *very* much with it. You don't have to go into a lot of prayers, just talk to God as you talk to Mummy and that's the way it should be. [Later heard him upstairs talking.] I said 'You were upstairs on your own, I thought you seemed bit worried' – 'Oh no, I just had a few things to tell God and I told him.' The other Sunday he was saying 'That priest was right, you know, God isn't a man that's floating about, he's inside you, and he's inside me.' He believes it, and he understands – he's got a wonderful idea.

'And it isn't that religion's thrust down him, cause it's not.'

In the same kind of way, mothers acknowledge that the philosophical problems that exercise their children are baffling to themselves also; or they may be taken aback by finding the child tackling eternal questions which are beyond their own awareness.

Not in paid work, husband a manager:
I was dishing the lunch up, and she started crying, she really did cry. I said 'What on earth's the matter, has something happened?' She said, 'Mummy, will you explain something to me?' She said 'What am I?' I said, 'What do you mean, what are you?' So she said, 'I look in the mirror sometimes, and I can see a face, and I know my name's Phyllis Dawson, but *what am I?*' I said, 'I don't know what you mean, Phyllis.' So she said, 'Well, I'm nothing really, am I?', she said, 'All I am, I've got a body standing up, and I've got a face, and I've got a name', she said 'but other than that I'm nothing'. Do you know, for a child of that age! – and I thought, 'what is she talking about?' [There followed a long discussion about the soul.] I was getting in such a muddle, I didn't know how to explain it. And the child was really breaking her heart, so I said 'Have you been reading something?' She said 'no', she said, 'I was sitting upstairs last night looking in the mirror, and I couldn't go to sleep afterwards thinking about it.' The way she was talking, it didn't seem natural for a child that age, it did really worry me.

Not in paid work, husband a tobacco-worker:
Well, he sometimes asks, you know, 'Who made God?' And a Jehovah's Witness came to the door and he asked her that, but she's never been back since. It's awkward to explain to a child. He's got a child's Bible that more or less explains, you know, how the *world* was made – but it puzzles all of us.

Before finally drawing together the threads which are the warp and weft of communication, we should briefly mention here one more form of parental behaviour which we regarded as anti-communication: teasing which went beyond gentleness. This topic was raised following a brief discussion of quarrels, bullying and teasing in the street and school: 'Do you tease N yourself at all? In what sort of way?' As one might expect, perhaps, mothers were more inclined to describe at length their husbands' teasing, which they often felt 'went too far'; however, we had not directly included fathers in the question, and therefore only coded answers concerning mothers, the criterion being that they knew the child minded being teased. 27% of mothers were prepared to admit this; class and sex differences did not reach significance except that rather more girls' mothers than boys' desisted from any teasing at all, even gentle teasing (52% girls, 42% boys ★★).

There is, of course, a very extensive area of communication between parents and children which we have barely touched on as yet: the whole question of how mothers communicate to the child what they often describe as 'a sense of right and wrong'. Here too there is an element of anti-communication – the use of idle threats which are intended to compel the child by virtue of his vulnerability to being bluffed. Some parents would also regard another form of disciplinary strategy as anti-communication: the use of physical force. These and other communications such as punishment, reasoning and appeals to the other spouse will have to wait until the next chapter.

Meanwhile, we can summarise degrees of communication outside the disciplinary area in terms of an index of communication between mother and child. Not all the items that make up the index have been discussed at length. This index is different from most of those we have devised, in that negative scores – denoting 'anti-communication' – have been included; five points are therefore added to each score in order to prevent negative total scores.

How this index is made up is shown in Table 6.4, while an analysis of high and low index scores appears in Table 6.5.

TABLE 6.4 An index of communication between mother and child

Based on:	Criterion for scoring	Score
26. Reaction to 'tiffs and upsets between friends'	M offers advice	+ 1
37. 'Do you tease N yourself at all?'	More than gentle teasing	– 1
56. 'Do you feel you know about most of his thoughts and fears …?'	Mostly	+ 1
93. Re molestation: 'Would you explain anything about the sexual danger, or … better not to mention that?'	Not prepared to mention	– 1
117. Re homework: 'Who helps him most often when he needs it?'	Mother, or equal M and father	+ 1
122. Any special thing that gives M a lot of pleasure?	Companionship and rapport	+ 1
123. Does he show his affection to people?	N spontaneously affectionate	+ 1
124. 'Do you find it easy to show him you love him?'	M spontaneously affectionate	+ 1
126–7. Does M talk a lot to N … discuss serious things?	Much conversation including serious	+ 2
	Much casual conversation	+ 1
143. Telling basic fact of where babies come from	No information from parents	– 1
143. Does he understand father's part in reproduction?	No, wouldn't tell if asked	– 1
144–5. Information re menstruation	Wouldn't tell yet	– 1
169. What makes N really angry – how does M get him back to normal?	M coaxes and reasons	+ 1
	(Add 5 to prevent negative score)	+ 5

Note: Possible score range 0–14; actual score range 2–13.

TABLE 6.5 High and low scorers on the index of communication between mother and child

	Social class					Summary		
	I&II	IIIWC	IIIMan	IV	V	M.class	W.class	Overall popn
	%	%	%	%	%	%	%	%
High scorers (9 or more)								
Boys	51	39	18	31	10	45	20	27
Girls	54	49	36	47	26	51	37	41
Both	52	44	27	39	18	48	29	34

Significance: class trend ↘ ★★★★   m.class vs w.class ★★★★
boys vs girls ★★★★

	I&II	IIIWC	IIIMan	IV	V	M.class	W.class	Overall popn
Low scorers (6 or less)								
Boys	23	35	52	42	70	29	52	46
Girls	14	16	32	31	39	15	32	28
Both	19	26	42	36	55	22	42	37

Significance: class trend ↗ ★★★★   m.class vs w.class ★★★★
boys vs girls ★★★★

It can be seen that boys' sparseness of communication with their mothers, as compared with girls', is much too great to be compensated for by the slightly superior level of conversation with their fathers (Table 6.1). This difference is a good deal more marked in the working class than the middle class, and recalls with new force the working-class saying:

> A son's a son till he gets him a wife
> Your daughter's a daughter for all your life.

In certain ways the index of communication both replaces and resembles the index of child-centredness which we used at 4 and 7 years, and which no longer seemed so appropriate at 11. Communication, like child-centredness, taps the mother's wish to take the child seriously as a person in his own right, whose self-hood is worthy of respect: whose 'basic considerability' includes rights to information, the right to have his dignity respected (and not brought low by unkind teasing), and a valuation of himself as someone worth both talking to and listening to. Thus the communication index measures quite directly the messages the child receives which identify him to himself as a person of worth.

Because both child-centredness and communication indices are concerned with messages which are reiterated through every part of the child's contact with his mother, rather than merely evaluating specific strands of their relationship, even small class differences would 'matter' in real terms. The kind of differences we see here represent massive inequalities which befall the child through the accident of social class, and this must at the very least be a deeply divisive aspect of children's experience. How far this and other differences also have effects on the individual child's competence is an issue we shall return to in Chapter 8.

Notes

1 For this reason, we would not advise the questions that make up specific indices being used as a straightforward tool for measuring the topic of the index; they need, we believe, to be embedded in a much more extensive conversational interview in order to elicit trustworthy information.

2 At 7, 10% of children (no class differences) were 'often' reluctant to go to school, and an additional 36%, with certain class differences, were 'sometimes' reluctant; not all reluctance, even among the 10%, was anxiety based, however. At 11, 93% of children were rated as either 'very happy' or 'happy enough' at school; whereas at 15–16 only 69% were rated as 'very happy' or 'happy on balance' at school, and a strong class trend was seen from 80% in Class I and II to only 50% in Class V.

References

Illich, I. (1975) *Limits to Medicine: Medical Nemesis, the Expropriation of Health*, London: Calder & Boyars.

Newson, E. (1978) 'Unreasonable care: the establishment of selfhood', in G. Vesey (ed.) *Human Values* (Lectures for the Royal Institute of Philosophy), Hemel Hempstead: Harvester Press.

Newson, E. (1982) 'Child and parent, school and culture: issues of identification', in M. Braham (ed.) *Aspects of Education*, Chichester: Wiley.

Newson, J. and Newson, E. (1976) *Seven Years Old in the Home Environment*, London: George Allen & Unwin.

Newson, J. and Newson, E. (1984) 'Parents' perspectives on children's behaviour at school', in N. Frude and H. Gault (eds) *Disruptive Behaviour in Schools*, Chichester: John Wiley & Sons.

7

MAKING GOOD

'If you haven't got a working relationship with your child by the time she's 11 ...'

At any stage of childhood, from 12 months to 12 years, it makes sense to mothers that we should ask them to consider issues of socialisation, moral understanding and control – whatever words they may prefer to use in discussing these questions. At 12 months, even if a mother thinks the baby 'can't really be naughty at this age', she still wants him to understand the word 'No' and, for his own safety and that of her possessions, to respond to it. By 4, the use of nurseries for some and the approach of school for all gives some urgency to the need for the child to accept ordinary social and group demands which are not tailored to his own idiosyncratic wishes; while his growing verbal sophistication creates new issues of falsehood, defiance and 'cheek'. At 7, these issues remain, and there is a marked increase of conflict surrounding 'not doing as he's asked' as opposed to 'doing what he's not supposed to do', reflecting the greater demands on the child for specific kinds of behaviour.

As the child moves into his twelfth year, discussions about his socialisation become in some ways more reflective, in other ways and for some mothers more desperate. To a certain extent, small misdemeanours have always raised questions of principle: 'a small lie can lead to a big lie'; 'if he thinks he can get away with that now, what'll he be like when he's 16?' At 11, the principle is the more urgent because the mother has now been hammering away at it for a long time without apparent success.

> **Barry's mother at 4:**
> [On whether smacking does any good] Sometimes I begin to wonder. I think it does *later on*, if you know what I mean. At this age I don't think it's doing a lot of good. But I think that you're kind of moulding them now, and it's

sinking in, so that a bit later on … I mean, if I thought that when he were about 7 or 8 he were going to backchat me like he does now, and I thought smacking would stop that, I'd half-kill him *now*, you know what I mean?

Barry's mother at 7:
Cheekiness? You're joking, are you? It's horrible. 'Shurrup – shut yer gob' – oh yes, he's had many a smack for that. I've told him I'll send him to boarding school – he says 'You haven't got enough money'. I say, 'I'll go out to work *all day* to keep you there!' Oh, I go very dramatic! I mean, I'm looking ahead a couple of years – what's he going to be like then if I don't stop him now?

Barry's mother at 11:
I'll stand back-answering so much, it all depends what attitude it's done at me, same as I say; but if he comes as I call *mouthing* manner, you know, then I'm liable to pick me hand up and … you know Barry, it's his face, you can half kill him anywhere else, but if I pick me hand up near his face, I can more or less just tap his face; I mean he's getting as wide as what I am, kind of thing, but I'll go for him then over that, and bad manners if he insists on carrying on.

In the same breath, and not quite inconsistently, the mother may also make allowance for the changing status of the child as he moves towards adulthood: Barry's mother adds 'You've got to have a certain amount of that now, haven't you, you know what I mean?' (Indeed, by the time he was 16 she was secretly proud of the fact that he had picked her up and dumped her outside the back door during an argument!)

Misdemeanours at 11 are seen as important to the extent that they either threaten the kind of relationship which the mother expects with her child or illustrate the shortcomings which she is beginning to recognise in that relationship or in his total personality. Some mothers, in reflecting on their present attempts to influence the child in question, also express a disappointment with the way their own situation has turned out: whereas previously the future held possibilities of improvement, now they often seem brought face to face with the recognition that 'this is how things are and this is how they'll go on being now'.

Not in paid work, husband an administrative assistant:
I tell you another thing Andrea does, is not hear you. You'll talk to her and she won't take any notice, she gets smacked for that. She doesn't hear you. [I remember you saying when she was small that she just closed her ears.] Yes, she does, just closes her ears, she's terrible for that. Mind you, *he's* just like that, my husband, I fall out with him for not answering. He'll sit there glued to the television, and it doesn't matter what I say, he never hears me; and *she* doesn't. They're all the same, they never hear what I say, so I get a bit mad then, you know, because I've been sitting here all day on my own, and then when they come in I want to talk, and nobody wants to listen. He'll smack the kiddies

for that, but he does it himself … It's annoying when you've spoke and nobody hears you, especially when you've said it three times or four times and they still haven't heard you, you know, you feel like screaming. And yet you say something in the same voice … 'Oh, talk to yourself!' I say, you know, and they'll hear that! But they can't hear what you ask them to do. Mind you, I think he shuts his ears sometimes when he doesn't *want* to hear me, you know. I think he does it on purpose, he says he doesn't, but I think he does.

Part-time playgroup leader, husband a manager:
[Biggest fault?] I don't know if it's how she might try to cope with a difficulty, or perhaps *not* try. We have this conflict over the piano. She never practises. Sometimes she seems sort of vacant, and I think that's when I get cross with her. I say, 'Oh, aren't you *wet*!' It's not good, because it's not good for her self-esteem, but I just can't help it. That's the thing that makes me crossest; if I think she's not bothering to tackle something that I think she should. I know with the piano, you see, that if I don't say 'Have you practised?', she won't do it. So, you know, the responsibility is mine … It's such an all-embracing fault, isn't it?

Not in paid work, husband a professional engineer:
He just won't give up. He goes on and on to finish the argument. [Father:] He will have to learn when he gets older to compromise a little bit. I used to be fond of saying in fun when he was younger, 'He'll either be a captain of industry or he'll be in prison.' There's no middle of the road ever. It's this lack of being able to see the middle way, it's all black and white. He doesn't seem to understand shades of grey.

We have argued elsewhere (Newson, 1978) that the long-term nature of the parental role induces in parents both a sense of their ultimate responsibility for the proper socialisation of the child (which from time to time will imply urgency), and at the same time a notion of *gradual* development towards that final goal. There is for many reflective parents a complication in terms of causality. Implicitly, by accepting parental responsibility they accept the idea of causality in child-rearing: that the means they use to socialise the child will have an effect. At the same time, partly *because* of the complex and drawn-out nature of child-rearing, much of what they do is done through faith and hope, and even when they have done it they find it difficult to be certain how far they actually influenced outcomes by their actions. At 11 they have enough experience of child-rearing, perhaps, to realise how little they can be sure of; they also know there is still some way to go, and that some kind of action continues to be demanded of them.

Not in paid work, husband a postman:
As I say, a lot of it's me, you know, when I'm turning her off. I know it's me at fault half the time. [Do you mean that there's things that she does which

get on your nerves a bit perhaps, and you feel that they're not real faults?] Yes, because every child I speak to, they're the same. And as I said, when they get over one, they've got another one. As the years have gone by, I've thought to myself, to think I used to get on to her for that, and she's really changed, and she's gone to something else. But now I think, well, *should* I get on to her for this appearance thing, will it make any difference to her, will it, in a few more years – will she get better through me telling her about it, or will she just come tidy of her own free will? Is it *worth* getting on to her for? But I still do get on to her.

The changed perspective of the parent in terms of the stage the child has reached in his life also changes the function of certain interview questions. At earlier stages, we introduced questions on the mothers' pleasure in and expression of affection for the child, specifically in order to start from a basis of warm feeling, so as to enable mothers to face the questions that followed which were designed to elicit criticism and descriptions of conflict. (We were unsuccessful, of course, in the case of those mothers who could think of nothing about the child that gave them pleasure, and their criticism was the starker for that.) At 11, questions about pleasure and affection seemed much less separable from socialisation as a whole: again, the child seemed to be perceived as a highly integrated personality rather than as a collection of pleasures and problems.

Nonetheless, it seemed useful to focus the mother on different potential areas of conflict in turn, as a springboard for the more general questions of how she actually dealt with conflict at this age. The topic of 'arguments and disagreements' was introduced as follows:

149. We're interested in the sorts of things children argue about at this age – is there any special thing that causes a lot of disagreement between you and N?

We then proceeded to specify particular areas: the child's conscientiousness in doing household jobs and keeping his own things tidy; coming home by a certain time, bedtime; clothes, hairstyle and make-up; smoking, drinking and drug-taking; envy of other children's possessions; envy of what other children are allowed to do (see Appendix 1 for wording of these questions). The results perhaps have some interest as delineating danger zones for parents bringing up 11-year-olds. These areas of conflict are illustrated below in the order of frequency with which they were described as causing conflict; they are not, of course, mutually exclusive. The introductory question also attracted, from 40% of mothers, answers that were not in the specific categories that followed: these were extremely idiosyncratic, the most recurrent being quarrelling with siblings (5%) and various forms of 'cheek' (3%).

1. Envy of what other children are allowed to do (Q. 158): 65%, sex and class differences not significant.

Not in paid work, husband a tradesman in own business:
Oh yes, yes, we've had that occasionally. Oh, there's very crafty little moves go on there, yes. I've learned that lesson, because we had a fishing episode on Saturday afternoons when the boys was down at the Trent – my heart was in my mouth all the time. But I thought, well, if Martin's mother says he can go, it must be all right for Simon to go. And I met Martin's mother and we had a few words, and Martin was only going because I allowed Simon to go! So after that I've become wise, sort of …

Part-time dinner-lady, husband a driller:
Many a time, yes, yes. I just say 'Well, I'm not so-and-so's mother, am I? I'm your mother.'

2. Bedtime (Q. 154): 50%, sex and class differences not significant.

   Not in paid work, husband a machine operator:
   Oh yes, Hamish'll stay up till it's, till the spot on the television goes – even the news or the epilogue, if it's not turned off. I have to turn the television off to get him to bed. At one time we used to take the aerial out and tell him it wasn't working.

3. Keeping own things tidy (Q. 152): 47% overall; sex differences not significant. There is a slight suggestion of a class trend (I & II 56% to V 42%), which is perhaps the result of more possessions at the upper end of the scale; middle class vs working class shows no significance. Untidiness, incidentally, is more often named as the child's 'biggest fault' than any other single item – but because parents chose fairly idiosyncratic things as the 'biggest fault', this still only amounts to 10% of children overall.

   Not in paid work, husband a clergyman:
   Yes, the state in which she leaves her bedroom, which usually resembles a tip which has been stirred with the biggest wooden spoon possible. The fact that she will wear as many clean cardigans in the week as she can lay her pretty little paws on, and leave the dirty ones anywhere she happens to drop them. Untidiness generally, I think. A lack of personal fastidiousness too, which I find surprising in Stephanie, because outwardly she's very fastidious; but she will leave dirty socks and dirty pants lying around her bedroom, which Beth [12] would never dream of doing.

4. Envy of other children's possessions (Q. 159): 38%, sex and class differences not significant.

   Not in paid work, husband an engineer:
   Pets. She'd like a pet, you see. Her friend's got a pet. And she says 'She can have things, and I can't.' And I say, 'Well, you've got a brother, and she's got no brother.' And she says 'Well, I'd rather have a dog than a brother.'

Travel agent, husband a representative:
Well, I try and tell them this is a fact of life. I see people with better clothes and smarter cars than me, and this sort of thing – you have to accept this, don't you?

5. Clothes (Q. 155): 34% overall; no significant class differences, but there is more conflict with girls than with boys (42%:25% ★★★).

Doctor, husband a doctor:
She hates nice clothes. She hates dressing up. [Do you have arguments about that?] Yes. She would go out visiting in the same filthy jeans that she would come in from the garden, it wouldn't worry her.

Part-time cleaner, husband a cycle packer:
We went to town last week, we got trousers, she's got a pair of boots. Trousers tucked in her boots! I said to her, 'I'm not joking, you look like Farmer Jane.' So she says 'I'm with it now.' So I says 'Looks to me as though you've passed it.' [You might not like them, but you would let her wear them would you?] Well, I think, she's in uniform all week, she might as well show off. But she overdoes everything, Anne does.

6. Hairstyle (Q. 156): 32%, sex and class differences not significant.

Machinist, husband a postman:
That's argument number one! He likes it long – he doesn't like B___. School because you have to have it cut, and if I left the combing to him he can make it that it doesn't touch his collar so he won't have to have it cut. He'd got to have it long like that or a skinhead, and I wouldn't tolerate that, so I'm letting it grow and grow until he gets detention, hoping that will cure him.

Not in paid work, husband a policeman:
Oh yes, we're always arguing about her hairstyle – she wants it long and I say 'Oh, your hair!' – 'Oh, it's fashionable, it's fashionable, you're old fashioned!' We do get a bit of friction there.

7. Coming in on time (Q. 153): 24% overall, no significant sex difference, slight suggestion of a class trend (I & II 17% to V 30%).

Secretary, husband a chemist:
I know jolly well she doesn't listen. I think all children are conveniently deaf at some time or other. She has a lot of freedom to come and go within certain rules and limits, and if you say 'Now you must be back, Marilyn' and you give the reason why, she comes in quarter of an hour late, 'Well I forgot.' That makes me cross.

3% of girls were having conflict over wearing make-up and 3% of children (rather more boys than girls) were regularly in trouble over smoking (although there were probably as many parents who were in trouble with their children for the same reason!). 6% of children were not involved in arguments or disagreements about any specific thing.

'He's nearly as tall as I am … it's a bit difficult, sometimes, thinking of the right punishment …'

By the time we had identified these various foci of conflict, each time also asking the mother how she did or would react in these situations, the topic had often proceeded beyond simple disagreement to the point where punishment was being invoked. We have discussed the role of punishment in child-rearing at some length in previous books (Newson and Newson, 1968, Chapters 13 and 14; Newson and Newson, 1976, Chapters 9 and 10) and will not repeat the argument here. As in previous discussion, we are not defining punishment in terms of *any* aversive stimulus; this could include the mother merely asking the child 'Have you thought about whether that's a good idea?' and thus would make nonsense of the *social* implication of punishment. We are taking the social implication as crucial, and defining punishment in terms of a more powerful person imposing sanctions on a less powerful person, either in order to change that person's behaviour on this occasion, or to demonstrate superior power in the hope of changing it on the next occasion. Thus punishment, as we saw at 7, invariably demonstrates inequality of status and almost invariably humiliates in the process; while some punishments are explicitly designed to humiliate.

The question of disagreement was raised at Q. 149, and it was not until Q. 170 that we explicitly asked about punishment: 'Now that N is 11, are there any punishments you use when he's naughty?' Again, the general question was followed by prompts as to whether various specific non-corporal punishments were used, and we finally turned our attention to corporal punishment at Q. 175 – by which time it had very often been mentioned already.

One problem in discussing punishments, whether smacking or non-smacking, is that it is difficult to measure their severity very accurately, and indeed they are likely to vary in severity from one tine to the next. It was clear that a punishment such as 'sending to bed' could also be of a different order from one mother to another, as is illustrated in the first category below. Even so, it seemed worthwhile to have some idea of the repertoire of punishments being used, along with their frequency, despite the caution which needs to be exercised in interpreting these findings.

In terms of their meaning to parents and child, it also seemed necessary to distinguish more precisely than some researchers have between different kinds of isolation (sending to bed, sending out of the room – the latter often isolating the mother from child rather the child from mother), and between different kinds of deprivation (pocket money, sweets, TV). Having prompted these separately, as well as whether certain threats were used as sanctions, we found 14% of mothers using non-smacking punishments other than those we had prompted (usually in addition). None of these individually reached a frequency as high as 10%, and almost all were some other form of deprivation – usually treats, outings and 'special' activities, though one mother broke a child's cherished model and another withdrew maternal services. These last are of interest as idiosyncratic ways of 'getting to' the child, but not typical as actions; they do typify, however, the fact that mothers who punish are exercised as to how to find a punishment that will make an impression.

Part-time dinner-lady, husband a driller:
He said he wasn't going to school, and I said he'd got to go, you see, and I did break one of his models up [child's special talent is making model ships]. Mind you, I was sorry after, but it was the first thing I knew that'd hurt him that way – and of course now I say to him 'You know what happened the other day!' you see, and of course he's quite wary of it now. I thought, I've got to do it to show him, cause I tell you, he thinks the world of his models, he does really. I mean, I didn't like doing it, but I thought, well, here goes. [Did you threaten him that you were going to do it?] Yes – I said 'Before I have any more trouble with you, Philip, I'm going to break a model up.' [And he went on persisting, did he?] Yes, so I had to just break one up. Course, he didn't like it. So I said, 'Now, you remember, won't you?' And he's sort of took care since.

Part-time mender, husband a supervisor:
He couldn't care less whether he has pocket money or whether he don't; but I can threaten him more by saying to him, 'All right, dirty football clothes, dirty gym shoes' and all them sort of ... 'I'll leave all them, and you can go to school in them' – and I think that upsets him as much as anything.

As with foci of conflict, we will present the non-corporal punishments in order of frequency, and will illustrate them at the same time. They are not, of course, mutually exclusive, unfortunately for the children.

1. Sending to bed early (Q. 172): 52% overall. This is more used for boys than girls (58%: 46% ★★★), and more for working class than middle class (55%: 45% ★★). Benjamin Spock, as one middle-class mother reminded us, is against associating bed with punishment.

    Part-time ironer, husband a lorry-driver:
    [Would you send him to bed if it was during the morning?] Oh yes. [How long would he have to stay?] All day. [He gets undressed?] Yes. [What would he be sent to bed for?] Swearing.

    Not in paid work, husband a labourer:
    [Bed early?] Yes, send her up to her room. Trouble is, with her, she'll always find something to do up there. So it's no way of punishing her!

2. Sending out of the room (Q. 172): 31% overall. There are no sex differences, but a strong class difference: 51% of Class I & II mothers use this, Classes III WC to IV descend gradually 33% to 27% and Class V show 18% (trend ★★★★). Middle class differs from working class (42%: 27% ★★★★). The main objections to this punishment and to the previous one are logistic: how to prevent the child from either returning or finding interesting things to do elsewhere. However, democratically-inclined mothers are often mainly concerned to put space between themselves and the child, rather than finding a punishment as such, and this may be a reason why Class I and II mothers are particularly likely to employ this strategy.

    Part-time playgroup leader, husband a manager:
    I tend to use banishment – you know, if I get so cross with them that I can't stand them, I say 'For heaven's sake, get out of my sight before I murder you' – you know – 'Go up to your room and stay there until you feel better or until I feel better.'

    Not in paid work, ex-husband a Class III manual worker:
    I put her outside, I forget what it was about, but she was really showing off: I says, 'Right, my girl, you can go go outside and cool off. I put her outside and you never heard anything like it – she kicked and banged and thudded at that door so that I had to fetch her in.

    Part-time cleaner, husband a train driver:
    She won't go – will you? [to Vicky]. I tell you, these kids nowadays have got a mind of their own. We were told by my mum, and we used to have to do as we were told.

3. Depriving of television (Q. 171): 25% overall. There are no class differences, but boys receive this punishment slightly more than girls (29%:21% ★). Again, there are logistic problems in that if the television is turned off this deprives the whole family, while if the punished child is sent out of the room his attempts to get back may spoil other people's TV-watching; also, as a morning punishment it may have to be postponed. The transcripts therefore tend to show attempts at this, rather than regular 'successful' use. Of course, sending to bed early also deprives the child of television.

    Part-time sales representative, husband a teacher:
    No, because I've tried it but, you know, I get over these things and by television time I'm not cross any more. That's why I smack – I do it at the moment, and then it's finished with, you see.

4. Depriving of pocket money (Q. 171): 22%, no class or sex differences. This is regarded as an effective strategy; some readers may remember that for some children pocket money was instituted in the first place in order to have a

convenient sanction. Adam at 7 'very rarely' got his pocket money because he failed to stay good enough; he still has this problem at 11.

Secretarial teacher, husband an insurance inspector:

Yes, it's a laugh really, because Adam has pocket money from us when he's good, so he doesn't have any. I know that sounds terrible … he just loses the lot. Stop their pocket money – that hurts them more than anything. You've got to hit them personally – their pocket money's their independence, isn't it? If they've got nowt of their own, I think that hurts more.

5. Threatening to leave the child (Q. 173): 17% overall, differences not significant the number being small. This is clearly a different kind of sanction from the preceding ones, in that it is not only a threat but an idle threat. The proportion using this at 11 is almost exactly the same as that at 7, and presumably it has become habitual for many, with the result that it 'goes in one ear and out the other'. Roy's mother has been threatening that she'll 'go back to Ireland and leave you with your Dad' since he was 4: 'I say I'll never come back. He doesn't believe me now, cause I've done it for years; they say "You never *do* go".' However, there are still children who are upset by this threat, and the child's reduced credulity may be offset now by his greater experience in the community of families whose mothers have left them.

Not in paid work, husband a crane driver:

Oh yes, many a time. I just say, 'When you come home tonight, I won't be here.' He'll say, 'Why, where're you going, Mam?' – and then he'll say 'I love you' – you know? Many a time I do say that, when they're all on together, you know – 'Oooh, I've had enough, I won't be here when you come home from school.'

Not in paid work, husband a tobacco blender:

I have done – I've threatened to walk out on them. And then when I did put me coat on to go to the greengrocer's, they both screamed. I'd only got me coat on!

6. Depriving of sweets (Q. 171): 13% overall, no significant differences. Oddly enough, this traditional sanction is not much used; perhaps sweets are nowadays seen as a part of food, which is extremely rarely withheld. One mother explained that 'If I stop sweets one day, she might be tempted to accept them from somebody else, and I don't like to think of her doing that'; it may be that the fierce warnings that mothers give about 'never taking sweets from strangers' do make them feel that children should have a dependable supply of their own.

7. Keeping in (main source Q. 170): 12% overall. This may be a minimal figure, the result of our not having prompted this punishment. 15% of boys are kept in compared with 10% of girls (not quite significant at 0.05), and presumably it is a more severe punishment in relation to boys, who expect to be 'off out'

more. There is a class trend (★★★), Class I and II mothers being unlikely to use this punishment (only 4%).

8.   Threat to send the child away (Q. 173): 11% overall. Like threats to leave the child, this is a similar figure to that found at 7. Class differences are in fact great enough here to reach significance: the trend runs from 6% in Class I and II to 16% in Class V (★★★★, middle class vs working class ★★★). This threat is particularly upsetting to children whose fathers have left and whose mothers threaten to send them to their fathers – presumably with some credibility. Other relatives are less commonly threatened than fathers: obviously it helps if there is an element of unpleasantness in the person chosen, though if there *is* such a convenient person the threat might carry more weight than the anonymous 'Home' (which perhaps is why some homes, such as the Gordon Boys' Home, traditionally recur as names in such threats).

> **Not in paid work, husband a joiner:**
> Oh yes, time upon time. I've even packed her bag, and it upset her. It's put her right again. She'll say 'Oh Mam, I don't want to go anywhere!' And I say 'Are you *sure*?' – cause I *would* send her away for a day or two – say to my parents. They're getting on in years, aid they're *very* nasty [i.e. bad tempered]. I say, 'I'll send you to Granny', and she says 'Oh, not that!'

Some mothers have given up the threat since 7 because the child was more upset than they intended; Shaun's mother used to threaten to put him in a home, but no longer does so because 'I think he got a bit … he felt I didn't want him, sort of thing'. Other mothers are in fact now closer to the process of care proceedings, and their children are aware of this; Paddy's mother often threatens that he'll go, and has invoked her social worker to back up the threat of sending them away: 'I've threatened them all this morning to have Mrs Welton and put them all in a home.'

It must be emphasised that mothers who threaten in these two ways do not necessarily think that it is justifiable to do so: some are as disgusted with themselves as Felicity's mother below. However, to the extent that the child does experience this kind of statement, which the mother may not feel able to withdraw, and to the extent also that there is a large body of mothers who cannot imagine themselves ever saying such a thing, whatever the stress, it seems correct to categorise mothers on what they do rather than what they wish they did. This, indeed, is a good example of how sensitive interviewing can enable a person to discuss actions of which she is ashamed, and hence give us much better insight into what goes on than observation could ever do.

> **Part-time machinist, husband a cook:**
> Both; which I honestly think is very wrong, and I bite my tongue off after I've said it. I definitely think it's wrong, because things like that play on children's minds. But I don't know, sometimes, especially if you're not feeling too good and then they start and that. And I have – I've got to be truthful

– I've said it – both – horrible for saying such a thing. Each time I've said it, I've felt horrible, you know. Because I think it's cruel really. [Do you think they do take you seriously?] Oh, I think Felicity – because you can tell by her face; she does her *best* to get back in your good books again, she'll do anything to get back with you again, you know. Straight away she does, she tries her utmost to smooth things over and see that you calm down. [When you say that you could bite your tongue when you've said it – would you in fact *tell* her you didn't mean it, or not?] No – not after I'd said it, I wouldn't go back on it, no; because I think other little things that you say to them, she'd think, oh, she didn't mean that … I wouldn't sort of tell her I *wouldn't* send her away. But if I sort of *think* when I'm shouting at them, I don't say it. [You don't always think in time?] Well, that's it, sometimes if you get yourself het up, you just can't, it just comes out, and that's it.

9. Threat of authority figure other than father (Q. 174): 10% overall. Boys are threatened in this way more than girls (14%: 6% ★★★) and there is a steady class trend from 6% in Class I and II to 16% in Class V (★★★). These figures are perhaps cautious, as there are some veiled threats that involve another person: for instance, when Paddy's mother threatens to 'have Mrs Welton' the social worker and 'put them all in a home', is this a threat of an authority figure or not? Similarly, a mother may give *as a reply to this question* that she would 'not threaten – perhaps say that I would come down and *discuss* it with his teacher' while admitting that this would have the effect of a threat on the child. Teachers and policemen, as at 7, are often *not* threatened because 'you never know when you're going to need them sort of people', but they are still the main authority figures mentioned.

The use of external authority figures has steadily reduced over time, from 22% at 4 (almost entirely policemen) through 18% at 7 to 10% at 11. The sex/class/time effect is particularly clear in Class V where 40% of boys were thus threatened at 7 and 23% at 11, compared with 13% of Class V girls at 7 and 9% at 11. One problem for mothers who wish to use this threat is that the children now know better.

Part-time clerical worker, husband a presser:
No, well it wouldn't be much use with the teacher because he's just like a friend to her – and the policemen are so darned friendly around here with the children, that you just couldn't.

However, for those children who are beginning to get into some degree of trouble outside the home, presumably the threat of authority could carry some weight.

Not in paid work, husband a bricklayer's labourer:
You can get the truth out of Katrina. I've only got to threaten her with the police. She hates the police.

Part-time shop assistant, husband a driver:
If you frighten him or tell him you're going for the police, it will worry him – it doesn't p'raps frighten him as much as it used to do, but he will go a bit pale then, that's all.

Not in paid work, ex-husband a scrap dealer:
I threaten to have the children's officer down to have a talk to him about smoking.

Not in paid work, husband a gas labourer:
Yes I've done that. I'll agree on that. I've said 'If you don't do what Mummy tells you, Mummy will have to go to the probation officer and ask him if he could help me with you.' I have said that. I don't know whether that's right or wrong, I don't know.

The following threat includes the teacher as its object: the identification patterns are complex.

Not in paid work, husband a machine operator:
The other week he swore, and I said 'Right, I'm going down to see the teacher just to see what they *are* teaching you at this school.' I threaten him, but unless it was really desperate I don't think I would. I don't like getting him into any *more* trouble.

As on earlier occasions (Newson and Newson, 1968: 465–73), the interviewer was sometimes drawn into the teasing exploitation of chance opportunities which we have discussed before as a socialisation technique often used, as here, by mother and another adult in collusion.

Part-time cleaner, husband a quarryman:
She was very upset when she knew you was coming, she wanted to know what you wanted to see her about, she saw the letter. So Marion [elder sister] says 'That's with you having these few paddies – that's what the lady's coming for!'

'I say that many things, you know, she knows I don't mean it. That doesn't wash any more now.'

Threats to leave the child, to send the child away and to bring in an external authority figure have in common that, on the whole, they are not likely to be carried out, even though there may be enough examples of such things in the wider community to give the child pause. It is certainly rare that a mother actually intends to carry out the threat at the point of uttering it. It is thus a means by which the mother takes advantage of the child's uncertainty about what she might or might not do, in order to give him a sense of her power and subdue his will to hers.

Threats also have in common that they are a *verbal* means of disciplining the child in which words are deliberately used to convey a false impression, as opposed to being used as the agents of truth. To this extent they violate the ideal of truthful communication which even these same mothers subscribe to, and which they certainly hope for from the child to themselves.

Part-time cleaner, husband a labourer:

If I think she's told a lie and it could cause any trouble, I often say 'Oh, all right, get your coat on, you know where you're going', and she knows then, and she says 'I'm sorry Mummy', and she'll tell the truth then. [Where does she think she's going?] The police station.

There is another form of threat which also uses verbal means to invoke sanctions which the mother may have no intention of carrying out: the threat of corporal punishment *using an implement*. Obviously the use of an implement to hit the child is not necessarily an idle threat, and we shall return to the whole pattern of physical punishment in the remainder of this chapter. However, when we had asked about the use of sticks, belts, etc., we followed this with the question 'Do you ever *threaten* to use anything on him' and, if the mother said yes, we asked 'Do you reckon it may come to that, or is it just an idle threat?' 21% of mothers overall were threatening implements with no intention of using them, the class trend (★★★) being somewhat distorted by a heavy influx of Class III WC mothers threatening their boys (30%, compared with 16% of their girls – the only sex difference in the table).

At 4 years we devised an index of 'evasion or distortion of truth' and at 7 we used a somewhat similar index which we called 'bamboozlement'. The notion of bamboozlement proved an important one: defined by the *Oxford English Dictionary* as 'to deceive by trickery, hoax, cozen; to mystify', it was based on a series of idle threats plus the mother's attempts to conceal her ignorance if she did not know the answer to the child's questions; and mothers' behaviour in this respect was found in particular to correlate negatively within classes with children's verbal reasoning scores at 11 years. This question of outcomes we shall return to shortly. For the moment, it is worth looking again at an index of 'idle threats' at 11. It should be noted that these threats are made by the mother rather than the father: although we also asked questions about the father's threats, we did not feel the mother could reliably speak for the father on the question of whether his threats were idle or not.

Table 7.1 shows how the index of mothers' use of idle threats is made up, and gives a breakdown by sex and social class of the top quarter-plus of the population scoring on this. Because idle threats of this sort are not a common occurrence at 11, this group qualifies by scoring one or more items on the index list.

In the 'bamboozlement' index at 7, with its broader behavioural base and score range, scorers of 2 or more made up 29%. Comparing this group at 7 with the 'scoring' group at 11, the line-up is very similar, with a class trend and middle-class/working-class difference of equal significance, and non-significant sex differences;

TABLE 7.1 Mothers' use of idle threats at 11

Item								
Threatens to leave the child					Score	1		
Threatens to send child away from home					Score	1		
Threatens child with external authority figure (i.e. not father)					Score	1		
Threatens to use an implement in hitting child, and this is identified as an idle threat					Score	1		
Score range 0–4								

	Social class					Summary		
	I&II	IIIWC	IIIMan	IV	V	M.class	W.class	Overall popn
	%	%	%	%	%	%	%	%
Mothers scoring 1 or more idle threats								
Boys	22	12	30	34	41	17	32	28
Girls	16	23	31	27	33	19	30	27
Both	19	17	30	31	37	18	31	28

Significance: class trend ↗ **★★★★**   m.class vs w.class★★★★
Boys vs girls n.s.

37% of Class V mothers fell in the bamboozling group at 7, 15% of middle class and 34% of working class. Given that parents so often suggest that their children are 'too big to fall for that nowadays', the persistence of idle threats and their pattern across the sample is interesting, and indeed, persistence may be its destructive force. This topic is re-analysed in terms of its rather chilling cumulative outcomes in Chapter 8.

'I say "Roger, go. Because you know if I touch you once I shall really lay into you, so go for your own sake." And he goes, cause I know he will.'

In turning now to physical punishment, we have to remember first of all that smacking is seldom exclusively physical, in that it almost always takes place within, or as a culmination of, a barrage of words. Even the mother who says 'you can hear them in here falling out, and it really gets on my nerves, so I just come in and don't speak and just smack' in fact follows up the smack with a tirade.

At 11, the justifications of smacking which parents used at 1 and at 4, that the child 'doesn't really understand unless you smack', have now fallen away – as indeed they had by 7. At 7, however, the size-ratio of adult to child perhaps allowed habitual patterns of 'giving him a clout to help him on his way' to be maintained without the mother necessarily feeling the inappropriateness of her action, whereas the sheer stature of the child at 11 begins to make smacking feel more like fighting. Fighting with her child is definitely not the intention of any mother. The size of the child is often mentioned as one of the reasons for not smacking or rarely smacking at 11.

Physical size is also expected to imply maturity, and clearly mothers generally would like the child now to be amenable and reasonable towards what they see as their own reasonable demands. The problem arises when the child resists, and persists in resisting, these demands. At that point, the expected maturity of the child may be invoked either as a reason for not smacking or as a reason why the mother thinks the situation intolerable enough to 'have to' smack.

Shop manageress, husband a vehicle builder:
When you come before, I used to have a slipper hung up in the kitchen – not now. I think it's a bit too undignified now. I wouldn't say – I mean, if I really thought that a damn good slapping or something … but I can't see me doing it really, because I think if I can't talk to Edwina at this age, you know, then I would begin to lose contact with her altogether. I mean, because you can't hit them really later on, so you've to start to find a way, other than physical I mean; because you only smack them in a way when they're little and you're bigger than they are, but I mean it's not long before they'll be as big; and no, I would think I was failing somehow then.

Not in paid work, husband a clerk:
Mostly cheekiness, answering back. Well, I wouldn't have smacked her for that so much at 7, because I think at 7 they're sort of beginning to grow up and develop themselves, therefore it isn't cheekiness, it's sort of finding their way; but at 11 I think they should have sort of more sense. It's selfishness in a way – in abroad sense – she's cheeky because she thinks she can get away with it and be herself rather than give in to what *I* want.

Not in paid work, husband a plant driver:
I don't like to hit him but I have done. I'd sooner just, 'I'm not going to hit you – bed early tonight.' But it comes that many times – I'll say 'bed early tonight' – he don't *mind* going up to bed now. I'm just getting nowhere – I'm going to have to start hitting him. When he was as big as Sharon, I'd class them as perfect. I could have had a dozen, they were that good, him and Beverley. But right now – well, he's all I can manage completely. I'm not saying out of hand, owt like that. He seems as if he wants to be the centre of attention, he talks bossy, he's like that all the while.

Table 7.2 compares the frequency of smacking at 7 and 11 years. The way the data are arranged is slightly different at the two ages. At 7 the main source of 'frequency' information was the question 'How often does N in fact get smacked?', father and mother not being differentiated in this question, while by a later question

TABLE 7.2 Frequency of smacking at 7 and at 11 years (overall population)

Smacking frequency	Age 7	Age 11		
	By mother/father %	By mother %	By father %	By either %
1+ per day	8	3	1	3
1+ per week, less than 1 per day	33	12	4	15
1+ per month, less than 1 per week	28	22	10	22
Less than 1 per month or never	31	63	85	60

Sex differences:				
Smacked 1+ per week				
Boys	52 ★★★★	19	5	22 ★★★★
Girls	41	13	3	14

Social class:	I&II	IIIWC	IIIMan	IV	V	M.class	W.class	Overall popn
	%	%	%	%	%	%	%	%
Smacked 1/week + at 7	29	36	43	39	56	33	44	41
		(trend ↗ ★★★★ m.class vs w.class ★★★)						
Smacked 1/week + at 11	6	15	18	22	32	10	21	18
		(trend ↗ ★★★★ m.class vs w.class ★★★)						

we ascertained that mothers smacked more frequently than fathers in 79% of cases. At 11 we asked for a frequency estimate for each separately, and later asked more general questions about disagreements between parents on child-rearing and dis- cipline. The columns offering a direct comparison in the table are thus the first and the last.

It can be seen that twice as many children at 11 as at 7 are being smacked rarely or never, and less than half as many are smacked as often as once a week or more. As at 7, mothers are doing more smacking than fathers. Various reasons are given for this: that father deliberately does not because if he did he would hit too hard; that father is too 'soft'; that mother is more often there; and, an extension of this last, that father objects to being brought in as executioner following conflicts that 'belong' to the mother. These attitudes are all illustrated below.

Not in paid work, husband a driver:
Ooh, my husband wouldn't, no. No, that time when he belted him [for breaking and entering], he [i.e. father] cried. He said 'I wish my hand would drop off'. He don't, cause he always says 'My hand's a lot harder than yours.'

Canteen assistant, husband a boiler-maker:
[Mother:] Yes, he's too soft, he's far too soft with her. It's me that's got to do it all. [Father:] Well, that's the mother's job, isn't it? Father's the provider, mother's the corrector and educator. [Mother:] No, she should have a good hand off you now and then. I think so. [Father:] Don't believe in it, duck. Only did that once. I was working down pit, and I was as tired as anyone that came up; and she'd saved it up till I came, in: 'She's been a naughty girl and she's done this …' And if there's anything I hate, it's this. Because I reckon a child should be punished on the spot, not the threat hanging over her head for hours. So I walloped her – and she's got a very sensitive skin – two minutes later my wife came raging, 'Look what you've done, big finger marks.' And I swore blind I should never hit her again. And I was only doing what she told me. I told her there and then, I said 'I shall never hit her again' – and I haven't done.

Part-time packer, husband a driver:
Daddy doesn't seem to want to hit them. He says he isn't with them all day, and then he doesn't want to come home at night, and hear this and that, and then have to start and hit them.

The table also shows sex and class differences in smacking frequency. At 7, boys were smacked more than girls, and smacking increased at the lower end of the social class scale. These differences persist at 11 despite the diminished frequency, and in fact the *proportional* differences between middle class and working class have increased since 7: twice as many working-class mothers as middle-class mothers now smack their children once a week or more at 11.

A check on frequency was made by devising an index of smacking frequency based both on differential scores according to the overall frequencies given by the mother (information in Table 7.2), and on her 'smacking' replies to questions which sought her strategies in specific situations of conflict. Similar results obtain. Smacking does not increase markedly with family size, and this relationship is only evident at all in working-class families.

'I wouldn't smack in anger, I think it's good to discipline a child …'

The notion of *formality* in smacking is one which we have addressed before, and it clearly has significance in evaluating how far the mother is committed to smacking as punishment – a justified and considered act – or whether she finds herself committing an act of violence as a result of emotional stress when she would not do so in, as it were, her right mind. This is one reason why the 'barrage of words' in which smacking takes place is important: it identifies to the child what the mother thinks is right and proper behaviour on her part, as opposed to deplorable though perhaps inevitable behaviour. In so far as the mother *intends her behaviour to the child during conflict to have an effect on his moral development,* her inclusion of violence in that behaviour and her evaluation of the significance of that violence, must be incorporated into his moral learning.

There are a number of ways of getting a purchase on the notion of formality. One is to look at whether the mother tends to smack in anger or (as one mother said, rejecting it) 'in a calculated way'. 71% of mothers who do smack, do so only in anger, while 26% smack simply as a punishment; class and sex differences are not significant. The two attitudes are expressed below:

> **Clerk, husband a chief clerk:**
> It's only when they've worked me up that I will lash out at them. And as I say to them, 'If you're going to get me so mad, you've got to expect it.' They should see. I say to Curtis afterwards when it's all over, 'You should *know* that when you're working me up it only ends one way, and you're intelligent enough to *realise* that's how it's going to end up.'

> **Voluntary worker, husband a journalist:**
> I'm not quickly aroused to anger. I wouldn't *like* to smack in anger. I'd use it as a measured punishment.

An extension of the difference can also be seen in the mother's attitude to the aftermath, for the formality of smacking would be undermined by expression of regret. The first mother below is an 'angry' smacker who is correspondingly sorry – the second is a formal smacker complaining of her husband's attitude.

> **Not in paid work, husband a foreman:**
> It's usually my temper afterwards you stand there feeling a bit tearful, 'Oh dear, I didn't ought to have smacked him' … we usually end up 'Oh, I'm sorry, love.'

> **Not in paid work, husband a manager:**
> He's smacked them, and then he goes back upstairs and loves them! He can't bear to see them crying. I say 'A lot of ruddy good *that's* doing them!'

The use of an implement for smacking also has a more profound significance than the increased pain of any one blow – though obviously that is one intended consequence. To own a specific implement in the first place – like the slipper that

Edwina's mother used to keep hanging in the kitchen (p. 154) – announces, in advance of any conflict, the mother's avowed intentions. We also pointed out at 7 that the *slowing-up* of punishment invests it with formality, whether this consists of threatening the child 'Wait till I get you home' and punishing on arrival there, baring the child's bottom, or fetching an implement: in each case, the intentionality of the act has to be maintained through the preparational pause – although it is also true that the pause itself may contribute to the impetus of the drama for the parent as well as the child.

We have not distinguished between actual implements used; cane, strap or belt and slipper are the most common. It would be unwise to dismiss the painful potential of slippers; one mother showed us her slipper, which turned out to be a wooden exercise sandal, and many slippers have wooden heels.

> **Mender, husband a supervisor (two children):**
> Mostly a slipper. Well, long trousers and that, your hand don't seem to do any good; but I just take me shoe off, and 'one!', it seems I get through. I did have a cane at one time, and then, same as I say, I found the slipper very effective, which is always handy and I seem as if I get me results. [This is Barry's mother, pp. 00–00; at four she was using a hairbrush, which she liked because it had a curved back which fitted the curve of Barry's bottom. We must emphasise that Barry's mother is a woman of strong and attractive personality, who throughout has achieved a very warm and friendly relationship with Barry.]

> **Not in paid work, husband a foreman (six children):**
> I don't use a stick but I've always kept a strap, and if I think they're arguing I just go to the drawer and it's usually enough – if I take it out, they stop. I've always kept that.

> **Not in paid work, husband a labourer (nine children):**
> Well, I just carry it around my shoulder [strap] – when they come home from school at 4 o'clock – and then they know they have to be quiet.

> **Part-time cleaner, husband a labourer (eight children):**
> Anything I've got in me hand – the broom, mops, chairs …

The threat of an implement seemed to us to belong on the same dimension as its actual use, again for the reason that the mother thereby stated her intentions formally, whether or not the threat was actually carried out. Table 7.3 shows mothers' use or threat of implements for hitting the child, distinguishing between actual use at 11, serious threat (where mother was expecting that it 'would come to that'), and idle threats, where she was not actually expecting ever to use an implement on the child.

TABLE 7.3 Use or threat by mother of an implement for corporal punishment

	Social class					Summary		
	I&II	IIIWC	IIIMan	IV	V	M.class	W. class	Overall popn
	%	%	%	%	%	%	%	%
Currently used:								
Boys	12	18	15	10	29	15	16	15
Girls	5	2	3	1	11	3	3	3
Both	8	10	9	6	19	9	10	9

Significance: class trend non-linear *** (large rise in Class V) m.class vs w.class n.s.
boys vs girls ****

Note: If father's use of implement is taken into account to give percentages for 'use by either parent', percentages only rise by 2–4 except for boys in Class V, 36% of whom have an implement used by one parent or the other.

	I&II	IIIWC	IIIMan	IV	V	M.class	W. class	Overall
Serious threat:								
Boys	5	5	7	4	10	5	7	6
Girls	0	0	5	3	0	3	3	2
Both	3	3	6	3	5	3	5	5

class. trend n.s m.class vs w.class n.s.
boys vs girls*

	I&II	IIIWC	IIIMan	IV	V	M.class	W. class	Overall
Idle threat:								
Boys	8	30	22	26	16	18	22	21
Girls	8	16	24	25	17	12	23	20
Both	8	23	23	26	17	15	23	21

class trend linear ↗ *** m.class vs w.class *
non-linear *** boys vs girls n.s.

	I&II	IIIWC	IIIMan	IV	V	M.class	W. class	Overall
Neither implement nor threat:								
Boys	73	47	54	56	38	61	53	55
Girls	87	82	67	71	67	85	68	72
Both	80	65	61	63	52	73	60	64

class trend ↘ **** m.class vs w.class ***
boys vs girls ***

Again we need to compare the use of implements at 7 to put this into perspective. At that age, only 25% of parents neither used nor threatened to use an implement; 22% had already used one. Thus, while perhaps the majority of psychologists would feel that our 35% of mothers either using or threatening an implement on 11-year-olds was an unacceptably violent picture, it is at least a minority group and less than half the size of the same group at 7. There is an exception to this decrease, however: in Class V, actual use of implements by one parent or the other has *increased* for children generally from 17% to 25%, and in the case of boys from 25% to 36%.

One further measure of mothers' belief in formal punishment can be found in their attitudes towards the school's use of such sanctions. The acceptance of a right of teachers to hit the child at all implies acceptance of formality of smacking, since even where school staff are allowed to hit children, this is supposed to be done on an entirely formal (i.e. recordable) basis. In our question we made doubly sure that formal corporal punishment was understood by asking 'Do you think teachers should be allowed to use a cane or a strap on children of N's age?', together with further questions about whether this had happened to their child, whether it had upset him and whether the mother had complained (or would complain if it did happen).

53% of mothers overall think that teachers should be allowed to cane children of 11, and a further 5% would object to their own child being caned but think caning should be available to teachers. There are no class differences here except that Class III WC mothers of boys in particular rise to 74% expressing unreserved approval. Mothers of girls generally are less inclined to approve of teachers caning.

We are now in a position to evaluate the child's overall experience of formal corporal punishment, in terms of an index drawing on attitudes and behaviour of the mother, and behaviour reported of the father. This index is made up as shown in Table 7.4.

Table 7.5 shows high and low scorers on the index of commitment to formal corporal punishment. It can be seen that social classes differ mainly in terms of Class I and II being isolated from the rest. The second major finding here is the punishing attitude of Class III WC mothers to their boys; although there is a sex difference that holds throughout, Class III WC show the one majority group leaning strongly towards formal punishment, in respect of boys only (54%), with twice as many boys as girls being affected.

'That's what we strive for – to bring them up into decent people'

The majority of parents feel that both of them are involved in striving for the child's socialisation; but we saw at the beginning of this chapter, in the quotation from Andrea's mother, how discussion of the child's shortcomings can quickly spill over into focusing on those of the father and on the mother's general dissatisfactions with her situation. This area seemed important enough, for the mother's experience of child-rearing and for the child's experience of being reared, to address it directly. We asked 'Is there any (other) way in which you disagree with your

TABLE 7.4 Index of commitment to formal corporal punishment

Item	Criterion	Score
Mother's mood when smacking	Simply as punishment	3
	Either above or in anger	2
	Only in anger	1
	Doesn't smack	0
Implement use by mother	Currently used	3
	Serious threat	2
	Idle threat	1
	Neither threat nor use	0
Implement use by father	Currently used	2
	Threat only	1
	Neither threat nor use	0
Mother thinks teachers should cane	Yes, no reservations	2
	Yes, but not her child	1
	No	0

Note: Actual score range 0–10. Possible score range 0–10.

TABLE 7.5 Parents scoring high and low on the index of commitment to formal corporal punishment

	Social class					Summary		
	I&II	IIIWC	IIIMan	IV	V	M.class	W.class	Overall popn
	%	%	%	%	%	%	%	%
High scorers (4 or more)								
Boys	21	54	42	38	35	37	40	39
Girls	13	23	28	30	29	18	29	26
Both	17	39	35	34	32	27	35	33
	Significance: class trend non-linear ★★★			boys vs girls ★★★★		m.class vs w.class n.s.		
Low scorers (0,1)								
Boys	36	17	22	24	27	27	23	24
Girls	48	30	26	40	37	40	30	33
Both	42	24	24	32	32	33	27	28
	Significance: class trend non-linear ★★★			boys vs girls ★★★		m.class vs w.class n.s.		

husband about how you should deal with N?' and found it possible to distinguish between major disagreements and minor disagreements. 54% of mothers (class range 52% to 56%) had no disagreements in this area worth talking about and the only sex differences appeared in the top and bottom classes, where there were more likely to be disagreements over boys. 29% of mothers overall were having minor disagreements with their husbands over bringing up the 11-year-old, and these were more common further up the class scale (trend ★★★); 11% were having major disagreements, and conversely these increased towards the lower end (trend ★★). The sex differences mentioned above were reflected for Class I and II in the area of 'minor disagreements' (more about boys), but for Class V were distributed between major and minor, both showing rather more for boys. The quotations that follow are examples of disagreements in the two categories.

Minor disagreements

Instructor, husband a representative:
[Father:] There is only one disagreement that we have. My fad is that they should be quiet at the table – my wife thinks they should be allowed to say odd things. [Mother:] You know, they just sit there like mummies – I think they should be allowed to say the odd thing, providing they don't go mad and just talk and don't eat.

Part-time typist, husband a clerk:
I suppose we have arguments, theoretically you're not supposed to have, but we do. My husband insists that they eat everything put on their plate, so we argue about that, you see … I think you can get far more obedience and respect by showing a bit of love than by frightening them, but he doesn't agree. You see I had that upbringing – my husband thinks I adored my father, actually I was frightened you see.

Not in paid work, husband a burglar:
Well, he don't like him to stop up late at night. I keep him up for company because I'm on my own. He shouts at Godfrey and tells him to go up to bed when he comes in. I say, 'Don't shout at Godfrey, cause it was me that kept him up.' I don't like sitting on my own at night – I like one of them up.

Not in paid work, husband a labourer:
There's only one thing that I get on to Jim for. You see he worships Verity. Well, this shows you how much he loves her. If I say to Verity 'Go and do the pots', and say she's not done them straight away, and I say 'Now you'll get a good hiding if you don't do it now, go and do what I say', if I get angry with her – he'll run to the sink and do them! He'll say, 'You go out, Baby, I'll do them'. That is wrong. To me it is – I know he's doing them for her, but she's got to understand the way of life in a home. But she doesn't. And what's her husband going to say?

Major disagreements

Part-time assembler, husband a packer:

Oh, we disagree such a lot – we do disagree. My husband – he don't talk to him enough – he's very – he shouts and shouts a lot, you know, if he wants something doing, he doesn't give them time to get up and do it. He'll say 'Come on, come on', you know, and I think it's a way of badgering – and he's only too ready to give them a smack, sooner than explain or talk to them like I do. I talk Nicky round, but his dad wouldn't, he'd just smack him. Or ... Nicky answers back, but he's trying to explain why he's done this thing, if you understand me, but in the *way* he's doing it – he's shouting and bawling his explanation out, but to his daddy he's answering back, and he'll smack him. I agree he shouldn't speak to his daddy in that way, but at the same time his daddy should hear him out. We do disagree ever such a lot with the children.

Not in paid work, husband a clerk:

We have a terrific amount of arguments, and this is one of the biggest bones of contention between us – the fact that he will not, when they're cheeking me, he will not stand up for me or discipline them. I don't like it. In fact I don't think it's fair, to be honest, I can yell till I make myself ill, and er ... I'm sort of a bit shaky and really upset, and swallowing me tablets – I mean it's neither good for me nor them.

Part-time ward orderly, husband a miner:

It was gone midnight, and he came in grinning, and he said 'I know you're mad, but wait till you hear what I've got to say.' Well, his dad never stopped, he just gave him the biggest hiding I've *ever* seen. Well, I can't bear that, I was pushing him and saying 'leave him, leave him!' There'd been an accident, and he'd been up to the hospital with someone and had to wait ... I said 'You should have *waited* until he stopped talking', I mean it seemed such a terrible thing ... when he does punish him it's awful and I can't bear it. We do argue about it I think his Dad wants to keep him straight, I'm afraid he had a strict upbringing, and he says 'It never did us any harm, it kept us straight'. If he got into trouble or had to go away, I don't think he'd ever forgive him, *never*. I sometimes think he's a little bit too ... I don't suppose he is really, in this day and age ... a little bit too hard, like his dad, ooh dear – ruled him with a rod of iron! He's not as bad as his father, but it's there. And he wants Bernard to be straight, I can understand that [quotation much shortened].

Among parents who do have disagreements over the child's upbringing, three-quarters of their children know they disagree, but more working-class than middle-class children know (***). This class difference is confirmed by parents' answers to the following question: 'Some people say that parents should always back each other up, even when they really disagree; and some think that a child should be able to appeal to one parent if it thinks the other one is being unfair. What do *you* feel about that?' 65% of mothers overall think that parents should maintain a united front, but this rises to 75% in Class I and II and falls to 60% in Class V. In some ways this is a little surprising, in that one might expect the 'united front' attitude to be backed up by authoritarian beliefs, while the child's right to appeal might seem a democratic value.

Part-time check-out operator, husband a draughtsman:
Well sometimes I don't agree with what my husband thinks as regards things concerning Anita. Naturally I don't say so in front of the child. At the time, what my husband says goes, but after, I can talk to my husband about it and see if we can come to a different agreement.

Part-time market research interviewer, husband a police inspector:
Well, I would always back my husband up in front of him, I think, or not say anything; but if I felt he was unfair, I'd tell him afterwards about it, but I think it would undermine his authority if I did it in front of Dick. We've often had an argument afterwards, 'Why the heck did you ever do that?' – then it starts! I've given up trying to be the perfect parent years ago!

Part-time assembler, husband a packer:
Well, I don't think, any child would like to think both parents are of the same frame of mind and he can't go to one or the other.

Part-time cleaner, husband a labourer:
I think a child should know if parents disagree. Life isn't a bed of roses. If you always agree in front of the children and disagree behind the scenes, they'll never know what life really is.

The emphasis in the first two quotations – that the child's point of view would be represented privately anyway – is very typical of the majority view, and perhaps mothers feel that this justifies what they might otherwise see as disloyalty to the child. A strong source of resentment for many mothers is their husbands' occasional or repeated failure to back them up, so their wish to be backed up themselves may lie behind their willingness to support their husbands.

Throughout parents' discussion of socialisation runs the strong thread of an awareness of the need to look ahead. We have already pointed out that parents have in common this sense of their own responsibility for final outcomes, which in the end defines their need to treat individual events in ways that they believe will serve the desired result. The dilemma of parenthood is that parents (perhaps mothers in particular) have expectations and hopes of remaining friends for life with the child whom they are curbing and frustrating: it takes a great deal of confidence in one's ability to outweigh the negative by the positive *in the child's eyes*, in order to be unreservedly happy with one's role as keeper of the child's conscience and monitor of his behaviour. This is especially a dilemma to mothers who are committed to the idea that smacking is necessary: 'I think to myself sometimes, is she going to look back when she's sixteen or seventeen and think "Well, that was my childhood, and it was all smacking" – you know?'

In a long-term survey we have the advantage of being able to collapse time and consider some of the outcomes in these same children even as we describe the parental attitudes and behaviour that attempted to influence what was to happen in the future. In Chapter 8, we shall make use of this time perspective.

References

Newson, E. (1978) 'Unreasonable care: the establishment of selfhood', in G. Vesey (ed.) *Human Values* (Lectures for the Royal Institute of Philosophy), Hemel Hempstead: Harvester Press.

Newson, J. and Newson, E. (1968) *Four Years Old in an Urban Community*, London: George Allen & Unwin Ltd.

Newson, J. and Newson, E. (1976) *Seven Years Old in the Home Environment*, London: George Allen & Unwin Ltd.

8
STYLES AND OUTCOMES

It would be difficult to agree upon a defined point in a person's life when child-rearing (in terms of socialisation by parents) comes to an end and the outcomes can be identified. Growing up in Western society is marked more by a series of shifts into adulthood than by a grand initiation in which childish things are formally left behind. Moreover, once we take into account the contextual web of family, class and culture – and especially when we also remember the extended time-perspective which informs the parent–child relationship – the search for discrete causes of discrete effects seems more like a nostalgia for psychology's own adolescent excesses in the happy hunting-grounds of weaning and toilet training.

Further, the notion of the child as a passive *tabula rasa* waiting to receive the parental imprint has become less and less convincing when socialisation is increasingly seen as a process of negotiation that has its roots in the intersubjective communications of lap and cradle (Newson, J. 1979, 1982). The child's status as contributor to his own socialisation brings a factor of idiosyncrasy into the equation from first to last (whenever that may be). As George Kelly (1955) points out, every individual 'contemplates in his own personal way the stream of events upon which he finds himself so swiftly borne': indeed, it is Kelly's invocation of a time-perspective which is both global and idiosyncratic that makes his model so relevant to the parental predicaments of child-rearing. Within these considerations simple causal predictive laws must be suspect.

Nevertheless, there is an expectation which parents and psychologists share: that parents' actions have an effect upon what the child becomes. The issues of whether their children will grow up to be satisfactory adults – whatever their criterion of satisfactoriness may be – is one which exercises all parents, and partly for the very reason that they do feel some degree of responsibility for outcomes. Similarly, it is because psychologists have some notion of causality that they – we – have been prepared to cope with all the inconveniences of longitudinal studies in order to follow the same children and parents through progressive stages of childhood, rather than being content with snapshot views of separate samples.

What do parents (and their professional advisers) expect to achieve in their children through their style of child-rearing? Where do they expect their influence to be seen? In one sense, they do expect to have an effect upon individual 'snippets' of behaviour: that is to say, on the whole they believe they can predict whether the child would, for instance, laugh at himself when a joke is played upon him, or avoid paying his bus fare if he gets the chance. However, their child-rearing efforts are not so much directed towards a series of responses in individual situations as to producing the *kind of person* who would acquit himself appropriately in whatever situation arose. Thus, if parents were to read here the (true) statement that 'there is a significant association (★★★★) between parents' high frequency of smacking and the child finding it difficult to apologise when in the wrong', they would undoubtedly find that an interesting connection; but few would say that they were deliberately trying to inculcate ready apologies through their chosen frequency of smacking, even though apology is highly valued by the whole parental spectrum. On the other hand, they do deliberately aim for children who in general terms 'know the difference between right and wrong', are kindly and thoughtfully disposed towards others and so on, and these qualities are clearly expected to show themselves in individual actions – in fact it is their children's actions in response to individual events which enable parents to monitor whether their own efforts are being successful, and which they cite to an interviewer as evidence of their more general statements about the child's personality, as we have seen throughout this book.

The *general* areas in which parents seem particularly concerned to have an effect on outcome are in moral development, personal adjustment, and academic competence or the realisation of intellectual potential. These three areas are also widely assumed (by psychologists, educationalists, politicians and the public at large) to be influenced by parental practices. In this chapter we shall therefore address ourselves to tracing connections between child-rearing styles and their outcomes in these terms. Because of the caveats we have already mentioned concerning the danger of over-simplifying the causal argument, it is necessary to re-analyse some of these data in rather different ways in order to make it as secure as it can be; the reader is still advised, in so complex an area as child-rearing, to interpret associations with caution.

Obviously there is an important difference between associations occurring together at one point in a child's life (such as the smacking frequency and apology data already quoted, both of which are drawn from the situation at 11 years), and associations of earlier practices with *later* outcomes; and this will be particularly powerful if earlier practices can be shown to be associated with related outcomes at *two different* later stages, which gives us some measure of the durability of the effect. This chapter will therefore to some extent de-focus from 11 years, and will both look back at child-rearing styles as early as 7 years, in order to relate them to 11-year-old outcomes, and look forward to later outcomes at 16 years, with an additional glance at further data going up to 20 years.

'Me husband's always said, if he ever brings the police or any trouble to this door, I'll swing for him ...'

Parents generally are perhaps less confident than they once were that their children will never bring trouble to their door. Awareness of the drug culture in particular, and what it can do to apparently well-brought-up adolescents, has undermined middle-class security considerably: 'you hear so many things, don't you?' is an expression of parental anxiety which is founded on newspaper items about the misdoings of the children of well-known establishment figures, reports that a highly respected local school has discovered drug-trafficking in its sixth form, and, still more worrying, the early warnings of problems being encountered by family friends – 'people like us' – whose children are only a little older than one's own.

The longitudinal data we shall now examine obviously have to be based on children who were not lost from the sample over time. Biggest losses were sustained between 7 and 11 years, but fewer at 11 and 16. 524 children can be followed from 7 right through to 16 years (and the further data do not depend on durability of the sample thereafter); 686 of those who were the subject of interview at 11 were still present at 16.

We have three means of measuring 'trouble' at the stages of 11, 16 and later adolescence. At 11 we devised an index of potential delinquency, hereafter referred to as 'Delindex', based on the child's reported behaviour; the questions and answers from which this index is derived are given in Table 8.1 and a social class analysis of the 22% higher scorers is shown in Table 8.2.[1] At 16, we constructed a 12-point scale to measure how 'troublesome' the child was in his parents' eyes, and on this basis were able to designate just over 25% of the sample as 'troublesome': the derivation of this index is given in Table 8.3 and the 'troublesome' group analysed by sex and social class in Table 8.4. Over the following few years, we were able to call on Home Office records to identify members of the sample who were indicted for criminal offences during their late adolescence; this information was obtained by 'sweep' methods at particular dates, and therefore unfortunately cannot be given in the form of 'by age 18' or 'by 20', since our sample has birthdates spanning more than three years. This merely makes our outcome data more conservative, however, in that our 'criminal record' group are those we know to have acquired this distinction by at-earliest 17 and at latest 20; there are undoubtedly others who would appear in later sweeps.

In defining both these indices of potential delinquency or troublesomeness at 11 and at 16 in the way we have, there are certain advantages and disadvantages. An apparent disadvantage might be that both are based on parental report, and that parents might not be very willing to present their children in a bad light. This might mean that we have missed some children who might have scored if their parents had been more frank. This very problem can also be seen as an advantage, however: if unfavourable evaluations are given by parents about their own children, presumably these evaluations are not lightly made, so that we can assume that both 'Delindex' and the index of 'troublesomeness' represent a fair degree of parental concern about the child's behaviour. The answers are given additional credibility, of course, by the fact that the interview was not seen by parents as being mainly directed to the child's trouble-making or delinquency, and was as much concerned to discover his good points as his bad; indeed, one mother who had been at first unwilling to be interviewed at 16, because there was a court case pending and she felt there was 'nothing but trouble to talk about', was persuaded by the interviewer's memory of Eddy's kindness to animals at 11, and after four hours talking about him was grateful that she had 'had to think about all the nice things again, because there are a good few, and I think I'd forgotten them, and you could have gone away thinking he was all bad'. We have made the point before that parents are much less likely to soft-pedal about problems if the eventual index data are not allowed to accumulate visibly before their very eyes. Further, longitudinal data have the advantage of referring to the child in the light of parents' attitudes and values *at the time of the interview*, and are thus not contaminated by hindsight based on knowing how things actually developed.

It is clear from the tables that children who, in their parents' eyes, get into the kind of trouble which will eventually attract formal intervention by external

TABLE 8.1 Derivation of 'Delindex' at 11 years

Based on question:		Coding	Score
10.	Is he one of those children who are always in hot water, or does he manage to keep out of mischief mostly?	Hot water	2
		Varies	1
		Keeps out	0
186.	Sometimes children of this age go through a phase of taking things that don't belong to them; have you had this at all?	Yes	1
		No	0
187.	Has he ever been in real trouble with school, so that you really had to speak to him seriously?	Yes	1
		No	0
188.	Has he ever played truant from school, so far as you know?	Yes	1
		No	0
190.	Has he ever got himself into trouble with neighbours?	Yes	1
		No	0
191.	... or the police?	Yes	1
		No	0

Note: Possible score range 0–7. 22% overall score 2+.

TABLE 8.2 Children who score 2+ on the Delindex measure at 11

	Social class					Summary		
	I&II	IIIWC	IIIMan	IV	V	M.class	W.class	Overall popn
	%	%	%	%	%	%	%	%
Boys	18	16	34	31	41	17	35	30
Girls	11	7	16	16	15	9	16	14
Both	15	11	25	24	28	13	25	22

Significance: class trend ↗ ★★★★   m.class/w.class ★★★★
boys vs girls ★★★★

TABLE 8.3 Derivation of index of 'troublesomeness' at 16 years

Based on questions:		Coding	Score
57.	Does he ever get involved in any fights?	Often	2
		Occasional or peripheral	1
		No/Don't know	0
58.	Risk of police involvement in fights?	Police or risk of	1
		No	0
65.	Any of his friends a bad influence on him? (re friends who: swear; fight; truant; are anti-parent; are anti-school; visit pubs; visit clubs; are delinquent)	2+ such problems	2
		1 such problem	1
		Not these problems	0
70.	Do you think he has a strong sense of right and wrong?	Definitely no	2
		Uncertain	1
		Yes	0
111.	Does he ever cut school?	Yes, often	2
		Occasionally	1
		No/Don't know	0
111.	Have there been any problems over that?	Formal trouble	1
		Not formally	0
138.	Can you mostly trust him to tell you the truth … sometimes tries to pull the wool over your eyes?	Frequent lies	2
		Occasional lies or might conceal truth	1
		Entirely truthful	0
			12

Note: Possible score range 0–12. 26% overall score 3+.

TABLE 8.4 Adolescents who score 3+ on the 'troublesomeness' measure at 16

	Social class					Summary		
	I&II	IIIWC	IIIMan	IV	V	M.class	W.class	Overall popn
	%	%	%	%	%	%	%	%
Boys	18	23	29	35	55	20	33	30
Girls	9	5	29	19	31	7	27	22
Both	14	14	29	27	43	14	30	26

Significance: class trend ↗ ★★★★   m.class/w.class ★★★★
boys vs girls★★

authorities are more likely to come from the lower end of the social scale. They are also twice as likely to be boys as girls at 11, although the girls are beginning to catch up by 16. At 11, the major difference is between middle-class and working-class children; by 16, the class trend is particularly marked, with middle-class children forming one comparatively homogeneous group, skilled and semi-skilled another, and the unskilled group outstanding as troublesome, with more than half their boys scoring in this way. This is in fact foreshadowed at 11 if we look at children who have already been in trouble with the police at that age: 5% of children overall, only 1% of girls, but 16% of Class V boys.

> He's *very* often in trouble. [What for?] Oh – breaking windows – arguing with neighbours – making noises. [Any trouble with the police?] Oh yes, he went with a gang of boys and broke into a caravan and took some sweets and things. [What happened?] Nothing, they just came and warned him. And he got in trouble for climbing on a factory roof. He got cautioned again, and a good long telling-off … [On probation in early teens.]

When the policeman dropped him here on the door, he ran that way so the policeman had to get back in the car and run round and get him again. We've had no end of trouble with him … [Is he worried about the trouble with the police?] No, that hasn't bothered him at all. He just says 'Oh, *I'm* not bothered. It was nice riding round in the police car.' [At 11 he had been in trouble a number of times but was said to have 'calmed down a bit except for his temper' at 16.]

It is worth noting in passing that, in contrast to the popular stereotype, mothers who work either full-time or part-time when the child is 11 are, if anything, *less* likely than non-working mothers to have children who score 2+ on Delindex; the differences are not significant, but their direction is of interest in view of the myths that circulate in, for instance, schools, which are often accusatory of working mothers.

The third measure of 'trouble', the criminal record acquired by 17–20 years according to the age of the individual when the last 'sweep' was undertaken, is shown in Table 8.5 in terms of social class, sex and family size.

TABLE 8.5 Children known to have acquired a criminal record during adolescence

	Social class					Summary		
	I&II	IIIWC	IIIMan	IV	V	M.class	W.class	Overall popn
	%	%	%	%	%	%	%	%
Boys	6	5	17	21	25	6	19	15
Girls	0	2	4	1	3	1	3	3
Both	3	4	11	12	16	4	11	9
Small families (1–3 chn)	4	4	7	6	12	4	8	7
Large families (4+ chn)	0	4	16	18	17	2	17	14

Significance: class trend ↗ ★★★★   m.class vs w.class ★★
boys vs girls ★★★★   large vs small families ★★★★

Note: The family size comparison is based upon subsamples of large and small families having an identical social class composition; the 'real' difference would be larger because more large families occur in social class V.

Clearly we immediately wish to know how durable these measures are in terms of predicting from one age-stage to the next: in other words, how far can we expect children who were among the 22% scorers on Delindex 2+ at 11 to be found among the 26% designated as 'troublesome' at 16, and how far does troublesomeness at 16 predict a criminal record by the end of the teens?

Of 11-year-olds scoring on Delindex 2+ 46% were 'troublesome' in terms of our index at 16, while only 19% of non-scorers on Delindex 2+ had become troublesome by that age. To put this the other way round: of those who were troublesome at 16, 40% had scored on Delindex 2+ whereas only 14% of non-troublesome 16-year-olds had scored in this way at 11. This is obviously a highly significant association (★★★★).

Among the 16-year-olds scoring as 'troublesome', 17% went on to acquire a criminal record within four years or less (remembering that this is a conservative estimate); while among non-troublesome 16-year-olds, only 5% acquired such a record. Again this association is well beyond chance (significance ★★★★), but of course we cannot conclude that 'formal' delinquency can be predicted with a high degree of precision simply on the basis of scores on the 'troublesome at 16' index. One obvious reason is that more children are rated as troublesome generally (26%) than actually achieve a criminal record (9%); but there is certainly considerable overlap between the minority group classified as troublesome at 16 and the even smaller group who earn a criminal record. Again to turn these figures round, of the criminal record group, 56% had been 'troublesome', while of the rest only 23% had been so rated at 16. There is considerable difference between boys and girls; of troublesome 16-year-old boys, 26% acquire a criminal record, whereas of trouble-some 16-year-old girls, only 2% do so.

'It's difficult to know what to do for the best, but I'm thinking of the future, you know ...'

We are now in a position to look at associations between child-rearing styles and measures of 'trouble', both within one age-stage, and from one age to another.

'Delindex at 11'

Taking first the age with which we have mainly been concerned in this book, it is worth looking briefly at associations between 'Delindex 2+' and the use of physical punishment which we discussed in the last chapter. Table 8.6 uses the overall (randomised) population to show how different features of physical punishment are or are not associated with the child's score on Delindex.

It can be seen in relation to the first three variables that mothers who punish more often or potentially more heavily are more likely to have children in the higher-scoring category of Delindex. At this stage the causality of such a finding is ambiguous: it could be that punishing parents produce naughty children or, equally, that naughty children drive their parents to adopt punitive means of control. The only secure conclusion to be drawn is the rather negative, yet still important, one that the traditional simplistic adage 'spare the rod and spoil the child' is clearly not supported by this kind of statistical evidence: we are *not* justified in advising parents that if they punish their children more severely, in the physical sense, this will prevent them from getting into trouble.

Of equal interest is the implication of the findings in relation to the last two variables. Parents who 'feel driven' to smack are no more likely to have naughty children than those who use smacking as a deliberate disciplinary strategy – which does slightly suggest that the second causal proposition above has low credibility.

TABLE 8.6 Physical punishment and Delindex 2+, both at 11

Punishment variable	Delindex 2+ children	Other children	Significance of difference
Child smacked 1+ per week	34%	11%	★★★★
Implement actually used	25%	9%	★★★★
Implement used or threatened	60%	33%	★★★★
Mother smacks only in anger, when 'driven'	70%	68%	n.s.
Mother used smacking as deliberate corrective (excludes 'none' and 'anger only')	25%	22%	n.s.

It also appears that the 'deliberately corrective' parents are not actually any more successful in producing 'good' children than those parents who have no reasoned intention of resorting to physical punishment.

Looking at the longitudinal data, there is still less support for the popular assertion that children these days get into trouble mainly because their parents have been too 'soft' with them. When these children were 7, we asked, as at 11, about frequency of smacking and use of implement. In addition we devised two indices: *mother's reliance on corporal punishment* (based on frequency, use of smacking in a variety of proposed situations, use or threat of implement, and baring the child's bottom for a smack); and *mother's acceptance of the punishment principle* (based on the mother's feelings and attitudes about smacking, her use of other punishments and her forcing of apologies from the child) (Newson and Newson, 1976). A further indication of maternal style at 7 was the 'index of bamboozlement'.[2]

'Trouble – 16'

It is interesting to link these measures with the child's behaviour nine years later, at 16, by looking at associations with the index of troublesomeness at that age, and this has been done in Table 8.7.

However, as we have seen in Tables 8.4 and 8.5, both troublesomeness and criminal record are strongly influenced by class affiliation as well as by sex and family size; it therefore seemed necessary to re-work the data in order to estimate which upbringing factors were related to these outcomes *after sex, class and family size had been allowed for.*[3] Styles of child-rearing are themselves, as we have seen, inextricably

TABLE 8.7 Child-rearing strategies at 7 years and 'troublesomeness' at 16

Strategy at 7 years	Children exposed to this strategy, later rated 'troublesome' (n = 134)	All children exposed but non-troublesome (n = 390)	Non-troublesome allowing for sex, class and family size (n = 134)
Child smacked or beaten 1+ per week	65%	43% (★★★★)	46% (★★★★)
Implement used by at least 1 parent	27%	20% (n.s.)	18% (n.s.)
Mean scores on index of mother's reliance on corporal punishment	4.01	3.09 (★★★★)	3.23 (★★★)
Mean scores on index of mother's acceptance of punishment principle	5.78	4.91 (★★★★)	5.09 (★★)
Scores 2+ on bamboozlement index (see p. 152)	46%	21% (★★★★)	26% (★★★)

bound up with these circumstantial factors. The crucial question is *what is it about social class* which determines that children become troublesome on a class-linked basis?

We can address this question by using two 'allowance' methods which form a check on each other: (1) by comparing all the criminal record children with a *weighted* sample, based on all the remaining children but weighted appropriately for class, sex and family size; or (2) by comparing all the criminal record children with a *matched* sample selected from the remaining children by matching, case for case, for class, sex and family size. (In theory the latter, using a matched *t* test, should be a more sensitive method, but of course the number of cases is also smaller.) However, if we are comparing troublesome children with non-troublesome children, it is neither necessary nor possible to use the matching method. Having used the matching method as a check where appropriate, we shall therefore only present here the results of the weighting method in both cases, for simplicity.

By analysing the data in this particular manner we are enabled to go beyond the well-established fact that there are very clear differences both in the prevalence of troublesomeness and delinquency, and in parents' choice of child-rearing strategies, when these are analysed in terms of social class. We would argue that *the differences between troublesome and non-troublesome children reflect differences in disciplinary philosophy and style* between individual families even *within* each social class group. In other words, we have analysed the data in this way so as to be able to identify any consistent pattern of relationship between how parents deal with children at 7 through 11, and how the children turn out at school-leaving age and later, independent of social class.

It will be seen in the remainder of the tables that allowing for these variables causes some apparently predictive factors to 'melt away', whereas others 'shine through' as *remaining predictive even when class, sex and family size are taken into account.* It is these child-rearing factors that must be taken seriously as having at least some causal significance in determining outcomes.

Table 8.7 illustrates child-rearing factors which do 'shine through' persistent when allowance is made for class, sex and family size ('CSFS'), together with one which showed no significant association in the first place. Although troublesome 16-year-olds are slightly more likely to have been hit with an implement at 7, this does not reach significance level. However, both mothers' reliance on smacking and their acceptance of the punishment principle at 7 are associated with troublesome 16-year-olds, and when CSFS is allowed for the association remains significant, though slightly weakened. The same is true of mothers' willingness to bamboozle their 7-year-olds (mean scores are not used here because of a skewed distribution, but show a higher and more durable significance value).

This last association is of particular interest because of speculations which we made as early as 4 years about the outcome of what then we called 'evasion or distortion of truth', which was the forerunner of the 'bamboozlement' index at 7. We suggested then that 'the mother is, in normal circumstances, the child's first experience not only of a loving protector but of someone in authority over him; and it is she who must *set the pattern* for his feelings towards others in such a position. The mother who upholds her authority by resorting to deceit cannot hope to succeed in this for longer than the limited period of the child's gullibility. […] He therefore learns at an early age that authority in the person of his mother, *despite her pretensions to having his own welfare at heart*, is yet not averse to using trickery whenever this suits her purpose of controlling him […] [this may] be generalised to colour his feelings and attitudes towards [later] manifestations of authority: school, police, social agencies, employers and so on' (Newson and Newson, 1968: 474–5). In these speculations, both at 4 and at 7, we explicitly linked these attitudes with eventual 'trouble'; and it is gratifying to find here at least one piece of positive evidence to confirm that hunch. We shall return to this at the end of the chapter.

Patterns of discipline are based in a wider context of a certain style of family life; for this reason, we undertook a similar analysis to relate more general lifestyle indicators at 7 to troublesomeness at 16. This analysis was not very productive in finding child-rearing factors which are predictive in their own right: child centredness, father participation and chaperonage of the child, all of which are strongly class-linked, lost their predictive power in relation to 'trouble at 16' once CSFS was allowed for; perhaps surprisingly, low level of general cultural interests as mediated by parents, the child's lack of competence in reading and writing and his dislike of school at 7 were more firmly predictive of trouble at 16 (straightforward differences ★★★★, ★★★★ and ★★★ respectively, all ★ for weighted sample).

More predictive still was one of our temperament/personality indicators at 7: the index of temperamental aggression. This defines children in terms of being outdoor rather than indoor types, very or rather destructive with toys, having quarrels that come to blows, rough-and-tumble games at first or second choice out of three categories of games, don't-care attitude to being smacked and frequency of getting into a rage; and scores above the mean on this index at 7 were found to be positively related to trouble-16 (★★★★, CSFS allowed for).

These findings are simply a collection of bits of statistical evidence, and perhaps it is best to regard them as building bricks from which a theoretical edifice may eventually be constructed. The associations from 7 to 16 are of course particularly interesting for showing factors already visible nine years before the outcome (although we have to remember that what was going on at 7 in child-rearing terms is likely to be consistent with the mother's style through the following years). The five-year gap between 11 and 16 gives us a further opportunity to confirm predictive factors, and these are shown in Table 8.8, which gives the 11-year-old data corresponding to the 7-year-old data in Table 8.7. It will be seen that the 'bamboozlement' index is replaced by that of 'idle threats', and it might be argued that the child is more likely to realise at 11 that these are indeed idle. Additionally we have an item recording whether the father is the main (corporal) punisher of this child as opposed to the mother.

The results relating child-rearing at 11 to outcomes at 16 serve to confirm and extend the general pattern relating child-rearing at 7 to these outcomes (Table 8.7). In particular, frequency of corporal punishment continues to be associated with later troublesomeness, and use of an implement begins to show its own effect at this age. Fathers who hit more than mothers are very much in a minority at this as at every age (7% in a random sample), but they all but treble in percentage so far as children who become troublesome are concerned.

TABLE 8.8 Child-rearing strategies at 11 years and 'troublesomeness' at 16

Strategy at 11 years	Children exposed to this strategy, later rated 'troublesome' (n = 168)	All children exposed but non-troublesome (n = 518)	Non-troublesome allowing for sex, class and family size (n = 168)
Child smacked or beaten 1+ per week	26%	14% (★★★★)	16% (★)
Implement used by at least 1 parent	22%	9% (★★★★)	12% (★)
Index of mother's commitment to formal corporal punishment, high scorers	23%	21% (n.s.)	23% (n.s.)
Mean scores on composite index of corporal punishment based on above three measures	3.97	2.69 (★★★★)	2.90 (★★★★)
Scores 1 or more on index of idle threats	55%	33% (★★★★)	36% (★★★★)
Father hits N more than mother does	13.2%	4.6% (★★★★)	4.7% (★★)

Family lifestyle indicators at 11 were similarly tested for association with troublesomeness; low scores on the indices of communication between mother and child and family cohesion were both associated with 'trouble-16' (★★★★) but neither association persisted when CSFS was allowed for. Associations between 'trouble-16' and low scores on father's participation and chaperonage did not reach significance. Once again, outside the area of disciplinary strategies the most significant association that persisted when CSFS was allowed for was with a temperament/personality index: this was the index of 'amenability' at 11, based on whether the child tended to agree or not with his mother's demands, whether he was easy or touchy, moody or not, took out his upset feelings on himself or others, reacted aggressively or not when feeling foolish, blamed others or not for his own faults, and whether he had shouting rages. This index shows no significant class differences; and scores in the lower third of the population predict troublesomeness at 16.

Again, an interesting association was found between 'trouble-16' and poor adjustment to school at 11, as measured (a) by whether the child in his mother's opinion had, on balance, disliked primary schooling and (b) by whether he had had difficulty with one or more of his teachers at primary school. Both these remained significant (★★★) when CSFS was allowed for. Equally interesting is that the mean verbal reasoning quotient (VQR) at 11 had been 92.4 for the 'trouble-16', but 96.9 for the CSFS weighted sample of non-troublesome children.

'Basically I believe in honesty, and yet … um … on the other hand …'

Before looking at associations with the eventual acquisition of a criminal record, and because this chapter is perhaps indigestibly statistical, it is worth reminding ourselves of the people behind the tables of categories. At 11, trouble with the police rarely consisted of much more than 'a good talking-to'; but we thought it useful to impel mothers to think about their own role in such a situation. Having asked about actual 'trouble', we continued: 'This one might be a bit difficult – do you think you'd tell a lie in order to save him from that sort of trouble?'

This was one of those questions for which we had not the least idea either how individuals might answer or how the answers would break down. In the event, 76% overall thought they would not tell a lie, 17% thought they might well (including a policeman's wife), and 7% (including a JP) qualified their answers to such an extent that it was impossible to determine the category. Looking at the social class breakdown, at first sight there appear to be no class differences at all; but in fact this only applies to the definite answers of 'Yes' or 'No', and there is a clear class trend for mothers further up the social scale to be uncertain whether or not they would lie (12% in Class I & II, 2% in Class V, ★★★★).

On the whole mothers did find the question difficult, even though most of them came to a conclusion on it; they were widely agreed that they would not shield the child if drugs were involved, but usually had to think hard about their attitudes in other situations. Few were as immediately definite as the Class III white-collar mother who said 'That's not difficult at all. I know most certainly that I wouldn't lie.' Among the majority group who were against lying, a major reason was that the child would find out, hence (a) contradicting the mother's teaching about telling lies, and (b) making him believe he was invulnerable.

> Gosh! You see, how could I, when I've told him you must tell the truth? You did say it was difficult! I don't *think* I would tell a lie. I think I would want him to accept whatever he'd done but I would always love him, and I think that would be it. I'd say 'Well, you've been very wrong and we'll have to face it, but we'll face it together.'

> No, quite honestly, I don't think I *would* tell a lie, not if I knew that she'd done something. If I knew she'd done it, I couldn't tell a lie and say she hadn't. But if I didn't know, I'd rather believe her than the police, you know but I don't think I could say 'she wouldn't do a thing like that' or anything, if I knew she had. No, because I think that would start her off on the wrong track altogether.

> No, no – Anthony'll tell you that [older brother] – he came home one night, didn't you, and he'd got some drink from somewhere, and he was only 14; so I *fetched* the police. I did. [What did they do?] Laughed at me! He said 'Put him to bed, and make sure he lays on his side so if he vomits he don't choke'

– and he says, 'I'll come back and talk to him in the morning.' And he came back the next morning and took him in the front room and gave him a good talking-to – said they'd take him to court the next time. I wouldn't shield them, not if I know they're in the wrong, because I think it saves them later on. If you let them get away with it, they'll do it all the more, won't they?

Mothers who reckoned they would tell a lie mostly thought they would do so out of maternal instinct, but one or two felt it would be a matter of needing not to shield the child, but to remain in control of how the matter was dealt with.

Well, what parent wouldn't? I think you'd sit there and lie till you were blue in the face for your children. I think you would. Because I think that's what loving children really means. You would do anything for them, and you would lay down your life for them if necessary. Yes, I think you *would* lie for them.

I would with the police – I mean you've got to side up with your own children, haven't you? Say he was with a group of boys and they double-dared him or something like that, and he'd done something wrong, I'd shelter him then.

I would, I would – I would certainly do that, because I would feel that most probably I could deal with it better than they could, or I would try myself out first. Knowing the child, I think I should know how to cope.

Some mothers distinguished between serious and trivial offences – in both directions, the serious offences (other than drugs) rather more often being lied about.

It all depends what she'd really done. Often I think the police – if they have done something really naughty, the police *should* know … so they won't do it again. [In what situation might you cover up for her, then?] If it was something really trivial.

I don't know – if he was going to come out best in the end, I don't think I'd tell a lie. If he was a real devil and always in trouble, then I'd feel I had to help him any way I could.

It depends – I mean, if the police came and caught him scrumping, no, I wouldn't tell a lie then because it's not a serious crisis, it's a thing that most children do. Well, I think every parent'd cover up if it was serious.

This was very much a question which proposed situations that needed considerable thought, yet might not, if they actually happened, allow time for thought. It was notable how many mothers used this as an opportunity for turning the matter over carefully in their minds. We will finally quote three who did not manage to come to a clear conclusion; in the first quotation, the daughter happened to arrive just before this question was put. The second and third mothers are both active members of non-Anglican religious communions.

[Lorraine:] I don't think Mummy would. You know, she'd sooner me learn. [Mother:] I don't know – it's a thing you see. [Lorraine:] You never know until it happens. [Mother:] A mother's instinct is to protect a child and I think it is ... you know ... sort of ... I'd maybe tend to. I couldn't tell you. That's a question I wouldn't like to say. [Lorraine:] No comment!

No. *Probably* not. Well, it would depend. I don't know, it's so difficult to know exactly what the situation was. I'm in favour of law and order *up to a point*. On the other hand, I think you can make too much of bringing people to justice, it can often make it worse than if you turn a blind eye I think the community ought to be able to take a fair amount of ... what would you call it? Experimentation, if you like. I think you could *make* a child criminal by bringing him face to face with authority in some situations. If she got herself into a position where the police were involved, I don't *think* I would tell a lie – I don't know. I would be on her side, obviously, in that she would need recourse if she were in trouble. She might be as perplexed as I was. It's often a question of getting to the facts, I think. And I think the most help a parent can be in a situation like that is to see that there isn't any misunderstanding, and that what is *thought* to be true *is* true. So you would want your child to be truthful in those circumstances, cause I think the police are fairly ready these days to pick up people, and I should want to know what they thought she thought. I would *hope* that I could talk about it calmly and try to get to the bottom of it, instead of rushing in ...

Oh dear. Now you *are* asking. Well, I think I should have to bring it out into the open, don't you? – I mean, for his good. I would have to make him see he'd done wrong, wouldn't I? I'm sure I should tell them a few *white* lies, though – to put him in a good light, you know. I mean, if it was really serious it would have to be brought out, but at the same time I would want to ... well, butter them up, shall we say! It's a *very* difficult question – I don't know – let's hope and pray it doesn't come to the police.

The question was still theoretical for most of the mothers, although, as we have seen, some children had already tangled with the police and Paddy's mother was prepared to admit that she had 'screened him once or twice'. We have no way of knowing what mothers did when their adolescents eventually came up against real trouble in the form of criminal charges; but it is to those whose charges were upheld that we now turn.

Criminal record

Since only 9% of our sample had acquired a criminal record during the limited period that we are so far able to cover here, we would not expect to produce a great deal of predictive data at this stage. Although one might suppose that acquiring a criminal record at an early age was a significant achievement, we do not yet know what it signifies: we have not had time to discover whether early attention from the

TABLE 8.9 Child-rearing variables at 7 and 11 years and eventual criminal record

Variable	Children who attained a criminal record before 20 (n = 67)	All remaining children (n = 697 at 7, 713 at 11)	Sample of 'no-record' children allowing for class, sex, family size (n = 67)
Child smacked or beaten 1+ per week at 7	73%	47% (★★★★)	56% (★)
Mean scores on father participation at 7	4.93	5.73 (★★★)	5.69 (★★)
Child smacked or beaten 1+ per week at 11	40%	14% (★★★★)	17% (★★★★)
Score 4+ on overall index of commitment to formal corporal punishment at 11	51%	26% (★★★★)	24% (★★★★)
Score 1+ on index of idle threats at 11	56%	38% (★★★)	41% (p = 0.06) (★ on matched sample)
Mean scores on index of mother/child communication at 11	4.30	5.53 (★★★★)	4.82 (n.s.) (5.07 ★★ on matched sample)
Mean scores on father participation at 11	1.21	2.13 (★★★★)	2.07 (★★★★)
Mean scores on index of family cohesion at 11	4.59	6.59 (★★★★)	5.84 (★★) (★★★ on matched sample)
Mean VQRs (children) at 11	86.3	98.2 (★★★★)	91.2 (p = 0.06)

courts prevented or was predictive of our sample becoming established in a criminal pattern. Certainly we are beginning to meet a few whose tear-away days seem to be over, while one or two have been unavailable to us against their will.

The 'criminal record' children are strongly associated with CSFS as we saw in Table 8.5, but a few factors in their earlier life still 'shine through' when CSFS is allowed for. These significant factors are collected together in Table 8.9.

In terms of disciplinary strategies, the frequency and degree of severity of corporal punishment show the most outstanding association with later criminal record. Both at 7 and at 11, these retain significance even when social class, sex and family size are allowed for – at 11, to a very high level. The use of idle threats, taken with earlier results on this, must at least remain of interest although the findings are clearly not at all conclusive at this stage.

In terms of disciplinary child-rearing variables, it is notable that indices measuring intra-familial involvement with each other stand out as being negatively correlated with the acquisition of a criminal record. Mother–child communication at 11 shows this with a rather low significance level (on the more sensitive matched-pairs test); family cohesion is more marked as a contra-indicator; and father participation, with a moderate significance at 7, shows a high significance level at 11. It does seem incontrovertible, then, that children who acquire a criminal record before 20 have fathers who, from the age of 7 through 11, were less involved with them in non-disciplinary ways than were the fathers of 'non-record' children, *even when class, sex and family size are held constant.*

As a check on the validity of this last result, we also repeated the comparison tests at 11 after excluding all those children whose fathers were divorced, separated or dead by the time the children reached 16 years. With these cases excluded, the significant difference was still maintained (★★★); and it therefore appears that it is the *poor quality of the father's involvement in intact families* which is important in shaping up to a criminal record, rather than his absence or loss.

It is intriguing that, although the father's involvement with the child seems to be consistently related (from 7 years) to whether or not the child becomes delinquent, this only shows up clearly with those who acquire a criminal record, and not with those designated 'troublesome' at 16. This can probably be accounted for by the fact that children with a criminal record are mostly male, which is much less true of the group regarded as 'troublesome'. In other words, high father-participation seems to be a factor in keeping *boys* out of serious trouble.

On the whole, then, there is evidence that a well-integrated family background, in which both mothers and fathers are close to their children and do things together as a family, tends to act as a relative safeguard against children going off the rails later on, whatever the social class or family size. Of course there will be many exceptions to such a broad statistical generalisation. Predictions of this kind may also fail to stand up in times of rapid social change or in widely different cultural contexts; but those who believe that it is important for children to have a stable and secure family life may take heart from the fact that their intuitive predictions do bear some relationship to social reality. Contrariwise, the belief that more punitive parents would ensure less adolescent crime is clearly not supported by the data we have presented.

Looking at what parents say about problems at various stages of childhood, one at first tends to be overwhelmed by the diversity of individual conflicts between them and their children, and how these were eventually resolved. The conflicts we have seen at 11 are augmented at 16 by arguments over staying out late, homework and rival attractions, suitability of boy and girl friends and whether one should sleep/take holidays/stay at home alone with them, tastes in music and other things, importing the language of the peer group into the home, and so on. However, what ultimately seems to be important is the preservation of a degree of mutual respect as parents eventually concede to their children the right to follow their own interests and values, even when there is a risk that these will differ from the ones they themselves subscribe to and hoped their children would share. What seems to count is the ability of parents to dismantle the structure of their earlier disciplinary restraints more or less gracefully, so that these can in time give place to the kind of egalitarian and reciprocal relationships that are needed between adults co-existing within the same household. At 16 years, our protocols are full of crises and showdowns, brinkmanship and battles of wills which could at worst result in the child leaving home or the parents bringing in outside authority, or in permanent estrangement between parent and child.

Sooner or later physical punishment has to be abandoned as inappropriate; but sometimes parents only finally relinquish it at the point where it literally hurts them more than it hurts the child, where the child is manifestly bigger and stronger and seriously threatens to hit them back; or where parents are overwhelmed by the indignity of becoming involved in a stand-up tussle which they realise they cannot win except as an act of self-control on the 'child's' part.

Discipline can continue by the use of other sanctions, but these can only be effective if the young person recognises the fairness of the case being made against him, and therefore concedes the right of the parents to impose their views in the name of justice. If parents and children are to continue to live together for a while as adults, hard-line positions must be modified and compromises reached: the account of rights and duties, benefits and obligations must somehow be brought into a mutually agreed balance. The evidence suggests that parents who stress obedience to adult authority as an absolute value supported by physical punishment have children who, they admit, are more difficult to manage than those whose parents come to evolve a more democratic style of cooperation based upon mutual respect.

'If she wants to be on the floor and scream, who am I to deny the child the pleasure? She's got the choice, she can come and join the rest of us, nothing's stopping her.' (Isla's mother at 11)

Another way to approach the question of outcomes is to look at the whole spectrum of the child's characteristic ways of meeting and coping with the world and its demands, rather than just the items which denote real troublesomeness. Using data obtained when our children reached 16, we can look for associations between their attitudes and behaviour in this area at that age, and their mothers' child-rearing strategies at 7. The rather wide-ranging index we constructed for this purpose at 16 was originally intended to identify a dimension of adjustment–maladjustment; but we became unwilling to call it by this term, since it is difficult to judge how far a child's abrasive or conciliatory reaction to situations or demands is in fact well or ill adjusted to them. Nonetheless, there did seem to be a dimension which, in semi-operational terms, could be defined by the way the child seemed to swim with or against the current of life. To change the metaphor, some children seem to meet the world claws out, others purr their way through – yet who is to say whether the alley cat or the tame pussy is best adjusted? It seems more honest, therefore, to refer simply to an 'easy to difficult' continuum at 16.

Because we also wanted to be able to draw out two samples of our 'hundred most difficult' and 'hundred easiest' 16-year-olds (for follow-up purposes later), the index has emphasised definite scores on items indicating 'easy' at one end and 'difficult' at the other, and this gives a bipolarity to the measure which is rather different from the smoother continuity of other indices. The composite measure has an actual range of 0–28 points; it has a unimodal distribution which is positively skewed so that the modal score of 21 points is towards the 'easy' end of the scale. The mean score is 18 points (S.D. 5.3): high scores denote 'easy', low scores 'difficult'. The way the index is derived from the answers to questions at 16 is given in Table 8.10; for lack of space, the whole list of questions cannot be given here, but can be obtained on application. It will be seen that four of the items in the 'troublesome' index contribute to this more global one; but of course here their individual weight is very small indeed.

If high and low scorers on this index are defined as the 36% most 'difficult' and 37% most 'easy' 16-year-olds, an analysis by sex and social class shows no significant differences except a slight increase in difficult children in Class V (*). There is therefore no real need to make allowance for these in our comparison table, although we have done so as an additional check.

Table 8.11 shows those variables at 7 years which are associated with low and high scores on 'easy/difficult at 16'. Variables tested include measures of the child's temperament, family lifestyle, disciplinary styles and strategies, and items relating to school. Indices which have been tested for association but not found significant between 7 and 16 in relation to the easy/difficult index are *general cultural interests, child centredness, father participation, acceptance of the punishment principle* and *chaperonage*. The index 'easy/difficult at 16' is a finely-graded measure (since so many questions enter into it), and should therefore distinguish rather accurately between 16-year-olds; it is a substantial finding then, that no less than eight of our indices at 7 show predictive associations to a good degree of statistical significance.

The first three variables showing significant associations from 7 to 16 give evidence of the durability of temperamental features: amenable children and those who seem emotionally stable at 7 are also among the 'easier' adolescents, whereas temperamentally aggressive children at 7 are 'more difficult' adolescents. Still more interesting are the findings that show the disciplinary strategies of frequent smacking and 'bamboozlenent' (the latter not exclusively disciplinary) to be predictive of more difficult adolescents: it is notable how these two features in particular have more lasting power than parents really expect, and of a rather different kind.

The last two, concerned with school, confirm parents' own priorities. At 7, we suggested that in the first two years of primary school parents were mainly concerned that the child should be happy at school, whereas by 7 their anxieties became more closely focused upon whether reading and writing skills were becoming firmly established; these results seem to show that it is indeed of long-term importance that the child should be happily settled at school by 7, and also that he should be fairly competent in reading and writing by that age.

'We just want him to make something of himself if he can ...'

I think my husband would've liked them to be a bit more brainy, but I accept th't – what they are – if it isn't there, it isn't there, and I don't believe in trying

TABLE 8.10 An index of easy or difficult behaviour and attitudes at 16 years ('easy' scores marked E; 'difficult' scores marked D)

Abbreviated question (numbered as in interview schedule)	Answer to score
3. Calm and placid, or highly strung?	Highly strung, D
4. Usually falls in with demands, or tends to object?	Objects, D
5. Easy to get on with or a bit touchy?	Easy, E; touchy, D
6. Self-confident, or a bit timid?	Self-confident, E
7. Takes things as they come, or a worrier?	Worrier, D
8. Gets anxious with adults?	Anxious, D
13. Busy person or easily bored?	Busy, E
20. Day occupying self the way he likes best; putting a lot of effort into something.	*Same* activity cited for both, E
21. Putting lot of effort into something	Never does, D
30. Seems to enjoy taking responsibility?	Yes, enjoys, E
48. Quarrels with siblings?	Many, D
50. Might he lose touch in adulthood with sibling he now quarrels with?	Mother thinks yes, D
51. Finds it easy to make friends?	Yes, easy, E
54. Prefers special friend or big group or …?	Isolate, D
57. Gets involved in fights?	Often, D
58. Risks police because of fights?	Police now or risk, D
66. Is he moody?	No, E; very moody, D
74. Wants to tell about things/reserved?	Open, E; secretive, D
84. Gets depressed or anxious re own appearance?	Often, D
86. Easily gets depressed generally, or mostly cheerful?	Mostly cheerful, E; easily depressed, D
89. Prescribed tranquillisers in past year?	Yes, regular dosage, D
90. Nervous habits?	Two or more, D
93. Gets worried by his own illnesses?	Yes, D
94. Sick, dizzy, headaches (no obvious cause)?	One of these, *and* N worried, D
101. Last 2 years at school been happy ones?	Very happy, E; definitely unhappy, D
111. Does he ever cut school?	Often, D
112. Found school work boring/interesting?	Mainly interesting, E
132. Does he mind admitting he's in the wrong?	Doesn't mind
133. – find easy to apologise if at fault?	Yes, easy } two or three of
134. Can he laugh at joke against himself?	Yes, easily } these: scores E
132. Does he mind admitting he's in the wrong?	Does mind
133. – find easy to apologise if at fault?	Difficult } two or three of
134. Can he laugh at a joke against himself?	Can't laugh } these: scores D
138. Can you trust him to tell you the truth?	Frequent lies, D
143. Ever stayed out all night without warning?	Yes, D
145. Which family activities does N willingly join? (outdoor outings, indoor outings, anniversary gatherings, holidays away)	Three or more types, E

(continued)

TABLE 8.10 (Cont.)

Abbreviated question (numbered as in interview schedule)	Answer to score
150. Angry moods: how often? how long-lasting?	Never/rarely angry, for less than ½ hour, E; 1+ per week, for more than ½ hour, D
151. Ever really rude or abusive to Mother?	Never, E; often, D
162. What happens on a 'bad day' with N?	No bad days, E
163. If behaving badly/wrongly, anything M can do or say to make behave better?	Nothing effective, D
178. Anything about N that M wishes bit different?	⎫
179. Anything about M/N relationship M would change?	⎬ No to both, E ⎭
183. Which stage of childhood has M enjoyed most (baby years, 4–7, junior school years, senior)?	Senior or all equally, E

Note: Possible range 47 points; actual range 29 points. Most questions have more than two levels of coding.

TABLE 8.11 Variables at 7 years associated with 'easy/difficult' index at 16 years

Variable at 7	Mean scores on the 'easy/difficult' index at 16 (higher scores = easier)		Difference and significance	
	(Low scorers at 7)	(High scorers at 7)		
Amenability	15.93 (n = 203)	19.89 (n = 194)	+ 3.96	(★★★★)
Temperamental aggression	19.65 (n = 169)	16.27 (n = 159)	− 3.38	(★★★★)
Emotional stability	16.50 (n = 162)	19.39 (n = 154)	+ 2.89	(★★★★)
Frequency of smacking	18.66 (n = 258)	17.10 (n = 238)	− 1.56	(★★★)
Bamboozlement	18.50 (n = 381)	16.53 (n = 143)	− 1.97	(★★★★)
Home–school concordance	16.99 (n = 119)	18.91 (n = 183)	+ 1.92	(★★★)
Child's liking for school	16.75 (n = 148)	18.79 (n = 167)	+ 2.04	(★★★)
Reading and writing competence	16.74 (n = 142)	18.71 (n = 241)	+ 1.97	(★★★)

to push something into a child if they haven't got it. I mean, I don't believe in snobbishness with kiddies, 'I want my child to go to a certain school' – I don't believe in things like that. If they haven't got it, they haven't got it.

You see Lee was allowed to play, instead of being sat down and learnt. Well, the idea is that they learn through play; but to a child like Lee play is play, and he never learned through play. I think myself that they concentrate more on a boy that they think's going to be above average, and they push and push and push that child till they get it to where they want it. Now a child like Lee, that don't want to learn – that shows no *interest* in learning – they just leave him, and that's where I think the mistake were made in the first place.

We come finally to the question which might be thought more crucially important than any other: do child-rearing styles have an effect upon the child's competence in intellectual terms, and, in particular, can this effect be seen independent of social class, which we already know to show massive correlations with measure of intellectual competence? If so, what are the implications for the child's future?

We first addressed this question at the end of *Perspectives on School at Seven Years Old*, when we briefly presented data linking child-rearing styles and other variables at 7 with verbal reasoning scores at 11 years. In order to complete this discussion of longitudinal findings, we will return to that data, both to present them in more detail and to show how they mesh with other long-term associations.

When these children were 11, the '11+' school selection system was still in operation in Nottingham, whereby children in their last year at primary school were given verbal reasoning tests on two separate days in order to determine which of them should proceed to grammar schools, and which to the 'bilateral' schools which replaced (at least in name) the earlier 'secondary modern' schools. In Nottingham there was one (boys') comprehensive school only, serving an almost entirely working-class housing estate:[4] the 11+ tests in this catchment area served to stream these boys, a system nominally disguised by code letters but transparent to both parents and children. The verbal quotients for our sample were made available to us for research purposes, and have enabled this analysis to be made; the data used in this section thus have the advantage of being independently obtained and also independent of parental judgement.

The VRQs obtained on the two different test days correlate very highly, at 0.95, and we have therefore been able to average the two scores for each child in order to simplify the analysis given in Table 8.12.

To quote our comment on this table at 7: 'The differences in terms of social class are extraordinarily dramatic, particularly as between middle class and working class: how many educationalists would have predicted such a difference between manual and non-manual within Class III, for instance? Once again, the blunt instrument that we originally assumed the Registrar General's classification must be has turned out surprisingly well honed' (Newson and Newson, 1977: 187). The sex differences do not quite reach significance in this analysis, mainly because there are so few high

TABLE 8.12 Children who score 'high' and 'low' on verbal reasoning at 11 years

	Social class					Summary		
	I&II %	IIIWC %	IIIMan %	IV %	V %	M.class %	W.class %	Overall popn %
High scores (110 +)								
Boys	48	29	9	7	0	39	8	16
Girls	67	39	10	6	3	54	8	21
Both	58	34	10	6	2	46	8	18
	Significance: trend ↘ ****					m.class/w.class ****		
		between sexes n.s.						
Low scores (under 85)								
Boys	2	8	32	36	56	5	34	26
Girls	2	16	17	22	55	9	22	19
Both	2	12	24	29	56	7	28	23
	Significance: trend ↗ ****					m.class/w.class ****		
		between sexes n.s. (see text)						

scorers at all in the working class and so few low scorers in the middle class; if we look at mean quotients for boys and for girls overall, however, we find a mean VRQ of 93.6 for boys and 98.7 for girls, a highly significant difference (****). Family size is also correlated with VRQ, children from families of four or more children tending towards lower VRQs (boys ****, girls ***). These findings are given and discussed in more detail in the earlier book.

At the time we first presented the results in Table 8.12, we already were sure that 'to say that "verbal reasoning scores are associated with social class" and leave it at that will hardly do; [because] although we may have started out by defining social class, for simplicity and ease of replication, in terms of the Registrar-General's classification, we have seen that the life-styles which characterise different social classes, of which father's occupation is only one part, are far more complex, even when we only look at them from the vantage-point of child-rearing. In the end, the life-style defines the social class: father's occupation is merely a shorthand index to it which happens to be more reliable than most other indices that one might choose' (Newson and Newson, 1977: 187). Few of us nowadays can really believe in some dominating gene or pattern of genes which unerringly distinguishes the working class from the middle class in terms of intelligence or criminality; and standards of hygiene and nourishment do not now show such marked disparities, except for the poverty-trapped minority, as to account for findings like these. Given that such differences exist, and given that there are also considerable differences in

TABLE 8.13 Significant associations between high and low scores on index measures at 7 years and VQRs at 11 years

Index measure at 7	Mean VRQ at 11 for low scorers on index at 7	Mean VRQ at 11 for high scorers on index at 7	Mean VRQ for high scorers weighted for CSFS
Reading and writing competence	90.0 (n = 152)	109.2 (n = 238) d = + 19.2 ★★★★	101.9 (n = 152) d = + 11.9 ★★★★
General cultural interests	90.2 (n = 121)	109.0 (n = 179) d = +10.2 ★★★★	98.9 (n = 121) d = +8.7 ★★★★
Child's liking for school	96.8 (n = 142)	103.4 (n = 179) d = +6.6 ★★★★	103.0 (n = 142) d = +6.2 ★★★★
Home literacy	93.5 (n = 169)	107.4 (n=194) d = + 13.9 ★★★★	98.7 (n = 169) d = + 5.2 ★★★★
Bamboozlement (M uses this)	102.9 (n = 380)	92.6 (n = 149) d = − 10.3 ★★★★	97.7 (n = 380) d = − 5.2 ★★★★
Home–school concordance	94.0 (n = 123)	104.7 (n = 182) d = + 10.7 ★★★★	98.4 (n = 123) d = + 4.4 ★★★
Chaperonage	94.8 (n = 191)	100.9 (n = 144) d = + 6.1 ★★★★	98.3 (n = 191) d = + 3.5 ★★★
Child-centredness	93.5 (n = 173)	105.1 (n = 179) d = + 11.6 ★★★★	96.8 (n = 173) d = + 3.3 ★★★
Father participation	98.2 (n = 131)	100.9 (n = 236) d = + 2.7 n.s.	100.0 (n = 131) d = + 1.8 n.s.

Note: In general it requires a difference of 3 or more points of mean VRQ to prove significance.

lifestyle and life-philosophy which are reflected in what the child experiences, the crucial question must, once again, be asked: what are the 'special ingredients' in social class which determine a lower or higher competence-rating such as VQR, or a proneness to be troublesome or difficult, or to be labelled by society as, at least potentially, criminal? Unless we know the answers to such questions, our attempts to break down the barriers that the class system erects against thousands of children are at best bumbling and simplistic, and at worst cynically inept.

Table 8.13 is an attempt to draw, more precisely than in our earlier book, the lines of association between certain variables in the life experiences of our 7-year-olds and their VQRs as measured at 11 years. In the first column, mean VRQ scores are given for low scorers on the index at 7 years shown on the left; in the second, mean VRQ scores are given for high scorers on the same index, together with the difference and significance level. It will be seen that these are all at the 0.001 level with the exception of the last measure, which is included here for its own negative interest. In the third column, the figures for the high scorers have been weighted to allow for sex, social class and family size, so that the differences shown here hold *within class* and are therefore predictive without reference to class. These indicate which index measures might be regarded as 'special ingredients'.

This is a more rigorous statistical treatment than was used in our earlier account, which allowed for social class but not for sex and family size. This accounts for the slight reduction in significance level shown in this column for home–school concordance, chaperonage and child-centredness, which does not occur when class only is allowed for.

The findings are arranged in the table in order of magnitude of effect; it will be seen that this table is in fact a list of statistically significant predictors at 7 of VRQ measures at 11.

It is perhaps not surprising that the first four index measures in Table 8.13 are associated with higher VRQ, since these are all to do with variables more or less directly connected with how far school 'makes sense' to the 7-year-old in terms of home values and home activities. Reading competence for instance was, we found, of interest to almost all mothers, who, if they did nothing else 'educational' with their child, at least tried to monitor how well his reading was 'coming on' by 'hearing him read' occasionally. The child's liking for school was equally under scrutiny by mothers since they had to bear responsibility for getting him there; and our discussion of school reluctance, as opposed to real refusal, was mainly of interest in delineating mothers' normal strategies, not only in coping with unenthusiastic or actually malingering children, but also in negotiating tiffs and misunderstandings with the teacher which often she was probably not even aware of. 'General cultural interests' measured how far *parents* took children on outings of the kind which might equally be organised by school, and therefore paralleled and affirmed the school's extramural activities: cinema, concerts, theatre, museum or gallery, zoo or circus, shows, sporting events, and religious services, plus extra lessons such as dancing, music, sports etc.; while 'home literacy' was based on the child's ownership of books, membership of a library, and having a regular comic or magazine, plus the mother's habits of reading to the child, the type of material she read, and whether she ever consulted printed material in order to answer the child's questions. In short, whether the child feels at home in school is likely to have a good deal to do with such measures, and we can see how his verbal reasoning might be enhanced or depressed by what is going on in these areas. It is, however, of interest that home–school concordance, which measured home back-up of school of a perhaps slightly more direct kind than 'general cultural interests', is marginally less significant in association with VRQ.

Chaperonage, which measures the degree to which the child spends time under adult supervision rather than being 'off out' at 7, is an association which may well contribute a good deal to the superiority of girls over boys in verbal reasoning at 11 (which in the '11+' selection necessitated positive discrimination in favour of boys). In the final column, where sex as well as class is accounted for, the significance is reduced but still at an acceptable level. It is an intriguing thought that girls' verbal reasoning ability, like their accident rate, approaches parity with boys' only after chaperonage perforce decreases as a result of the logistics of secondary education.

Child-centredness, intended to measure treatment which would offer the child a sense of his own worth and 'considerability', was identified by us at 7 as 'a major social class differentiation in child-rearing practice'. The attitudes thus tapped both permeated the whole range of parental behaviour towards the child and showed a steep class trend varying from 60% highly child-centred at the top of the class scale to 16% at the bottom; 15% of middle-class mothers were rated low on child-centredness, compared with 40% working class and 57% in Class V. The fact that this measure holds good in association with higher VRQ scores when these massive class differences are allowed for gives great credibility to the idea that children with a poor sense of worth are defeated children who are, in Jerome Bruner's words (Bruner, 1971: 152), 'caught by a sense of powerlessness' and therefore, in his speculation, discouraged from problem-solving.

Yet it is to the index of bamboozlement that we must return with special interest. As we reminded the reader earlier in this chapter (p. 175), we have always seen 'evasion or distortion of truth' at 4, as well as 'bamboozlement' at 7 and idle threats at 11, as one element in the mother's disciplinary armoury which carried a long-term fuse that could cause a dangerous back-firing at a later stage: the inescapable fact that at some point the child would be too sophisticated to be bamboozled any longer, and would come to understand his mother's attempts for what they were. Moreover, because we have been concerned not with discipline alone, *but with the total pattern of understanding between mother and child* which we take to inform and underpin the whole socialisation structure, we have sought in these three indices to include not just the strategies which the mother would recognise as having disciplinary intentions, but other indicators of her willingness to put expedience and her own convenience or comfort before truth and honesty. Thus 'evasion or distortion of truth' at 4 included telling the child definite lies about where babies come from (to escape embarrassment) and slipping away without telling him when leaving him with a minder (to escape protest); while 'bamboozlement' at 7 included concealing her ignorance if she didn't know the answer to his questions (to escape losing face). It is an indication of the gradual falling of the scales from the child's eyes that the scope of these indices has become reduced at 11 to 'idle threats' alone, which the child still cannot be sure will not be carried out. The notion that attitudes permitting bamboozlement exert a destructive power against the child, as we have long suspected, is strongly confirmed by its appearance both as a predictor of lower VRQ *within class* and as a precursor of 'troublesomeness' at 16, also within class; and the latter is further confirmed by 'idle threats' at 11 as a precursor of troublesomeness.

It may be suggested that a difference of five points of VRQ (the figure for 'bamboozled' children when class is allowed for) is not something to get too perturbed about. At the time these measures were taken, when the child's academic future could directly depend on a few points on these same scores, the 11+ was indisputably a tool for class divisiveness and for the labelling of very large numbers of children as 'not good enough'. What that did to countless children's morale and feelings of self-worth has never been adequately documented. Because the 11+ as a generally used selection method is now past history (although certain local education authorities have been reported as seriously considering its reintroduction), we have not quoted in this book the extensive transcripts in which mothers described the anxiety and misery laid upon their children by this so-called educational process;'overnight she became a child we didn't know' was how one mother described the damage done by this explicit rejection, and adults who remember suffering it will testify with what bitterness the memory still returns. We cannot really be confident that all this is behind us now: as recently as 1983, an attempt was made to re-introduce the 11+ selection procedure in Solihull (and was finally abandoned after sustained parental protest) (Walford and Jones, 1986). The political climate of the eighties is such as to foster further similar moves. Without the 11+, selection is less blatant and more covert, as it becomes more a matter of knowing how to find one's way around an educational system; but children's permission to progress still hangs upon a series of cumulative decisions taken early in their academic lives and is grossly dependent in real terms on their place in the social class system.

Putting those five points of VRQ difference into perspective, this is a greater discrepancy than that for IQ of children exposed to lead pollution *even before class was taken into account* in the 1983 study which caused considerable national concern. If we are really interested in allowing children to 'make something of themselves', we cannot help but concern ourselves with the forces that work against that end.

Clearly, there must invariably be the problem in work of this kind that descriptive labels may be giving a spurious cohesion to psychological and sociological concepts which we are only able to measure in rather crude and indirect ways. As soon as we try to separate sociological and psychological explanations for outcomes, for instance, we find ourselves wading into a conceptual quicksand. Nonetheless, the risk is worth taking: at the very least because reliable long-term data of such depth and detail are, for good enough reasons, hard to come by. Yet repeatedly one has to remind oneself that the attempts made by psychologists to delineate and analyse patterns of child-rearing can never be either as subtle or as complex as child-rearing itself. This may, indeed, be the thought that helps longitudinal research workers to survive – and which, if we survive, will, we hope, carry us through to the next generation of 'our' children.

Notes

1 Some of these data have been published in Newson and Newson (1984: 99–116).
2 The 'bamboozlement' index at 7 is made up of six self-reported maternal behaviours: conceals her ignorance if she cannot answer child's questions; usually 'lets go' a threat once made; threatens with external authority (other than father); threatens to leave child; threatens to send child away from home; tells child she'll stop loving him if naughty. Two or more of these are scored by 29% of mothers overall (class trend ★★★★, range from 1% in Class I and II to 34% in Class V).

3 Strictly speaking, it is of course wrong to discuss such allowances as if we were able to 'control' for these factors (i.e. in terms of a formal experimental design in which child-rearing practices might theoretically be systematically varied to see what the outcome would be).
4 The Clifton estate.

References

Bruner, J. (1971) *The Relevance of Education*, London: George Allen & Unwin.

Kelly, G.A. (1955) *The Psychology of Personal Constructs*, New York: Norton.

Newson, J. (1979) 'The growth of shared understandings between infant and caregiver', in M. Bullowa (ed.) *Before Speech*, Cambridge: Cambridge University Press.

Newson, J. (1982) 'Dialogue and development', in M. Braham (ed.) *Aspects of Education*, Chichester: Wiley.

Newson, J. and Newson, E. (1968) *Four Years Old in an Urban Community*, London: George Allen & Unwin Ltd.

Newson, J. and Newson, E. (1976) *Seven Years Old in the Home Environment*, London: George Allen & Unwin Ltd.

Newson, J. and Newson, E. (1984) 'Parents' perspectives on children's behaviour at school', in N. Frude and H. Gault (eds) *Disruptive Behaviour in Schools*, Chichester: John Wiley & Sons.

Newson, J. and Newson, E., with Barnes, P. (1977) *Perspectives on School at Seven Years Old*, London: George Allen & Unwin.

Walford, G. and Jones, S. (1986) 'The Solihull Adventure: an attempt to reintroduce selective schooling', *Journal of Educational Policy*, 1 (3): 239–53.

9

'CHILDHOOD INTO ADOLESCENCE'

The importance of the parent's perspective

Charlie Lewis

Can a book written about 35 years ago be relevant to contemporary parents, psychologists and educators? Before I address this question, I must declare an interest and a position. I worked under John and Elizabeth Newson from 1977 to 1983, first as a Master's student training in Clinical Child Psychology, next as a PhD supervisee with John and then on an independent postdoctoral fellowship but still a member of their Child Development Research Unit. The CDRU was a lively place, with a constant throughput of families, journalists, visiting academics and clinical/educational psychology trainees. It might be assumed that such a busy and public centre of excellence would reflect the accepted canons of research and theory. However, the Newsons' approach to psychology was considered by many even in the same department to be at odds with that of the cutting edge of the discipline, with its emphasis on journal publications in which every point closely cites references to the continuing and new debates in the literature. In this chapter I will argue that their longitudinal study has had a lasting influence on policymakers and practitioners, despite the fact that it had limited implications for research and theory in developmental psychology.

The Newsons were more keen to present parents' perspectives on issues that emerged largely as a result of having their own three children. In methodological terms their longitudinal study drew from the tradition of ethnographic research conducted by sociologists such as Michael Young and Peter Willmott (1957) and the anthropologist and follower of Melanie Klein, Elizabeth Bott (1957). This was a time when 'child psychology' was dominated by psychiatrists, psychoanalysts, educationalists and other professionals (specialist social workers called 'child care officers', health visitors etc.). It was largely separate even from developmental psychology, which was conducted within experimental laboratories, notably by Peter Bryant and Jerome Bruner at Oxford. However, a few emerging psychologists with links to more clinical services were more like the Newsons – particularly Jack and Barbara Tizard in London, Ann and Alan Clarke in Hull and Rudolph Schaffer in Strathclyde, but each of these published mainly in academic journals and so worked more within the emerging experimental tradition. Even in the 1960s and 1970s the Newsons' work was hard to place in terms of how it contributed to the discipline of psychology; as the small number of footnotes in this book shows, their references to the psychological literature were few and they focused on issues, even if there was little or no 'academic' research on the topic. Those of us with one foot in the Newson camp but hoping to place another firmly on the academic ladder were always aware that their approach and their longitudinal study, in particular, were hard to place in terms of research examining the nature of parenting and its influence on children's development. The differences between the Newsons and the emerging generation of psychologists in the Nottingham department did not deter collaborations with its members, who were also mindful of the fact that it was John and Elizabeth (much more than their collective colleagues) who were focus of articles in *New Society*, the *Guardian* and the *Observer*, and that the CDRU was filmed by CBS, America's leading television news channel.

With these introductory comments in mind we can begin to interpret the contribution of this book. First, it is a statement of parenting through parents' eyes two generations ago. The children described here will be in their late fifties now and several will be grandparents themselves. Reading what the Newsons say and the extracts from parents are both fixed in a period of history that is obviously different from now, particularly in terms of the role of technology in homes and in individuals' daily lives. Second, *Childhood into Adolescence* is a reflection of the Newsons' approach to psychology. To develop a point made by Peter Barnes and Susan Gregory in Chapter 1, their earlier books, particularly *Infant Care in an Urban Community* (1963), reached a very wide readership of parents and professionals involved in early care. Not only was this 'a notable addition to the scanty information of the natural history and habitat of the human infant' (Kahn, 1964: 106), but also it highlighted the very interests that parents develop, often quite unexpectedly and with no preparation: their preoccupations with the infant's sleep, feeding and social development. At the age of 4, they were preparing the child for school and expressed their preoccupation with both releasing the reins and protecting the child against the world outside the home. The first three books were so successful and so 'free of jargon', as one reviewer put it, that they were republished in paperback by Pelican and reached a much wider readership.

Seeing 11-year-olds through the eyes of their parents

Childhood into Adolescence homes in on the difficult time for parents as the 11-year-old moves from primary to 'big' school, and from childhood into adolescence. The start of Chapter 8 states explicitly that childhood is marked by a series of gradual shifts into adulthood and not by a single 'crisis'. This comes across in several other chapters. The focus is very similar to that of more recent studies and resulting theoretical analyses that suggest adolescence is marked by a series of small changes rather than one single identity crisis (as suggested by the psychoanalysts Peter Blos, 1966 and Erik Erikson, 1968). In keeping with the research evidence, Coleman and

Hendry's (1999) much discussed focal model proposes successive negotiations with parents and peers and concerns with their sexual identity. The Newsons' natural history of the start of this stage of development presented in this book focuses on the same issues but the account is very different in tone, with a central focus on parents' observations of the challenges facing the 11-year-old and the changes in their own experiences. Given the pivotal age of 11, it is perhaps not surprising that the main preoccupation of the book is on transitions. There is a flavour of such change in each of the volumes of this longitudinal study as the Newsons reflect back to the preceding episode and project forward to the next.

The topics in the book can be divided into three types, concerning the timelessness of some parental concerns, the historical context of the study, and the relationship between the topics analysed here and longstanding issues in the research on preadolescents.

First, there are perspectives which remain the same despite social change. For example, 47 years ago these parents were preoccupied with the same problems – is their 11-year-old getting on with their friends? Do they fit into the peer group? Are they mixing with a child who might get them into trouble? Such issues preoccupy parents at any time but the Newsons explore the nature and extent of parental concern and this part of Chapter 3 is very revealing. There are two other themes that echo this continuity. First, the discussion on housework (Chapter 4) by children and teenagers continues to interest family researchers (e.g. Langford et al., 2001; Warin et al., 1999), who note the issues of children's compliance with, often gendered, domestic chores (Noller and Callan, 1991). Second, these parents report several timeless issues concerning controlling and disciplining their children. That one-third of parents, particularly those in the low socio-economic groups, make idle threats to their children and 18% use physical punishment seems consistent with the evidence today (Chapter 7). The mothers' descriptions of these threats and punishments, however, are intense and might raise some eyebrows. The very frequency of use of services such as Childline indicates that parents continue to threaten or use severe sanctions with their children. The longitudinal analyses of the effects of parental punishment (Chapter 8) fit squarely within a tradition that shows consistently that parental smacking (or 'spanking' in the US) is a predictor of negative outcomes in children. These are found even in a recent meta-analysis with 160,000 children (Gershoff and Grogan-Kaylor, 2016). What the Newsons add is not just another study showing the long-term correlates of parental smacking but that such physical punishment is one of a means by which parents' use of smacking is set within a context of threats and 'bamboozlement'.

Second there are topics in this book where there has been clear social change over the intervening time but which have distinct parallels with contemporary child-rearing. Every generation faces the problem of the balance between allowing children freedom to explore the world while needing both to protect and inform them. In the late 1960s and early 1970s these 11-year-olds were allowed free rein to visit friends and play in quiet streets, with little or often no chaperoneing (Chapter 3). Indeed, this was also reported at the age of 7. These friendships were often developed on the walk to school, or a local street during free time, and the geographical divisions of peer groups were bounded by 'big roads', which were thought too dangerous to cross. This seems to be different from the highly monitored and protected lifestyle of contemporary children, who are at home much more and are likely to be driven to school – not always the local one if parents think that a more distant choice is preferable (and they are successful in the lottery to secure a place). There is the same parental screening of friendship networks. However, young people live in a very different world and much of the parental screening and monitoring is increasingly done through electronic means (Luckerson, 2012).

Parental concerns also remain similar while the nature of the issues has shifted. Take, for example, the responsibility of informing the child about human reproduction and relationships. In the early 1970s, the liberalisation of sexual relationships was a hot topic in the press and cultural analysis but the parents expressed to the Newsons' interviewers deep concerns about how and whether their children should be informed and protected. Since that time the HIV/AIDS epidemic forced most Western democracies to emphasise safe sex and to provide parents and educators with information that could be life-saving. Yet the same tensions continue. In the UK, despite 25 years of discussion of these issues and an amendment to the statutory framework for sex education in the Learning and Skills Act 2000, this took until 2010 to implement and until 2017 for the Act to be extended to all schools (see e.g., Blair and Monk, 2012). In keeping with the accounts in this book, parents often leave it to the school to provide information to their children and the issue of the role of educators continues to be a heated tug-of-war between conservative and liberal forces. As a result, even today's emerging adolescents often reveal that they are largely ignorant of sexual relationships especially in social groups where the balance is tilted towards conservatism (Hurwitz et al., 2017).

The third theme in the book concerns perspectives the Newsons seem to bring to parenting that have only indirect relation to the existing popular debates and academic literature. Their approach to the child's entry into 'early adolescence' (the *Journal of Early Adolescence* has published papers on nothing but 10–14 year olds for over 30 years and other journals were reporting studies over a century ago) contains a number of differences from that literature. For example, much of the attention on temperament has been on how we measure it in this relatively mature group (e.g. Capaldi and Rothbart, 1992) or on continuing stability in the construct (e.g. Sylvester et al., 2018). Yet, the focus in Chapter 2 concerns *changes* in 'temperament' (taken by others to represent stable personality characteristics) between childhood (age 7) and preadolescence (11). The interviews suggest that while some children remain bloody-minded or shy at both periods, others are reported to show change – for example from placidity to extraversion or, more typically, to retreat a little into their shell with the emergence or expectation of puberty and/or the entry into secondary school. Such individual differences in changes that parents report add a dimension to the literature, or at least warn researchers and commentators that our focus on stability of psychological constructs often prevents us from seeing other perspectives.

Likewise, Chapter 4 on children's collecting activities is a short period piece, but one which may be of great interest to contemporary social scientists. That 58% of 11-year-olds collect something and their mothers' descriptions of their close attention to detail makes fascinating reading. The Newsons homed in on collecting items as a sign of a normative childhood activity and typical pattern of development. Chapter 4 dwells on the finding that several of these 11-year-olds have deep interests, including attachments to teddies or dolls that they would save in a fire above all other material goods. In addition, several have dedicated hobbies. Some 31% of 11-year-olds are described as being 'remarkably good with their hands' and '58% of all children do at least one of the activities involving carpentry, sewing, knitting and crochet, "tinkering with mechanical things" and writing stories'. While not central to mainstream theories of adolescence, these discussions have resonance with the writings of Mihaly Csikszentmihalyi, which suggest that in early adolescence the skills developed in a concentrated focus on such activities enable the child to develop the concentration and 'flow' that are critical to later adult skills (e.g., Kleiber, Larson and Csikszentmihalyi, 2014).

There is a side to these pre-teenage preoccupations with objects and activities that Elizabeth Newson, in particular, could have picked up on. As her career developed she became increasingly focused on work on the nature of autism, setting up a clinic in north Nottinghamshire for the National Autistic Society to continue her diagnostic work and to carry this on in her retirement. In this period three definitional criteria (communication problems, language delay/deviance, and restrictive and repetitive behaviours) were deemed to be central to the diagnosis. This has been narrowed down to two – the first two combined and the latter (American Psychiatric Association, 2013). Restrictive and repetitive behaviours have become more central in the diagnosis but paradoxically receive much less attention than research on communication. Chapters 3 and 4 of this book provide normative data that are very informative about the role of highly practised and repetitive behaviour in typical development. To my knowledge, none of the material presented in these chapters on children's deep interests and collections has fed into recent debates about diagnosis. Indeed, Elizabeth's attempt to describe a syndrome related to autism, Pathological Demand Avoidance (see e.g. Newson, Le Marechal and David, 2003) was only briefly mentioned (and wrongly) in this debate (Wing, Gould and Gillberg, 2011).

Theoretical and methodological contribution

In this final section I reflect upon why the Newsons' longitudinal study continues to have a lasting influence on discussions on parenting despite there being more extensive datasets (such as the 1958 National Child Development Study, the 1970 British Cohort Study, the Millennium Cohort Study (2000–1) and Next Steps (previously known as the Longitudinal Study of Young People in England (LSYPE) – 2004 on): www.cls.ioe.ac.uk) and a large number of reflections on childhood – we are now bombarded with advice and information about parenting and children's development.

This would seem unlikely given the structure of their approach. In this section I will outline four issues that prevent the study from being cited in the mainstream literature on families and child development before re-considering the impact of this book.

The first issue concerns the fact that the Newsons' books report the details of parents' reflections without much critical self-analysis. In this and all their books, they start a section with a summary of the sample's responses to a single general question or an amalgamation of questions. Having identified in Chapter 3, for example, that 80% make friends easily, 16% do not and 4% have 'real difficulty' orients us to the problem or concern faced by one-fifth of parents and very clearly in a few. Such data are very general and rely on the assumption that this distribution of answers is not simply a reflection of how the question can be interpreted differently.

Second, the statistical analysis relies on very simple tests that are usually not reported and so are hard to interpret. The simplicity is compliant with most author-ities on statistical analysis, such as the task force of the American Psychological Society, that the simplest analysis to test the hypotheses should be applied (Wilkinson et al., 1999). Nevertheless, an analysis conducted today would, most likely, take on a different form. One big difference is the complete absence of effect-size measures in their analyses. Contemporary statistical approaches would require the researcher to find the model that best fits the data (particularly in Chapter 8). Although John was a competent statistician, he used statistical analysis more as a guide to our understanding than an exercise in applying the hypothetico–deductive model. The notes at the foot of tables serve the same function as the quotations, largely to illustrate the *patterns* of data reported within them. The scales that John developed (e.g. 'Chaperonage', Chapter 5) are reported in terms of high and low scorers. While the class and sex of child differences are interesting, there is little access to the distributions of scores and no mention of statistical interactions that sometimes seem to be apparent in a table. Thus the statistical analyses are not amenable to further scrutiny.

Third, the emphasis was on communicating the main points to a general read-ership. This may not square with what the contemporary reader needs to know. We are not used to dividing scales into high vs low scorers, so this might not be the optimal way of showing, for example, class or sex differences. We are not given detail about the means and distributions of the scales, so the researcher in me is left wondering what else could have been extracted from the data. The longitudinal patterns on smacking, for example, could not, as reported, contribute to the already massive meta-analyses, and this has the effect of making the Newsons' findings stand apart from that literature.

Fourth, and perhaps most importantly, there is a consequence of their unwilling-ness to engage in academic debates and simply tell the story of parenting as it is. There is little reference to continuing reflection on the nature and validity of the evidence from particular methods. For example, in the 1990s Anthony Giddens (e.g. Giddens, 1998), then a close advisor to the Blair administration, prompted a keen debate about the democratisation of the family, reflecting upon the emergence of democratic roles and the exchange of information and therefore trust between family members. Giddens' theoretical reflections reopened debates about whether we should take family members' statements at face value. By implication this literature criticised the type of stance taken by the Newsons (although they did not feature in what was largely a sociological debate). In one of our studies, we examined parental accounts of openness and trust within families and delving more deeply into parents' accounts found several breaches of this trust. Parents admitted to looking in the child's diaries to discover how sexually active they are, or following them unobserved into town on a trip to ensure their safety (Warin, Solomon and Lewis, 2007). To overcome the idea of respondents and thus the researchers taking or accepting a particular stance, we also compared the mother's, father's and child's accounts of the same relationship. In doing so we were able to identify agreement or disagreement, framing such discussion within current debates about whether and how there can be several truths on the same experiences. Parents and children often described homework as a site of tension between them, but from very different vantage points (Solomon, Warin and Lewis, 2002). In the Newsons' account perspectives are explored but the respondent's (i.e. the mother's) is writ large.

However, there is a paradox in the Newsons' writing that I have never been able to reconcile. These books are apparently written for parents as a result of the interviews conducted parent-to-parent (mother-to-mother) and the authors appear to be reporting the 'facts' – how many members of each social group adopt a particular perspective. Yet behind each of these analyses are several unanswered questions – particularly why the Newsons were interested in following one line of enquiry and not several other possibilities, the way in which parents' answers are interpreted, and the influence of academic and popular debates and the references to these debates. Yet, if I were to put my money on a study or account of family life in twentieth-century Britain (and probably in international discussions) that will be referred to in 100 years' time, the safest bet would be on this one and not those published and discussed in 'high-impact' journals such as the American Psychiatric Association *Journal of Family Psychology*. Why is this the case?

What might be termed the Newsons' naive realist approach was an attempt to step back from the mêlée of contemporary social, psychological and political debates and provide a dispassionate account of the parent's perspective at each time point in the child's life. For example, they simply describe the teenager who 'brought an illegitimate baby into the home' to live with her parents (Chapter 2) to report a difference from the norm, but this does not question where the norm comes from or its validity. I remember announcing to John that my partner and I were expecting. His immediate, quizzical question as he looked over his glasses was 'Are you going to get married?' He didn't seem fazed by me replying in the negative – he was genuinely interested in the approach to family life, in this case by a member of the next generation in which cohabitation proliferated. This reflects a genuine openness to the possibility that a parent might see the world from a very different vantage point.

To adopt as neutral a stance as is possible requires great sensitivity on the part of the researcher. The Newsons' great strength (as well as their weakness, as suggested above) was that they continually ask questions which strike parents as being of importance, often expectedly as is the case with discussion about the child's temperament or inner life. Their keenness to understand parents' accounts of their children sets out explicitly to explore experience in its richness and complexity. The very differences between individual parents within and across social groups illustrate a diversity that so much 'academic' research and practice overlooks. It is not fashionable to reflect upon social class, but every chapter in this book identifies that the experiences of parents and their children are vastly dissimilar across the social spectrum.

The Newsons were able penetrate these issues because they asked questions that appeared to be open and naive, but which led the parent carefully into terrain that they might otherwise be guarded about. For example, they open with: 'I'd like to start off by asking you about what N is like now as a person; and some of the questions will be the same as last time, because we're interested in how much children change over the years, and how far they stay the same. Would you say that N has changed a lot since he was 7?' John and Elizabeth were fully aware that some parents could not remember even being interviewed before, despite receiving Christmas cards from the study team. Such questions re-establish continuity and rapport, inviting the parent to offer an account of their child with as little leading as possible. I remember that they spent hours addressing the possible ways in which a question should or should not be phrased. The trend in family research has been to increase reliability at all costs – to make sure that every participant gets identical questions and would answer the same again if asked twice. The Newsons placed much greater emphasis on *validity* – getting as deeply as possible without cajoling the parent into a particular position. The analysis of parent–child closeness in Chapter 7 is a prime example of this.

Conclusion

Behind what I have written in this chapter I have attempted to explore for myself why I, as an academic following in the Newsons' footsteps, chose, in many respects unwillingly, to take an alternative path to the one demonstrated by them. They were talented and influential enough to disregard much of the activity of their peers and to conduct a study that has, indeed, described the natural history of parenting in ways that outshine the literature that they avoided. This sets them apart from their peers and from contemporary (then and now) analyses of childhood, but they were able to present an account of family life that will be long-lasting, while others will fade into obscurity. For me, this explains the tentative, almost wistful final paragraph that they will publish – of Chapter 8. They fully acknowledge that their approach and methods were necessarily 'rather crude and indirect' but it is clear from reading this book, and particularly the whole series, that John and Elizabeth's individual style was in its openness much better able to reveal the 'subtle and complex' nature of parents at one point in history and perhaps across generations.

References

American Psychiatric Association. (2013) *Diagnostic and Statistical Manual of Mental Disorders (DSM-5®)*, Washington, DC: American Psychiatric Publishing.

Blair, A. and Monk, D. (2012) 'Sex education and the law in England and Wales: the importance of legal narratives' in R. Davidson and L. Sauerteig (eds) *Shaping Sexual Knowledge: A Cultural History of Sex Education in Twentieth Century Europe*, Routledge Studies in the Social History of Medicine. Abingdon: Routledge.

Blos, P. (1966) *On Adolescence: A Psychoanalytic Interpretation*, New York: Simon and Schuster.

Bott, E. (1957) *Family and Social Network*, London: Tavistock.

Capaldi, D.M. and Rothbart, M.K. (1992) 'Development and validation of an early adolescent temperament measure', *Journal of Early Adolescence*, 12: 153–73.

Coleman, J.C. and Hendry, L.B. (1999) *The Nature of Adolescence*, Hove: Psychology Press.

Erikson, E.H. (1968) *Identity: Youth and Crisis*, New York: Norton.

Gershoff, E.T. and Grogan-Kaylor, A. (2016) 'Spanking and child outcomes: old controversies and new meta-analyses', *Journal of Family Psychology*, 30 (4): 453–69.

Giddens, A. (1998) *The Third Way*, Cambridge: Polity.

Hurwitz, L.B., Lauricella, A.R., Hightower, B., Sroka, I., Woodruff, T.K. and Wartella, E. (2017) '"When you're a baby you don't have puberty": Understanding of puberty and human reproduction in late childhood and early adolescence', *Journal of Early Adolescence*, 37: 925–47.

Kahn, J.J. (1964) 'Review of *Infant Care in an Urban Community*', *Mental Health*, 106.

Kleiber, D., Larson, R. and Csikszentmihalyi, M. (2014) 'The experience of leisure in adolescence', in M. Csikszentmihalyi (ed.) *Applications of Flow in Human Development and Education*, Dordrecht: Springer.

Langford, W., Lewis, C., Solomon, Y. and Warin, J. (2001) *Family Understandings: Closeness, Authority and Independence in Families with Teenagers*, London: Family Policy Study Centre and Joseph Rowntree Foundation.

Luckerson, V. (2012) 'Should you use your smart phone to track your kids?', *Time*, 14 September.

Newson, J. and Newson, E. (1963) *Infant Care in an Urban Community*, London: Allen and Unwin.

Newson, E., Le Marechal, K. and David, C. (2003) 'Pathological demand avoidance syndrome: a necessary distinction within the pervasive developmental disorders', *Archives of Disease in Childhood*, 88: 595–600.

Noller, P. and Callan, V. (1991) *The Adolescent in the Family*, New York: Routledge.

Solomon, Y., Warin, J. and Lewis, C. (2002) 'Helping with homework? Homework as a site of tension for parents and teenagers', *British Educational Research Journal*, 28: 603–22.

Sylvester, C.M., Whalen, D.J., Belden, A.C., Sanchez, S.L., Luby, J.L. and Barch, D.M. (2018) 'Shyness and trajectories of functional network connectivity over early adolescence', *Child Development*, 89 (3): 734–45.

Warin, J., Solomon, Y. and Lewis, C. (2007) 'Swapping stories: comparing plots. Triangulating individual narratives within families', *International Journal of Social Research Methodology*, 10, 121–34.

Warin, J., Solomon, Y., Lewis, C. and Langford, W. (1999) *Fathers, Work and Family Life*, London: Family Policy Study Centre and Joseph Rowntree Foundation.

Wilkinson, L. and the Task Force on Statistical Inference. (1999) 'Statistical methods in psychology journals: guidelines and explanations', *American Psychologist*, 54: 594–604.

Wing, L., Gould, J. and Gillberg, C. (2011) 'Autism spectrum disorders in the DSM-V: better or worse than the DSM-IV?', *Research in Developmental Disabilities*, 32 (2): 768–73.

Young, M. and Willmott, P. (1957) *Family and Kinship in East London*, London: Routledge & Kegan Paul.

APPENDIX 1
INTERVIEW SCHEDULE

UNIVERSITY OF NOTTINGHAM
CHILD DEVELOPMENT RESEARCH UNIT
District ....
interviewer at 1 ....
interviewer at 4 ....
interviewer at 7 ....
interviewer at 11 ....
Date ....
GUIDED INTERVIEW SCHEDULE
(for mothers of children aged 11)

BACKGROUND
Child's full name ....
Address..
....
Date of birth .... *Sex: Boy / Girl*
Family size and position (for each child in family, indicate sex and age – include foster children, marked F, and deceased children, marked D)
Insert names if possible: ....
SEX ....
AGE ....

MOTHER Age ...... *not working / working part-time / fulltime / homework*
Occupation if at work ....
FATHER Age ...... *Precise occupation* ....

(i) Does he have to be away from home at all, except just during the day?

Home every night/up to 2 nights away per week/3 nights + per week/normally away/
separation or divorce/dead/other...
SHIFT WORK? YES/NO What shifts? ....

(ii) Has N spent any time in hospital since he was 7? (Details: age, how long, what
was wrong?)
(iii) Has he had any accidents in the last four years that needed stitches or medical
treatment?
(iv) And has he had any medical difficulties – asthma, diabetes, anything of that sort?

A. GENERAL PERSONALITY

1. I'd like to start off by asking you about what N is like now as a person and some
of the questions will be the same as last time, because we're interested in how
much children change over the years, and how far they stay the same. Would
you say that N has changed a lot since he was 7?

2. Is he a calm, placid sort of child, or do you think he's a bit highly strung?
Calm/varies/highly strung

3. Is he the sort of child who usually agrees with what you want him to do, or
does he tend to object to things quite a lot?
Agrees/varies/objects

4. Do you find him easy to manage now he's 11, or is he a bit touchy – do you
have to *feel* your way with him?
Easy/varies/touchy

5. Would you say he's a self-confident person, or is he a little bit timid about doing
things he isn't used to?
Self-confident/varies/timid

6. In general, does he take things as they come, or is he a bit of a worrier?
As they come/varies/worrier

7. Does he get anxious about whether he's doing exactly what's expected of him,
or doesn't he care very much what grown-ups think?
Anxious/varies/doesn't care

8. What about other children – does he worry about their opinion of him?
Yes/varies/no

9. Is he a daydreamy child, or does he always seem very down-to-earth?

Daydreamy/varies/down-to-earth

10. Is he one of these children who's always in hot water, or does he manage to keep out of mischief mostly?

Hot water/varies/keeps out

11. In his interests and attitudes generally, would you say he's more like a child, or more like a teenager?

Child/varies/teenager

12. Does he spend a lot of time on his appearance?

Yes/varies/no

13. Would you call him an indoor child or an outdoor child?

Indoor/varies/outdoor

14. When he has to amuse himself, is he a busy sort of person, or does he easily get bored?

Busy/varies/easily bored

B. SOCIAL RELATIONSHIPS

15. Does he enjoy being all on his own – does he like his own company?

Yes/varies/wants others

16. How does he get on with his (brothers and sisters) – do they play a lot together?

(If 2+ sibs) Which does he play with most?

17. *(If 1 sib)* Do they quarrel much?

(If 2+ sibs) Which does he have most quarrels with?

No sibs/no quarrels with sibs/some quarrels with....../many with.........

18. What's the main cause of quarrels between N and ....?

19. Do they tease each other much? What sort of teasing mostly?

Often/sometimes/no

20. Do you think there's a little bit of jealousy between them?

N very moderately jealous of ..../......... very/moderately of N/little or no jealousy

21. How does N get on with other children – does he make friends easily?

    Yes/not very/difficulty making friends

22. Does he like to be one of a crowd, or is he happiest when he's doing things with just one special friend?

    Crowd/varies/one special

23. Does he belong to a group of children who always go around together? *YES/ NO*

    Is that a real secret society or gang, with a special name and passwords and so on?
    Are there boys and girls in this society/gang?
    Do you know what they do?
    No group/casual group/organised both-sex group/organised single-sex group
    Name: activities:

24. Is there any child who you would say is N's 'best friend'?

    How long have they been close friends? *boy/girl*

25. Does he seem to be happy in this friendship, or does he often seem to get upset about it?

26. Do you do anything at all about these tiffs and upsets between friends, or do you think they're best left alone to work it out for themselves?

27. Does he play with children older than himself? *(family not counted)*

    How does he get on with them?
    Prefers older/OK with older/some difficulty (specify)/no play with older

28. Does he play with younger ones – does he get on well with small children?

    Prefers younger/OK with younger/some difficulty (specify)/no play w. young

29. What about babies – does he show any interest in them at all?

30. When he's with children of his own age, does he usually tell *them* what to do, or do they tell *him*?

    (If they tell him) Do you think he'd like to boss the others a bit more, or is he quite happy to be led by them?
    He's boss/give and take/child prefers to follow/wants to lead but fails/isolate

31. Are you happy about all his friendships, or do you think some of them have a bad effect on him? *(specify)*

32. Have you done anything about that?

    Forbid/criticise/divert from/nothing

33. Does he come in for any teasing or bullying outside, as far as you know?

    Prompt as necessary:
    What about at school? *A lot/some/NO*
    What about in the street? *A lot/some/NO*

34. Do you think there's anything you can do about that sort of thing if it happens?

    School:
    Street:

35. Some children seem to get very upset when they're teased, and others manage to laugh it off quite easily – what's N like about this?

    Specially sensitive & upset/reacts aggressively/manages/couldn't care less (note if school/ home difference in reaction)

36. Do you think being teased can teach a child anything – do you think it can ever be *good* for him?

    Do you think it can do him any harm?

37. Do you tease N yourself at all?

    In what sort of way?

38. Has the question of girlfriends/boyfriends come up at all yet – I mean is there anyone N feels a bit romantic about? *(If adult, on to Q. 40 and specify child friend)*

39. Does (the other child) feel the same way?

    Do they hold hands and kiss – anything like that?
    (If NO) Do you think he'd tell you if they did?

40. How do you feel about that – kissing and so on – would you expect girls and boys to be interested in each other in this sort of way at 11?

    (If NO) When would you expect it to start?

41. How does N get on with grown-ups – is he shy of them?

42. Does he seem to enjoy talking to grown-ups, or isn't he much interested in them?

43. Is there any grown-up whom N sees a great deal of – any friend, or relative, or neighbour, who might seem quite important to him?

    (Prompt if necessary: regular babysitter? help in the house? Exclude school teacher. Child should see adult at least 1 per week)

44. What specially brings them together?

    Does N like (this person) a lot? *YES/SO-SO/NO*

45. Do you think (this person) is good for N *in every* way, or is there anything you're not altogether happy about?

    (If applicable) What about (adult living in house)?

46. What's N like in front of a grown-up audience – at Christmas, say, would he stand up and sing a song, or recite, or do a little dance?

    Enjoys this/wouldn't mind/reluctant/refuses/hasn't, probably would/hasn't, probably wouldn't

47. Does he ever have play-acting games when he's on his own – using his imagination and talking to himself? *YES/NO Details – criterion is that child talks <u>aloud</u>.*

48. Does he mind you listening, or does he stop when you come in?

    Likes audience doesn't mind/prefers privacy/sometimes each

49. Does he ever let his imagination run away from him when he's telling you things?

    Is it mostly exaggeration of something true, or does he make up the whole story?

C. STRESS

50. Has he any fears or worries, as far as you know?

51. He used to ....

52. Some children this age worry a lot about dying – do you think that bothers N?

    (If YES) Is he afraid that any particular person will die?
    Do you know how that worry started?

53. Does he talk about God or religion at all – is that something that interests him?

54. Do you think he has any worries about that kind of thing?

    (If YES) What do you say to him about that?

55. What about the sort of things he sees in the newspapers, or on television – is he ever frightened by something in the news?

    (If YES) What do you say then?

56. Do you feel that you *know* about most of his thoughts and fears, or do you think there's quite a lot he keeps to himself?

57. Does he ever have nightmares, or wake up crying in the night?

58. Does he sleep well, on the whole?

59. Has he a good appetite?

60. What about the odd habits children pick up? Does he bite his nails, for instance – he was doing that when he was 7, I remember

61. *(HABIT FOLLOW-UPS)*

62. Does he ever clear his throat, or swallow, as a nervous habit?

63. Does he blink, or screw his eyes up?

64. Does he ever stammer or stutter when he speaks?

65. Is there anything special he does when he's anxious or overtired?

66. Have you noticed whether he .... at any special sort of time, or when he's in a particular mood?

67. Do you do anything to stop him .... *(specify)* or are you just expecting him to grow out of it in time?

68. Would you say he's a moody child at all – does he seem to change from being happy to being cross, without any special reason?

69. Does he ever have a headache or a temperature because he's anxious or excited? Is he ever actually sick out of excitement or worry?

70. Do you think he ever *pretends* to be unwell, so as to get out of something he doesn't want to do?

D. ACTIVITIES – INDEPENDENCE

71. We're interested in the things children do in their spare time. Has N any special interest that takes up a lot of his time?

72. Does he collect anything as a hobby?

73. What do you think is his most treasured possession – if there was a fire what would he grab first? *(Exclude humans and animals)*

74. Is he interested in making things? – for instance, does he

    Boy: do carpentry? tinker with mechanical things? Girl: sew? knit?
    Boy & Girl: make models or drawings or presents for people?
    What sort of things does he make?

75. *(If he does make things)* Do you think he's *unusually* good at doing things with his hands?

76. Does he write stories in his own time? *Often/occasionally/NO*

    – write letters for the fun of it? *(Thank you letters excluded)*
    – keep a diary or any sort of notebook at home? *(Specify)*

77. Does he do any dancing or acting or choir-singing in his spare time? *(lessons?)*

78. Does he have music lessons at all?

79. Does he belong to any out-of-school club, or church group?

    – Scouts/Guides or Cadets – anything like that? Sunday School? (Not RC)

80. Is there anything else you can think of that N does as a regular thing – any (other) special lessons or regular meetings he goes to?

    (If applies) Has he taken any exams/gone in for any competitions?

81. Does he have any regular pocket money of his own?

    Has he any regular expenses, like bus-fares, that come out of that? Do you buy him sweets, apart from any he buys with his pocket money?
    (Calculate pocket money he can count on each. week, from all sources: necessary expenses (school biscuits, fares, collections), add 1/– if sweets, apart from involuntary savings unless he has unrestricted access)
    Regular unearned spending power: .... per week

82. Could he earn extra money if he wanted to?

    Does he ever? (details) Average earned income: from home .... per week from outside .... per week

83. What is he like with money – is it 'easy come, easy go', or does he like to save up for something special?

    Spend within week/saves week/fortnight/longer
    What sort of things does he mostly spend his money on?

84. We'd like to know what sort of things children of this age do on their own. For instance, does he ever go on a bus on his own? *School only/other/no*

85. Would you let him go into town on his own – to the big Woolworth's, say? *(Meadows children only)* – to Boots in the Victoria Centre, say? *YES/NO*

86. Would you let him go to Wollaton Part/Trent Bridge embankment by himself? *Alone/with another same age/only with an older person*

87. Has he got a bicycle? *YES/NO (If YES)* How far is he allowed to go on it?
    Do you have any rules about which roads he can go on?
    Is he ever allowed to ride it after dark?

88. And when he goes to .... does that mean a journey of more than ½ an hour on his own? *Less/about ½ hour/more*

89. Has he ever managed a train journey on his own?

90. How do you feel about children going off to places alone – does it worry you at all? (In what way?)

91. How do you think you can protect a child from being frightened or harmed by someone when he is on his own?
    Have you discussed this with N at all? *YES/NO*

92. Have you explained (if it came up, would you explain) *why* it can be dangerous to go off with someone or get in someone's car?

93. *(If explanation didn't include sexual angle)* Would you explain anything about the *sexual* danger, or do you think it's better not to mention that? *Would/wouldn't*
    (If would) How would you put it, do you think?

94. Has the school talked to them about this, do you know?

E. SCHOOL

95. We'd like to know something now about how N's getting on at school – does he seem happy at school? *Very happy/happy enough/not very/strongly dislikes*

96. Which school does he go to now?...
    Type

97. Do you know yet where he'll be going next? *YES*........................*/NO*

98. a) Are you pleased about that, or would you rather he was going somewhere else?
    b) *(If dissatisfied)* Are you doing anything about it, or do you feel you just have to accept these things?

    If grammar school aspirations, ask (c), (d) and (e).

    c) Did you do anything at all to try and help him over the 11+?
    d) Did you promise him anything as a reward if he did well? *(Specify)*
    e) *(If YES)* Have you given it to him? *Yes/not yet, will/no, undeserved*

99. *If selection result still unknown*
    a) Where are you hoping he'll go? ....
    b) Is that where you think he *will* go?

    If grammar school aspirations, ask (c) and (d).

    c) Have you been doing anything to help him over the 11+? *(i.e. help with work)*
    d) Have you promised him anything as a reward if he does well? *(Specify)*
    e) Suppose he gets selected for a school you don't like – will you do anything about it, or do you feel you just have to accept these things?

100. What age do you expect N to finish school? ....

101. *(If 15)* Will you let him stay on longer if he wants to?
    YES/NO
    (If 16+) Do you expect him to go on to further education after that? *YES/NO*
    (If YES) What sort of further education do you think is most *likely* for N?

102. Do you and your husband agree on the sort of education you want for N?

103. In general, do you think the way they select children at 11 is fair?

104. Do you think the teachers at the junior school have a pretty good idea of how well a child is likely to do, or do you think it's easy for them to make mistakes?
    Teachers know/not infallible/often mistaken/favourites

105. What about N – do you think the junior school has given him a good start?

106. On the whole, have the teachers been understanding and sympathetic to him?

107. Does N like the teacher he has now? *YES/SO-SO/NO*

108. Suppose he came home and criticised the teacher to you – what would you say to him?

109. Suppose he told you the teacher has said something to the class, and you thought the teacher was wrong, would you say anything to N?

110. Some people think you should always back up the teacher to the child – how do you feel about that?

111. Have you yourself seen as much of the teachers as you would like, or would you prefer to talk to them more often?

112. How often are parents invited to the school?
   Prompt: to discuss N? .... *per year for concerts and things like that?* ....
   per year

113. Do you manage to get there almost always, or not very often?

114. Is there a parent/teacher association? *YES/NO/DON'T KNOW*

115. Do you feel that parents are made welcome in the school? *YES/not very/NO*
   What makes you feel that?
   (Prompt if necessary) Suppose you drop in, do they seem pleased to see you?

116. Does N bring home written reports? *3 per year/2 per year/1 per year/none*
   (If YES) Have you found them helpful? *Very/moderately/not at all*
   (If NO) Have you ever been up to school to discuss a report?
   (If NO) Do you think it would be helpful if he did?

117. Does N have regular homework at the moment? *Approximately daily/1–3 per week/occasional/NO*
   How long does it take him? ....
   Does he seem to need a lot of help with it? *YES/little/none*
   Who helps him most often when he needs it?

118. If he has homework at his next school, do you think it's going to be a problem getting him to do it properly?
   (Prompt as necessary) Do you think you'll have to keep on at him to get it done?
   Where will he do it, do you expect?

119. What do you think about homework in the last year of the juniors?

120. What about when they get to 12 or 13?

121. If you could choose, and it wasn't a question of money, would you like N to go to boarding school? *YES/NO*

   What do you think about boarding school for children of this age?

F. FAMILY AND INTERACTION

122. Can you tell me now about how you and N get on together – is there any special thing about him that gives you a lot of pleasure?

123. Does he show his affection to people, or is he a bit bashful about it nowadays?

   Would he give you or his Daddy a hug or a kiss without being asked for it? *Spontaneously affectionate/affectionate but shy/definitely reserved*

124. What about you – do you find it easy to show him you love him?

   Do you use pet names like 'darling' or 'love' or, 'sweetheart' when talking to him? (*'Dear' doesn't count*)

125. You've said what gives *you* pleasure about him, but you're his mother – what would an *outsider* say was his best quality, the best thing in his character?

126. Do you find you talk a lot to N, or aren't you really interested in the same things?

127. Do you discuss serious, grown-up things with him at all – is he interested in that? (What sort of things?)

128. What about N's Daddy – do they talk a lot together?

   What do they mostly seem to talk about?

129. Is there anything that you and N do together – making something? – going somewhere?

130. Do N and his Daddy do anything together, just the two of them?

131. Would you say he's closer to you or to his Daddy, now he's 11?

   Mother/father/about equal

*132. What about the things you might do as a family – (if 3+ children) – or several of you together? – for instance, do you ever manage a family outing to the seaside, or into the country?

   – go to a film together? – the theatre? – museums?
   – stately homes? – go swimming, or for a picnic?
   – any other sort of outing or entertainment?

*133. Do you ever read aloud or sing together as a family — anything like that?
*134. Do you sit down and play a card game or a board game together?

> * *132, 133, 134 activity must involve at least 3 people, including N. Also, in 132 mark 'E' if activity is experienced but doesn't meet this criterion.*

135. Do the children ever get up a family concert or a play?

136. Have they ever organised a little jumble sale, or some sort of fair among themselves?

137. What about holidays, did you manage a summer holiday out of Nottingham this (last) year? (How long? Where?)

138. Has N seen anything of the rest of England at all?

    What about Wales and Scotland and Ireland?
    Has he ever been abroad? (I suppose he hasn't been abroad?)

139. Do you find that N watches television quite a lot?

140. Sometimes children happen to see something on television, and parents wish they hadn't — what sort of things would you rather N *didn't* see?

141. *(If any reservations)* Would you *forbid* him watching if you knew beforehand what the programme was going to be like?

142. When he's been watching television, does he ever ask you questions that you don't really want to answer? (What sort of questions?)

143. You said last time that N knew where babies come from/didn't know yet where babies come from.

    Does he know now? *YES/NO*
    Did you tell him, or did he find out from somebody else?
    (If knows) Does he understand the father's part in starting a baby?
    (Prompt if necessary) Does he know how the seed gets into the mother?
    (If knows father's part) Did you tell him, or did he find out from somebody else?
    (If doesn't) Would you tell him if he asked you, or do you think he's too young?

144. *GIRLS*: Has she started her periods yet? *YES/NO*

    (If NO) Have you explained that this will be happening soon? *YES/NO*
    (If not) Will you tell her pretty soon, or will you wait till she does start?
    What do you think is the best way to explain?
    (Omitted .... present)

145. *BOYS:* Does he know about girls having periods? *YES/NO/DON'T KNOW*

     (If NO) Do you think you'll tell him about that yet, or don't you think he should know?

     (If shouldn't) Would you try to hide things like sanitary towels or Tampax from him, so that he wouldn't ask questions?

     (If will tell) What do you think is the best way to explain to a boy about periods?

     (Omitted .... present)

146. Of course, there's been a lot of talk on television about the Pill lately. Has he asked any questions about that? *YES/NO*

     (If YES) What did you say to him? *(If NO)* What would you say if he did?

147. Have you ever taken a book or magazine away from him because you didn't want him to read it?

148. Do you think parents *should* keep certain books from children of this age?

     What sort of books specially?

G. CONFLICT

149. We're interested in the sorts of things children argue about at this age. Is there any special thing that causes a lot of disagreement between you and N?

150. Suppose you ask him to do a little job for you – does he take a lot of trouble to finish it carefully, or do you think he'd let it slide if he could?

     Always conscientious/varies/lets slide

151. What jobs do you expect him to do for you now – I mean without being paid?

152. What about keeping his things tidy – are there arguments over that?

153. Do you expect him to be in by any special time? ....

     Does he complain about that?

154. Do you have arguments about bedtime?

155. Some children want to wear clothes their parents think are silly, or want more expensive clothes than parents can afford. Has that come up with N? *YES/NO*

     How did you settle it?

156. Has there been any argument about hair-styles or smoking (or make-up)?

157. Do you think any drinking or drug-taking goes on among the children N knows?

  Do you know whether he's ever been offered pep-pills, or anything of that sort?

  (Do you think he'd tell you about things like that?)

158. Does he ever come in and say 'So-and-so is allowed to do something, why can't I?'?

  What do you do? (What would you do?)

159. Does he ever complain that another child *has* something – more pocket money, or something like that?

  What do you do then? (What would you do?)

160. I asked you earlier on what was his best quality. What do you think is his biggest fault?

161. Do you think he would agree with you about that, or do you think he'd never admit it, even to himself?

162. Is he good at admitting when he's in the wrong?

163. Does he find it difficult to say he's sorry?

164. When he's upset, does he tend to take it out on other people, or on himself?

165. Suppose he's done something that's not wrong but just silly, and he's feeling he's made a fool of himself – how does he react, what does he do?

166. Does he ever blame other people for things that are really his fault – I don't mean telling lies about them, but just saying it was *their* fault?

167. What makes him really angry?

168. When he really is in a rage, does he show it by shouting and banging about, or does he have silent *sulking* rages?

169. How do you get him back to normal?

170. Now N's 11, are there any punishments you use when he's naughty?

171. Do you stop his sweets or television as a punishment?

  What about pocket money?

172. Do you ever send him to bed early? *YES/NO*

    – or just out of the room? *YES/NO*

173. Do you ever threaten to leave him, or to send him away from home?

174. Do you ever threaten him with the teacher or a policeman, or anyone else of that sort?

175. *(If NO and starred)* You used to do that when he was 7 – is there any special reason why you've stopped?

176. Does N ever/often get smacked nowadays?

    About how often does he get a smack from *you*?
    1+ per day/1+ per week/1–3 per month/rare/definitely never
    What about your husband? *1+ per day/1+ per week/1–3 per month/rare/ definitely never*

177. What sort of thing do you smack him for mostly?

178. Are you usually angry if you smack him, or do you smack him simply as a punishment?

179. Do you ever find you need to use a stick or a belt or anything like that?

    How often does that seem necessary?
    Do you use it on his hand, or his behind, or where? (On his *bare* behind?)

180. *(If no instrument)* Do you ever threaten to use something on him?

    (If YES) Do you reckon it may come to that, or is it just an idle threat?

181. And what about your husband – does he ever use a stick (belt, etc.)?

    (If NO) ... or threaten it?

182. Is there any (other) way in which you disagree with your husband about how you should deal with N?

183. Does N know that you disagree?

184. Some people say that parents should always back each other up, even when they really disagree; and some think that a child should be able to appeal to one parent if it thinks the other one is being unfair. What do *you* feel about that?

185. *(If 'back up')* Do you think Father should always back up Mother; or Mother should always back up Father; or is it just that whichever is dealing with the child should be backed up by the other one?

    (If 'appeal') Can you think of a situation in which you might back up your husband, *even though you thought he was mistaken?*

186. Sometimes children this age go through a phase of taking things that don't belong to them – have you had that at all?

    What did you do?

187. Has he ever been in real trouble with school, so that you really had to speak to him seriously?

188. Has he ever played truant from school, so far as you know?

189. Do you think teachers should be allowed to use a cane or a strap on children of N's age?

190. Has N had the cane or strap at school at all? *YES/NO/DON'T KNOW*

    (If YES) Did it upset him?
    Did you think it was right that it should have been used?
    Did you complain?
    (If NO) Would you complain if he did?

191. Has N ever got himself into trouble with neighbours or the police?

192. (This one might be a bit difficult) – do you think you'd tell a lie in order to save him from that sort of trouble?

193. Small children often seem to think their parents know everything and can't do anything wrong, and teenagers sometimes talk as if parents know nothing and can't do anything right. What stage has N got to?

194. Just two more questions, and for both of them I'd like you to look ahead. In ten years' time, he'll be 21 – what sort of job do you think he'll be in then?

195. He might well be married by that time. What do you think he'll be like as a husband/wife?

    HOUSING Modern detached/modern semi/older detached/older semi/old large terraced/terraced with bays/terraced without bays/self-contained flat/rooms/council on estate/council not estate/council flat/other ....

APPENDIX 2
SAMPLING AND STATISTICS

Editors' note

The manuscript that came to light in 2016 did not contain any appendices or other account of methodology and statistics. Much of what follows is adapted from Chapter 1 *and* Appendix II *of* Seven Years Old in the Home Environment *where John and Elizabeth Newson explain the conventions used in displaying the data in tables and providing the levels of statistical significance for differences and trends identified in the data. As the same procedures were applied to the data gathered at 11, the account remains broadly the same but with a specimen table from* Chapter 4 *of this book. We have sought to retain the original voice.*

Sampling

780 mothers were interviewed at the 11-year-old stage. Table A.1 shows the actual composition of the sample as a function of sex and social class, with, for comparison, the number that would be expected in a fully random (unstratified) sample of approximately the same size.

The discrepancies are partly intentional and partly due to adventitious factors to do with how the sample was originally drawn and then augmented to replace losses from the earlier stages. As in our previous studies, the avowed aim was to arrive at a stratified random sample using occupational social class as the basis for the stratification. The strategy was to include at least 100 cases in each of the numerically smaller class groups. The practical problem, both in choosing the sample originally and in making up for losses later, was that the records that we used for our sampling frame did not provide sufficiently accurate or up-to-date information about the father's occupation. In fact they would not have been expected to do so, since from time to time people change their jobs, and sometimes their occupational status in

TABLE A.1 Class/sex composition of interviewed sample: comparable with (bracketed) expected composition of unstratified sample

	I&II	III WC	IIIMan	IV	V	I&II, IIIWC	IIIMan, IV,V	Total
Boys	92	57	119	67	61	149	247	396
	(55)	(51)	(195)	(59)	(31)	(105)	(285)	(390)
Girls	84	61	104	81	54	145	239	384
	(55)	(51)	(195)	(59)	(31)	(105)	(285)	(390)
Both	176	118	223	148	115	294	486	780
	(110)	(101)	(390)	(118)	(62)	(210)	(570)	(390)
	14%	13%	50%	15%	8%	27%	73%	100%

consequence. The final confirmation of occupational social class could therefore only be obtained at the time of the interview itself.

The information contained in Table A.1 does, however, enable us to calculate corrected proportions for the sample as a whole and for various sub-groups (such as all middle-class children) by adopting an appropriate weighting procedure. Given that x% of actual respondents answer 'No' to Question Y in specified proportions according to social class, this procedure yields an estimate of what proportions would answer 'No' in a non-stratified random sample. The weighting was undertaken routinely, and thus the data tables throughout include totals in terms of proportions to be expected in a non-stratified sample with equal numbers of boys and girls, as shown in brackets in Table A.1.

Tables

In an effort to make the statistical findings easy to follow, the tables are set out in a standard form which is followed, more or less consistently throughout this volume. A typical example is shown below. These tables are normally used to show the percentage of mothers who answered some particular question in a defined way; but the method of presentation lends itself equally to the display of other information about the sample, such as, for example, the number of high scorers on some more sophisticated measure derived from combining answers given to a group of questions which contribute towards a single theme: these combined measures we shall refer to as indices, as we did in the books about the 7-year-olds.

In the left-hand part of this table, the results are broken down in two ways, showing the percentages for five different social class groups and for boys and girls separately; the bottom line shows proportions for boys and girls combined. Social class is, as previously, ascribed according to the Registrar General's classification, with the modification that Classes I and II (upper and lower professional and managerial) are combined, while Class III is divided into white-collar and manual

TABLE A.2 Children who own bicycles at 11 (Table 5.1 from p. 91)

	I&II	III WC	IIIMan	IV	V	I&II, IIIWC	IIIMan, IV,V	Overall popn
	%	%	%	%	%	%	%	%
Boys	85	70	50	54	34	78	49	57
Girls	67	51	47	39	22	59	43	47
Both	75	60	49	47	28	68	46	52

Significance: class trend ↘ ★★★★   m.class vs w.class ★★★★

Between sexes ★★★★

workers; foremen in industry are included in the III white-collar group, and class affiliation in any individual case is determined on the basis of whichever of the parents' occupations is higher in the class scale.

If the combined proportions for boys and girls increase or decrease consistently as a function of social class, this indicates a trend which can then be tested for statistical significance (Armitage, 1955). The results of this trend test are indicated at the foot of the left-hand side of the table in terms of *direction* (upward from Class I to Class V ↗, or downward ↘) and the degree of significance (★★★★ p <0.001; ★★★ p <0.01; ★★ p <0.02; ★ p <0.05). The test used also allows us to say whether there is evidence for non-linearity (in this table, not). In examining this half of the table, it is worth observing whether the boy/girl differences are consistently in the same direction throughout.

The right-hand part of the table first summarises the social class findings in terms of a broader comparison between middle-class children generally (Classes I and II, and III white collar) and working-class children generally (Classes III manual (skilled), IV (semi-skilled) and V (unskilled)). It should be noted that our sample, while randomly drawn with respect to all other variables except the exclusions mentioned above, is class-stratified: that is to say, it is weighted to include more of the low-frequency classes than would normally appear in a totally random sample. In the summary table, the data are statistically treated to represent the proportions *which would occur in a fully random sample* (given the original exclusions), so that it now takes into account the fact that, for instance, most of the children in the working class belong to the skilled manual group. Similarly, the percentage figures given in the final column on the right provide a weighted estimate of what the proportions would be in a random cross-section of the overall population (again, given these exclusions).

The middle-class/working-class comparison is also tested for significance, and the result given at the foot of this section. The overall sex difference is tested on the basis of the difference shown in the 'overall population' column.

Taking the specimen table for comment, we can see that, in the first place, there is a very marked downward trend in the proportion of children who own a bicycle as we move down the social scale. Proportions decrease at every level from 75%

of children in the managerial and professional group (Class I & II) to just 27% in the unskilled manual group (Class V). There is also some suggestion that the drop is not evenly distributed through the whole scale, the difference between Class III manual and Class IV being much smaller than that between any other two class groups. The sex differences are also considerable in each social class group, though that is noticeably less the case in Class III Man. From the summary table, we can see a clearly significant difference on this variable between middle-class and working-class groups as a whole.

Indices

Every individual question contributes something to our understanding of the child-rearing process; but it is only when several related questions are considered together, and a pattern is seen to emerge from the responses, that the interpretation can be more confidently stated. We may do this simply by juxtaposing responses; a more useful method in some cases is to group different but related questions to provide an accumulation of evidence on a given theme for any given mother/child pair. An index is constructed by assigning scores to responses and summing these to give an individual chid an overall score for that index. A potentially useful index is one which gives a reasonable spread of scores across the sample, and for the purposes of comparison it is desirable that the scatter of the scores should be similar. The index is operationally defined in terms of the questions that make it up; the label attached to it is an attempt to sum up this definition. Expressing the child's standing by this single figure allows for more complex statistical treatment of the data, including the calculation of the degree of association between the various indices.

Indices of this sort, if they can be assumed to be valid as measurements which meaningfully distinguish individuals along a continuum, can be cross-correlated one with another and subjected to other forms of more detailed statistical analysis which are not generally possible on a head-counting or percentage-taking basis. There are, however, a number of problems which tend to arise when moving from the non-parametric domain towards methods where measurements on continua are deemed to be appropriate. First there is the question of deciding upon the rules which should be followed when attempting to put together separate pieces of information in order to arrive at a new dimension. The difficulty here is that there is no infallible and universally applicable set of statistical rules for arriving at forms of measurement which will turn out to be both meaningful and useful in promoting a deeper understanding of the theoretical questions at issue. In particular, we have yet to be convinced that procedures which rely on the selection of a few items from a larger pool on the criterion of maximising internal consistency between the chosen sub-set have any intrinsic merit. We are, in fact, inclined to the opinion that, in interpreting the answers given to the sorts of questions we are asking, the most prudent course may well be to rely most heavily upon a reasonably direct evaluation of the first-order data: namely the proportions of mothers whose answers fall into categories which have been defined in everyday commonsense terms. In other words, the further we move from results which are directly and intuitively comprehensible, the less secure we ought to feel about the interpretations we are making.

In practice, therefore, what we have attempted to do in compiling our indices is to put together all those responses which seemed to us, *on the grounds of face validity*, to have some bearing on a more general underlying attitude or characteristic style of behaviour. The only serious technical considerations were that each index should, as far as possible, be based upon answers given to a variety of questions, preferably with a discernibly different specific content, and that each index should have a dispersion or scatter compatible with a score range of approximately ten points. In practice, this also generally resulted in a distribution of scores which was unimodal and approximately symmetrical, which makes it permissible to use conventional statistical methods when comparing means.

A further and related problem with continuous measures established in this way is to choose labels which adequately convey what is being measured. In particular there is a risk of reification: that the giving of a name to a constellation or pattern of answers may artificially establish in the mind of both investigator and reader a conceptual notion of greater salience and definition than is strictly justifiable in terms of the specific questions asked and the way the actual answers are coded. Simply the use of a quantitative scale of assessment is likely to suggest that it is possible, merely through a refinement of technique, to measure an abstract conceptual notion with the same accuracy and precision with which we measure the physical properties of real objects. It is a comfortable and rather dangerous human propensity to impose patterns of perceptions and then to manipulate the patterns as objects in their own right; to press the analogy, the organisation of a constellation of items into a plausible whole is not totally unlike learning to see a particular patterns of stars as a Great Bear or (alternatively!) a Plough.

Thus we invite the reader to scrutinise carefully the questions which any index comprises, together with the way in which they are scored, rather than to rely uncritically on a summarising label. These questions define the dimensions we use.

Other conventions

Certain conventions which we have adopted in our reporting need to be re-stated. All forenames used, both of members of the sample and of people to whom they refer, are of course pseudonyms. In the case of the 780 children, a name once ascribed is not used for anyone else in the sample: so that, for instance, 'Vicky' at 11 is the same child as 'Vicky' at 7, 4 and 1. We have found it necessary to duplicate siblings' names, though within families each retains its pseudonym through time. We have not usually thought it necessary to disguise names of places and shops.

It goes without saying that nothing has been added to quotations from transcripts; occasional repetitiousness has been abridged, and in a few cases sentences have been reordered to avoid confusion on the reader's part.

The interview schedule which forms the core of the interview is given in full in Appendix 1. It should be borne in mind that this schedule has been devised to be used by highly trained interviewers, and *not* as a straightforward questionnaire. While we do not object to its use in whole or in part by other research workers, we would also suggest that this should not be done without consulting the account of our interviewing method (Newson and Newson, 1976). In particular, we would explicitly condemn any use of the questions which contribute to our index scores out of the context of the whole interview.

References

Armitage, P. (1955) 'Tests for linear trends in proportions and frequencies', *Biometrics*, 11 (3): 375–86.

Newson, J. and Newson, E. (1976) 'Parental roles and social context', in M. Shipman (ed.) *The Organisation and Impact of Social Research: Six Original Case Studies in Education and Behavioural Sciences*, London: Routledge & Kegan Paul (reprinted as a Routledge Library Edition, 2017).

APPENDIX 3
LOCAL AND TOPICAL REFERENCES

This Appendix comprises three alphabetically organised lists:

1. Places and institutions in and around Nottingham which are referred to in the text.
2. Nottingham dialect words and phrases used in everyday speech.
3. References in the text which were current at the time the fieldwork was being conducted and may now benefit from an explanation.

Places and institutions

Arkwright Street – the road between the Midland railway station and Trent Bridge, regarded by some as a 'rough' area.

Bramcote Lido – a swimming pool on the south-west side of the city.

Carrington Lido – an open-air swimming pool in the suburb of Carrington, north of the city centre. It opened in 1937 and closed in the late 1980s.

Clifton – a large estate of council houses on the southern fringe of the city.

Clumber Park – a park near Worksop, about 25 miles north of Nottingham. Formerly owned by the Dukes of Newcastle, it has been maintained by the National Trust since 1946.

Colwick Woods – an extensive area of parkland on the eastern side of the city, with recreational facilities.

Gordon Boys' Home – a home for 'destitute boys' which was founded in Nottingham in 1885 and closed in 1965.

Mablethorpe – a resort in Lincolnshire and one of the nearest accessible stretches of seaside; popular with holidaymakers from Nottingham.

Nottingham Castle – a 17th-century palace on top of a large rock in the centre of the city, the site of a former medieval castle. The building became the first municipal museum of art in England and is set in gardens and terraces which are a popular place for leisure and recreation.

Radio Nottingham – one of the early local radio stations in the UK which started transmission in about 1968.

Sunshine Corner – may have been a Sunday School run by the Salvation Army in Sneinton.

Trent Bridge – the bridge over the River Trent carrying the main road out of the city to the south-east, leading initially to West Bridgford. The cricket ground and Nottingham Forest Football Club ground are adjacent to the bridge.

Trent Bridge embankment – a riverside walkway in the region of the bridge.

Victoria Centre – a large, covered shopping centre built between 1967 and 1972 on the site of a former railway station, close to the city centre.

Wells Road – the road leading out of the St Ann's district.

Wollaton Park – a large area of parkland to the south-west of the city with a lake and a natural history museum housed in the 16th-century Wollaton Hall. A popular place for recreation.

(The big) Woolworth's – a large (by the standards of the day) F.W. Woolworth shop near the city centre.

Nottingham dialect words and phrases

call – run down, revile, usually to someone else, e.g. 'I don't like to call my mother, but she was a hard mother to me'

duck – a friendly form of address or greeting to either gender, often preceded by m' e.g. 'can I help you, m'duck?'

fussy – enthusiastic

mardy – whining, cross, making an (unnecessary) fuss

mester – man; husband, e.g. 'How's the mester?'

nasty – bad-tempered

owt – anything, e.g. 'that's not got owt to do with it' (pronounced oat)

road – used instead of way e.g. 'any road' – anyway

tap – smack, hit

us – our, e.g. 'we had us tea'

Contemporary references

Green Shield stamps – small green stamps which were given by some shops in return for purchases. They were stuck into books which, when full, could be accumulated and exchanged for a wide range of goods from a Green Shield shop, of which there was one in central Nottingham.

oral contraception – the contraceptive pill had started to become available, on prescription, from the mid-1960s. It was regarded with suspicion by some.

Puffin Club – a children's book club linked to Puffin Books (part of Penguin Books); subscribers received a monthly magazine and had the opportunity to attend book-related events.

TV Times – the magazine listing programmes on ITV (cf. *Radio Times* which then only provided details of BBC television and radio programmes).

Women's Movement – the mid-1960s saw the beginning of the second wave of feminism in Britain. The Women's Liberation Movement expanded feminist discussions to equality in marriage and the workplace; sex and sexuality; and violence against women.

INDEX